On War
Although I was once an active member of the Palestinian resistance and the wife of a Palestinian commando, I have to admit: I hate war. I cannot imagine losing more friends and family in yet another battle. And, late at night, I imagine that our opponents in these conflicts share my grief. I have to admit that they, too, have lost children, women, and young men in the prime of life.

On Peace
Both Arabs and Jews are human beings. Both are entitled to a dignified life. The time has come when this bloodshed must stop. We all have lives. We have families and homes. We care about the future of our children and grandchildren. The end of the occupation and the termination of hostilities mean that Arabs and Jews will need to accept the idea of living alongside one another. We have done this before 1948, and we can do it again. It is not impossible. The experts can decide on the details of a solution. What I know is that we need to accept one another, one person to the next. This is the foundation. This is the basis of peace.

—*Reem al-Nimer*

I have asked my friend Sami Moubayed to explain how my book came to be written. See his sketch, "A Trendy Café near Rue Hamra."

At the most literal level, let me say that I wrote "Curse of the *Achille Lauro*" to tell about the interplay of two very different Palestinian lives. My husband Abu al-Abbas came up hard in a refugee camp in Damascus while I was from a wealthy family in Beirut. I also wanted to sketch a portrait of my husband. He was more complex than the hero described in the Arab newspapers or the villain who was portrayed in the western media. And, when it came to the *Achille Lauro,* I wanted to repeat his apology for a military operation gone awry:

"What of Leon Klinghoffer?" my husband asked. "What did he do wrong?"

The war between Israel and Palestine has waged hot and cold for nearly seventy years. Our differences with the Israelis should have been resolved long ago. As my husband phrased it, "The time for fighting is past."

—*Reem al-Nimer*

A Trendy Café near Rue Hamra

I FIRST MET REEM AL-NIMER AT A TRENDY CAFÉ wedged between the American University of Beirut on the bluff above the Mediterranean and Lebanon's famous Hamra Street. This was in September 2012.

I am an historian and political commentator. Reem is well known in the Arab world as the wife of Abu al-Abbas, a prominent Palestinian general who died in 2004. I am from Damascus—and my country was up in flames. She is from Beirut—and her native Palestine had been on fire for sixty-four years. Still, the point of our talk was not war . . . but peace. Reem wanted to tell her story, a long and quirky tale of her journey from youth to wisdom. Along the way, she grew from an earnest desire to oppose Israeli military action with force to an understanding that war, in the end, does not create the desired result. It takes reconciliation to make peace.

Even though Reem al-Nimer had lived through eleven wars, she nevertheless spoke with high optimism. She had seen horrible things, she had lost friends and relatives, and yet she was willing to put the past in its place and to turn a new page in life. Her eyes sparkled and she seemed certain that sometime soon there would be peace in the Arab world. Her outlook required the ability to look past the current obstacles. It required confidence, and courage. Reem al-Nimer had all three.

Reem could see that one day Palestinians and Israelis would "work together, pray together, struggle together, go to jail together, stand up for freedom together." The future belonged to both peoples, in concert. Before any of this happened, of course, Palestinians and Israelis needed to stop killing one another. Reem thought that normal, healthy national pride had mutated into patriotic rhetoric that trapped the region in a cycle of violence and revenge. The impulse for martyrdom among Palestinians and cachet of military prowess among Israelis had been encouraged to the point of national self-destruction. As Reem told me, "It's better to live, than to die, for your country!"

Reem had a project in mind: She wanted to create a book about her life—and her husband's life. She asked me to serve as her writing coach, and I agreed. We spent nearly two years taking the world apart and then putting it back together. We discussed everything from the right of return of the Palestinians to Muslim history to Buddhist thought. As an Arab living in a country bordering Palestine, I have always been close to the Palestinian cause and have written extensively about Yasser Arafat. As Reem began to unfold her story, I found that Arafat played a central role. Reem knew Arafat well.

She had served in Arafat's Fatah organization under the umbrella of the PLO (Palestinian Liberation Organization). I also learned that Reem had served in a succession of other Palestinian groups, had lived through the Israeli siege of Beirut, and had witnessed or participated in the major events of Palestinian history since the 1960s.

Reem grew from a carefree teenager with a rich dad into an activist, a commando, and the wife of a prominent military leader. After her husband's death in 2004, she devoted the bulk of her time to helping her children make the transition into the working world, to establishing homes, to beginning families. And now she would like to do what she can to help Palestinians and Israelis overcome their differences and live with one another.

The role of mediator was a familiar one for members of Reem's family going back at least two centuries. Prior to World War I, the al-Nimers had helped locals deal with their Ottoman overlords. This was the Ottoman system: local rule through notable families. The al-Nimer family home in Nablus performed many of the functions we now associate with city hall, the county court, and the local unemployment office.

In 1986, Zafer al-Masri, her uncle on her mother's side, was assassinated in Nablus while acting as mediator. Zafer was an official in local government who served ordinary people in his area. Most of their problems could not be resolved without the consent or acquiescence of the Israeli occupation authorities. The situation left Zafer exposed. He knew this, but he also knew that residents needed the help of local government to survive.

Reem is just beginning to develop a public role as a peace advocate and her ideas are still being formed. Yet the kernel of her thinking is bedded in rich soil: her family's tradition of cooperation, problem solving, and mediation.

As she enters the public arena, Reem faces what seems an impossible obstacle. Her husband, after all, was the one who planned the *Achille Lauro* operation that failed so spectacularly in 1985. The operation became notorious and, adding to the irony, this rather awkward and regrettable incident has been kept alive in public thought as the subject of an opera: John Adam's *The Death of Leon Klinghoffer*. The recent plan of the Metropolitan Opera to perform this opera in New York with simulcasts to movie theaters around the world provoked protest among Jewish groups. *The New York Times* ran a feature article, an editorial, and a fierce letter to the editor by the Klinghoffer family in response to the editorial. In the meantime, Palestinians responded with . . . silence.

The military operation, as planned by Reem's husband, used the Italian cruise liner simply as a means to transport four commandos to an attack on a military target at the Israeli port of Ashdod. The point of the operation was to elicit public sympathy for the Palestinian cause as four young men battled and presumably lost their lives to the far superior Israeli forces. Instead of self-sacrifice, however, what resulted was the death of a tourist taking a cruise—a man who just happened to be elderly, wheel-chair bound, an American, a Jew, the member of a prominent and politically active family, and a resident of New York, the media capital of the world.

Rather than running from the *Achille Lauro* incident, Reem could see that the only possible way forward was to begin her dialogue where the public reporting had left off: with Palestinians in general and her husband in particular tagged as "terrorists." Reem knew that she would have to repeat her husband's apology for the death of Leon Klinghoffer. She knew that she would have to point to her husband's evolution from a fighter to one who accepted peace. And she knew that none of this would be quite enough . . . simply because nothing she could do would remove the *Achille Lauro* from public consciousness.

Still, Reem sensed a possibility here. For, in this conflict, it is very difficult to find anyone whose hands are not stained. Some are marked by their own actions, many more by association. Perhaps, if she spoke with the deep humility of a woman whose shortcomings-by-association had been well established in the media, she could say a few words and others would catch her meaning and then step back from the brink. Reem felt that there was no other way.

In this book, Reem al-Nimer tells the story of her growth over thirty years' time and the parallel evolution of her husband. Violence, she learned, is not the way. Violence is counter-productive.

After Reem and I had been speaking for an hour or two, our café became crowded. Some were grad students from AUB. Some were interns from the nearby hospital. Others were young bankers or sales staff from clothing stores on Rue Hamra. It was time for us to leave, but Reem had one more thought. "To move forward," Reem said, "Palestinians and Israelis alike must acknowledge our shortcomings. And then, without fear, we need to step into the future."

—*Sami Moubayed*

To the memory of my father, Rifaat al-Nimer, my uncle Zafer al-Masri, and my husband Abu al-Abbas: three brave and selfless men who lived and died for Palestine. To the soul of my dear mother Rabiha al-Masri, who left us in December 2013 as this book was being polished.

To my brother Rami and his wife Malak who selflessly runs the Unite Lebanese Youth Project (ULYP), an educational NGO in Beirut. To my sister Rana, who carried on my father's legacy through the Rifaat al-Nimer Foundation.

To these dear children: Louai, Reef, Khaled, Omar, and Ali. Abu al-Abbas loved you all and would have been proud of you today.

Curse of the *Achille Lauro*

Curse of the *Achille Lauro*
A Tribute to Lost Souls

By Reem al-Nimer

Curse of the *Achille Lauro:*
A Tribute to Lost Souls
© 2014 Reem al-Nimer
Cune Press, Seattle 2014
First Edition
2 4 6 8 9 7 5 3

Hardback	ISBN 978-1-61457-077-6	$34.95
Paperback	ISBN 978-1-61457-078-3	$21.95
Kindle	ISBN 978-1-61457-082-0	$ 9.99
eBook	ISBN 978-1-61457-079-0	$ 9.99

Library of Congress Cataloging-in-Publication Data
Al-Nimer, Reem.
Curse of the *Achille Lauro* : a Tribute to Lost Souls / by Reem al-Nimer.
pages cm
Includes bibliographical references and index.

ISBN 978-1-61457-077-6 (hardback : alkaline paper)
ISBN 978-1-61457-078-3 (paperback : alkaline paper)
1. *Achille Lauro* Hijacking Incident, 1985. 2. Terrorism--Mediterranean Region--History--20th century. 3. Asymmetric warfare--History--20th century. 4. 'Abbas, Muhammad, 1948-2004. 5. Generals--Palestine--Biography. 6. Jabhat al-Tahrir al-Filastiniyah--Biography. I. Title.

HV6433.M4A4 2013
363.325092--dc23
[B]
2013033358

Photo Credits:
Cover: Palestinian flag by Garyck Arntzen.
Added Credits: See "Notes on Illustrations"

Select titles in the Bridge Between the Cultures Series:

Curse of the Achille Lauro: A Tribute to Lost Souls - by Reem al-Nimer

The Plain of Dead Cities: A Syrian Tale - by Bruce McLaren

Gulen's Dialogue on Education: A Caravanserai of Ideas - by Tom Gage

Syria - A Decade of Lost Chances: Repression and Revolution from Damascus Spring to Arab Spring - by Carsten Wieland

The Ottoman Mosaic: Exploring Models for Peace by Re-exploring the Past
by Kemal Karpat and Yetkin Yıldırım

Steel & Silk: Men and Women Who Shaped Syria 1900 - 2000 - by Sami Moubayed

The Road from Damascus: A Journey Through Syria - by Scott C. Davis

www.cunepress.com | www.cunepress.net | www.cunepress.info

Find a Glossary with names from Palestinian History mentioned in
The Curse of the Achille Lauro: www.cunepress.com ("Free")

Contents

Table of Illustrations   11
To the Reader   12
Preface   14
- 1982 - 1985: Two Men with Contradictions

C-1 Something Went Horribly Wrong   17
- We Are the World
- 1985: A Rendezvous with Fate
- Arafat & the *Achille Lauro*
- The Law of Unintended Consequences

C-2 Aboard the *Achille Lauro*   28
- The Plan
- Dust vs Elegance: A New Explanation
- Myths about the *Achille Lauro*
- Abu Ammar Takes the Mic

C-3 Mubarak Gives Us a Ride   35
- F-14 Tomcats
- Saved by Italian Prime Minister Bettino Craxi
- Persona Non Grata

C-4 Abu al-Abbas: A Rebel with a Cause   41
- 1948: The *Nakba*
- 1951: Life in the Camps
- 1963: Revolt of the Schoolteachers
- The Palestinian Underground
- 1968: Working as a Schoolteacher

C-5 Rifaat al-Nimer & Our Family   53
- Rifaat's Early Life
- Rifaat's First Banking Job
- My Mother
- Our Family after the 1948 War

- Rifaat's Career in Banking
- 1968: Sweet Sixteen

C-6 Operation Gamal Abdul Nasser   64
- 1961 - 1966: The Palestine Liberation Front (PLF)
- 1977: Abu al-Abbas Revives the PLF
- 1979: Operation Gamal Abdul Nasser

C-7 My Life in Politics   70
- 1970: Flirting with Fatah
- 1971: The PFLP
- 1972: The PRFLP
- Mohammad & Ali
- 1973: The Egyptian Students' Movement
- 1974: Mohammad and I Decide to Marry
- Mohammad Is Kidnapped

C-8 Dark Skies   82
- Causes of the Civil War, Briefly
- 1974: The Arab Communist Organization
- 1975: My First Child
- Ali Is Executed
- A Desperate Proposal
- I Will Take You to Mezzeh!
- Safe in Baghdad
- I Meet Abu al-Abbas

C-9 Our Time in West Africa   94
- 1976: Finding Work in a New City
- 1978: A Gift from My Uncle
- 1980: Return to Beirut
- Divorce
- My Life in Ras Beirut
- 1981: The PLF Flies into Israel
- I Meet Abu al-Abbas and His Family
- 1982: Dating Abu al-Abbas

C-10 The Lebanese Civil War: 1975 - 1982   104
- 1975 - 1978: Background & Early Years
- 1978: Israel Invades Lebanon
- 1982: A Second Israeli Invasion
- Life in Beirut under Israeli Guns
- Back and Forth to Homs
- A Favor for Hafez al-Assad
- An Assassination Attempt
- An Escape to Syria
- Dancing on the Quay
- Massacre at Sabra & Shatila
- 1983: A Tête à Tête with the *Mukhabarat*

C-11 Life in Baghdad   124
- 1985: Our Villa Near Abu Nuwas Street
- 1986: Zafer al-Masri
- 1986: An Interview with NBC News
- The PLF in Baghdad
- 1987: The First Intifada
- 1988: A Feud Ends

C-12 The Jerusalem Sea Operation   131
- 1988: Arafat's Honeymoon with the US
- Gaddafi Makes Contact
- Why Gaddafi Wanted to Strike Israel
- 1989: A Project in Libya
- 1990: The Jerusalem Sea Operation
- Reasons for the Jerusalem Sea Operation
- A Telephone Number

C-13 Early Retirement   142
- Teach the Children
- 1990: Iraq Invades Kuwait
- 1991: Surprise, Surprise!
- The Children Return
- 1991: The Madrid Conference

- 1992: Crossing Uday Hussein
- 1993: Plastic Explosive in Kuwait City
- 1993: The Oslo Accords
- An Evening with the Arafats
- Finding Jobs
- 1996: Arafat Calls a Meeting
- 1996: Abu al-Abbas Travels to Gaza

C-14 A Final Journey to Palestine   157
- 2000: Twenty-four Hours on the Road

C-15 The Iraq War   161
- 2001: The Middle East Conflict Comes to America
- Oil & Water
- Life on Abu Nuwas Street
- 2001: The US Invades Afghanistan
- 2003: The Iraq War
- Escape, Or Not
- A Trip to Nowhere
- Apaches
- US Detention
- Yarmouk

Epilogue: A Note on Terror   182
- Zafer al-Masri: The Death of a Good Man
- A TV Movie Starring Karl Malden
- 9/11

Resources
End Notes   188
Notes on Illustrations   191
Glossary*   (See cunepress.com/free)
Further Reading   192
Index   194
Acknowledgements   199
Author   200

*See www.cunepress.com. Click on "Free" in the header.

Table of Illustrations

0.1	Reem al-Nimer and Yasser Arafat in Tunis, 1985	14
4.1	PFLP poster commemorating the *Nakba*	42
4.2	Abu al-Abbas as a college student	47
5.1	Rifaat al-Nimer holding Reem as a baby	53
5.2	Rabiha and Reem, 1954	56
5.3	A young Reem dancing in the sand, 1956	56
5.4	Reem dancing in restaurant, 1956	56
5.5	Rifaat and Rabiha cruising on a lake, 1957	57
5.6	Reem cruising on a lake, 1957	57
5.7	Reem and Rabiha in their Ras Beirut home, 1966	60
5.8	Reem with a Marlboro, 1968	62
5.9	Reem at Victoria College, 1969	62
5.10	Victoria College closeup	63
6.1	PFLP 10th anniversary poster, 1977	65
6.2	Newspaper report of the Abdul Nasser Operation	68
7.1	PFLP poster	72
7.2	PFLP logo	72
7.3	PLO logo	73
7.4	Fatah logo	73
7.5	PLF logo	73
7.6	PFLP-GC logo	72
7.7	Poster photo of Che Guevara by Alberto Korda	75
9.1	PLF poster: "Operation Martyr Kamal Nasser"	102
9.2	PLF poster: "Heroes of the Kamal Jumblatt Operation"	102
9.3	Reem al-Nimer	103
10.1	Cover of a PFLP publication	106
10.2	Legends of the resistance	108
11.1	Abu al-Abbas in Baghdad, 1986	125
11.2	Abu al-Abbas and Reem in their villa in Baghdad, 1986	125
11.3	Reem, Ali, and Abu al-Abbas at a wedding in Baghdad	126
11.4	Zafer al-Masri	127
15.1	Abu al-Abbas in US detention, 2003	175
15.2	Reem and her sons with Rocky the dog	176
15.3	The casket of Abu al-Abbas: Yarmouk refugee camp, March 2004	179
15.4	Reem at her husband's funeral in Yarmouk	180
16.1	January, 2004. A letter from Abu al-Abbas to his youngest son Ali	183
16.2	The casket of Abu al-Abbas is raised by the crowd in Yarmouk	186
16.3	Reem al-Nimer	206

To the Reader

Mohammad al-Abbas was given the name Muhammad Zaidan (also transliterated from Arabic as Muhammad Zaydan or Zeidan) at birth and is listed under this name in Wikipedia. Friends and family referred to him as Abu Khaled (the father of Khaled, as is customary in Arab society). Or they used his *nom de guerre* Abu al-Abbas (often spelled phonetically in news reports as Abul Abbas). It is the latter form that we use in this book almost exclusively. Abu al-Abbas was a Palestinian military commander who became active in the 1970s—and should not be confused with the contemporary leader of the Palestinian Authority, Mahmoud Abbas.

In the late 1980s, Abu al-Abbas became a media figure that was sought after by *CNN*, the *New York Times*, *NBC*, and others up to the time of the Iraq War in 2003. One of his more memorable interviews was with Christiane Amanpour.

Abu al-Abbas was physically imposing, a large man whom the *Telegraph* would describe as "bold and charismatic." I was his confidant, his wife, and the mother of his children. We were together from 1980 until his death in US custody in 2004.[1]

Abu al-Abbas had strong links to Yasser Arafat, chairman of the Palestine Liberation Organization (PLO). Although the two men had many differences, Abu al-Abbas regarded Arafat as the historic leader of the Palestinian Cause. For his part, Arafat endorsed Abu al-Abbas as the military face of the Palestinian resistance at some times and then, at other times distanced himself. Arafat tended to favor Abu al-Abbas when talking to Arab audiences and often put him at arm's length when talking to western audiences. Never, however, did Arafat restrict the access of Abu al-Abbas to the media. Although many of the military operations of Abu al-Abbas failed to attain their tactical objectives, they were nevertheless effective statements of resistance that drew attention to injustice in Palestine. Even his opponents conceded that, as a media figure, Abu al-Abbas was highly successful in putting a Palestinian perspective into the public arena in the US and Europe.

The interest of the international media in Abu al-Abbas was based on a single event. In 1985 Israel and the PLO were engaged in tit for tat attacks (a similar pattern of attacks had been going on at various levels of intensity since the creation of the State of Israel after termination of the British Mandate in 1948). When the Israeli air force dropped bombs on Tunis, aiming at the PLO headquarters, more than 200 civilians were killed. In response, Arafat chose to retaliate by giving Abu al-Abbas the green light for a rather unorthodox operation.

The plan was for several young Palestinian fighters to disguise themselves as tourists and to travel from Alexandria to the Israeli port of Ashdod on an Italian ocean liner. Once on land, they were to attack Israeli troops guarding the harbor. Hardly had the ocean liner left port when the young men were discovered—and their plan utterly fell apart. In the absence of instructions for this eventuality, they took control of the ship, demanded the release of fifty Palestinian prisoners in Israeli jails, and directed the ship to sail to the Syrian port of Tartous. When the Syrians refused permission to land, they returned to Port Said, Egypt. At this point Abu al-Abbas approached the ocean liner in a speedboat and instructed the hijackers to surrender without harming any more passengers. Soon after, they left the ship and placed themselves in Egyptian custody. In the middle of their zig zag course across the Eastern Mediterranean, they killed an elderly man in a wheel chair: sixty-nine-year-old Leon Klinghoffer, a New York Jew.

The point of the attacks in 1985 was international media and the sympathy they could elicit for the Palestinian Cause in the West. By this measure, the *Achille Lauro* operation must be regarded as one of the least successful military actions in Palestinian history. The PLO paid blood money and apologized to the Klinghoffer family for their loss. Later, Abu al-Abbas also made clear that Palestinian military operations should never target civilians—even though some of his past military actions had crossed this line. The *Achille Lauro*, as it turned out, had the unintended and surprising side effect of raising the visibility of Abu al-Abbas among Arabs. This deeply flawed and overtly unsuccessful operation established Abu al-Abbas among Palestinians and other Arabs as a champion.

Over the years, Abu al-Abbas evolved. Eventually, he accepted and in so doing legitimized the Oslo Peace Accord of 1993 which recognized Israel's right to exist. Thanks to his notoriety as a military commander, Abu al-Abbas's endorsement of Oslo was key to giving this agreement traction and credibility among Palestinians. One could argue that the death of Leon Klinghoffer on the *Achille Lauro* shocked the world so deeply that it marked a turning point for the combatants—who could not deny that the humanity of ordinary people trumped any pretext for violence.

As for his personal reputation and the verdict of history, Abu al-Abbas was well aware that nothing he could do or say would outweigh a single event: He was cursed by the *Achille Lauro*.

Preface
1982 - 1985: Contradictions

Tunis. 1985.

"Get ready. We leave to Yugoslavia in one hour!" Yasser Arafat announced.

Yasser Arafat, whose *nom de guerre* was Abu Ammar, was the leader of Fatah—a group he helped to found in 1959 with several Palestinian professionals working in the Arab Gulf. Arafat was also head of the Palestine Liberation Organization (PLO) which had been created January 17, 1964 by the Arab League in Cairo. Power rested less with the Palestinian National Council (PNC), than with its eighteen member Executive Committee. Arafat served as Chairman of the PLO Executive Committee from February 1969 until his death in 2004.[1]

On this morning in Tunis, Arafat was speaking to Abu al-Abbas, leader of the Palestine Liberation Front (PLF) and one of Arafat's top lieutenants: the previous November Arafat had publicly elevated him to membership in the PLO Executive Committee.[2] At the time, Abu al-Abbas and I had been happily married for nearly five years. Arafat and Abu al-Abbas were based in Tunis, and Yugoslavia was one of their many communist allies during the Cold War. It was 9:00 AM and they were scheduled to take off aboard a private plane at 10:00 AM. Abu al-Abbas groaned as he quickly got dressed, complaining,

Yasser Arafat and Reem al-Nimer in Tunis, 1985.

"These rollercoaster journeys with Arafat are just too much. We rush from one place to another, and he wants to finish everything and meet everyone in a matter of hours. He lives off a plane, and we don't even get the chance to eat or rest properly when flying with him." Arafat had promised that they would be back in Tunis by early evening.

Abu al-Abbas returned home to our two story villa at twilight as expected—completely exhausted. He immediately went upstairs to take a shower, while I went to the kitchen to prepare a meal. True to his reputation, Arafat had not given them a moment to rest or even to eat. I arranged an unusually large tray of dishes. When walking through the garden, I glimpsed a big black cat sitting there, staring at me with two large eyes that shined in the dim light from the terrace above. Although I have carried AK-47s in my life and engaged in my share of Palestinian adventurism, I was nevertheless ailurophobic—I had an irrational fear of cats. Screaming like mad, I dropped the huge tray, and everything upon it was smashed to pieces. Upstairs, Abu al-Abbas heard my shrieks and the sound of shattering glass. As far as he was concerned, the Israelis had just landed a commando force in our patio and I was being held from behind with a bayonet to my throat. He grabbed his sidearm, rushed out half-naked, and pointed it right at me. "What's wrong?" He froze, finger on trigger, ready to shoot.

"Ehhhh . . . *habibi* . . . it's a cat!"

"What?"

"It's a big fat cat."

"A *cat*? All of that noise was because of a miserable cat?"

Abu al-Abbas went *majnoon*, as we say—completely crazy. He waved his rifle in the air, "I swear to God that if this happens again, I won't think twice before shooting. This is outrageous! You are married to a Palestinian commando, Reem! You cannot do something this crazy."

This story speaks to the contradictions in my character. In my youth I helped to train Palestinian *fedayeen* or commandos. With a partner, I planned military operations including an attack in Damascus on the Syrian Ministry of Defense. I have been WANTED by the intelligence agencies of Lebanon, Syria, and Israel—and there was also that incident in Cairo. I have been smuggled through borders on fake passports more times that I can count. And I have lived through eleven wars. Yet here I was, rather foolishly, terrified at the sight of a small whiskered animal. But that was me, a bundle of contradictions.

I was born into Palestinian notability, yet lived my life in camps, slept in caves, and counted communists as my friends. I hate dictators, as did my husband, yet he was protected and financed at various times by Saddam Hussein, Muammar al-Gaddafi, and Hafez al-Assad. On the battlefields of south Lebanon, I have held the wounded in my arms as they whispered their last words, glanced toward heaven, and then departed this life. Yet I nearly faint when I see a cat.

Despite his reputation, my husband was a soft man at heart. The Israeli intelligence service Mossad had put a price on his head, yet Abu al-Abbas had a fear—not of combat or jail or assassination—but of water and swimming. He acquired this phobia as a child. Once, while his mother was bathing him in a small pond in the Palestinian camp of Neirab near Aleppo Syria, he nearly drowned. I only discovered his phobia late into our marriage—after he had mercilessly poked fun at my cat-phobia.

After Abu al-Abbas tried to dodge a missile during the Lebanese Civil War and came away with a head wound that scarred his head, the Soviets sent him to USSR for medical treatment. Part of the treatment required him to relax in a large tub of warm water, with water jets spraying his body while he was massaged by a Russian physiotherapist. The Russian in question was in her twenties, a tall voluptuous blonde who seemed impressed with this wounded hero from a faraway war. "I will go in with you," I said. He curtly refused, giving me a look that said, "She's going to teach me Russian and I don't want to be embarrassed in front of you"—or some other spin of the sort that husbands pull out of their back pockets in situations like these. In truth, of course, he was hiding his water phobia. A little later, I heard noises that seemed to indicate that language study had gone too far. I threw open the door—only to see the brave Palestinian commando, collapsed in the tub like a teabag. The Russian kept replenishing the tub with warm water. Whenever the water came too close to his face, Abu al-Abbas writhed and clawed at the edge of the tub like a little child who feared he was drowning.

"So much for cat-phobia," I said to him, unable to wipe the smirk off my face.

This book tells the unusual story of a couple who were highly compatible and complemented one another perfectly—yet occasionally broke out in fierce disagreement. We shared a love of Palestine and of our children and of quiet conversation in the middle of a world that at times seemed to have gone utterly mad. We shared a love of every innocent being on earth, everyone who loved their homes and families and who longed for justice and redemption—without exception. Our time together speaks of forbearance, honor, good faith, and chivalry. This is the story of my life with Abu al-Abbas.

1
Something Went Horribly Wrong

Tunis. October 7, 1985. 8:00 AM.

I WOKE UP EARLY, MADE COFFEE, and gathered the morning newspapers, and sat on the small balcony of our house above the garden. We were living in Tunis, along with other exiled Palestinians. (In 1982 the Palestine Liberation Organization (PLO) had been forced to leave Beirut.) The house where Abu al-Abbas and I lived was a cozy two-floor villa in al-Manzah al-Khames, a residential compound in the heart of the Tunisian capital. The house was given to us by the PLO and was located next to the Palestinian news agency. It was a simple yet functional temporary home for our small family. What mattered was that it suited my husband's work, the military struggle for the liberation of Palestine. Abu al-Abbas and I had been married for three years. A few days earlier, and like any young couple, we had quarreled, and he had left the house in an outburst of temper. I had no clue where he had gone. I was angry and insisted to myself that I did not even care.

We Are the World

I flipped through the international papers and magazines, reading snippets of news here and there. "Nothing about Palestine," I muttered to myself. Ronald Reagan was in the White House and civil war was raging in Lebanon. International media was interested in Michael Jackson's rise in the pop music industry. Two years earlier Jackson had splashed into public consciousness—his Ed Sullivan moment, so to speak—when a Motown TV special aired in front of forty-seven million TV viewers, and Jackson rocked the house with a performance of *Billie Jean* that included a killer dance move, his distinctive moonwalk. Just this year, in March 1985, he released *We Are the World* which ultimately sold twenty million albums and was featured in a Pepsi commercial that traveled around the globe. Where in this coverage was anything to be heard of Palestine or the Arabs? We were ants in a land of giants. How could we hope to put our case for justice in Palestine before the world if we had to compete with a slender young man in sequins and the world-beating media power of major corporations such as Pepsi?

Our small TV set was tuned to *Rai Uno*, which beamed into Tunisian homes, during this pre-cable era, thanks to our proximity with Italy. Although none of us understood Italian, we often watched it because the channel was more colorful, flashy, and informative than strictly controlled state-run Tunisian TV. *Rai Uno* was our only televised access to the outside world. The phone rang, and Khalil Abdul Rahman was on the other end of the line.

Khalil was the Palestine Liberation Front's representative in Cyprus, someone who my husband trusted and liked. (The PLF was a Palestinian resistance group that was represented on the PLO's executive committee by Abu al-Abbas.) *"Wane al-rafiq?"* he asked. "Where is the comrade?" He was rather impatient, skipping the customary small talk. He seemed agitated, tense. *"Mabarref,"* I murmured, "I don't know." On the TV screen in front of me were big bold leaders flashing in Marlboro red: BREAKING NEWS. I of course couldn't understand a single word, as everything was in Italian. But I did recognize the brochure of the Italian cruise ship, the *Achille Lauro*, when they flashed it on the screen. Apparently, somebody had hijacked the luxury ship during its twelve-day journey from Genoa, Italy, to Ashdod, Israel, and taken its passengers hostage. I had seen the exact same brochure before—in my house—on the coffee table next to my bed. Abu al-Abbas had brought several copies home, and it never occurred to me to ask why they were there. Looking back now, nearly thirty years later, I am not sure why I never asked and why he kept them so carelessly lying around the house. He certainly wasn't preparing to take me on the cruise, since the security requirements of his job prevented him from such indulgences. Was he trying, however, to send me a message? Was he trying to tell me, "Pay attention to the *Achille Lauro!*"

"Wait . . . wait," I yelped at Khalil. "I know that ship. I've seen the brochure!" I was pointing frantically to the screen. He must have smiled on the other end of the phone, "That's it! This is our operation! Thank you." If the ship's brochure was lying around in our house, Khalil reasoned, then Abu al-Abbas was definitely behind its capture. He hung up, leaving me completely in the dark. Still, I felt in my bones that this ship would change our lives forever.

1985: A Rendezvous with Fate

The *MS Achille Lauro* was a luxury cruise ship based in Naples, Italy that engineers started working on in 1939. Outbreak of the Second World War interrupted the ship's construction, and it was not put into operation until July 1946, originally named after the grandson of its founder, *Willem Ruys*, who had been killed during the war.[1] In 1965, she was sold to the Flotta Lauro Line, or Star Lauro, (now MSC Cruises) and renamed the *Achille Lauro* (after the company owner). Extensively rebuilt and modernized after an August 1965 aboard explosion, the *Achille Lauro* entered service in 1966 carrying passengers to Sydney, Australia. It was converted into a cruise ship in early 1972. Shortly afterward, however, she suffered a disastrous fire. A 1975 a collision with the cargo ship *Youseff* resulted in the sinking of the latter, and another aboard fire in 1981 took her out of service for a time.[2]

On this day in October 1985, the *Achille Lauro* was sailing the eastern Mediterranean, toward Port Said in Egypt, before docking in the Israeli port of Ashdod. Four of Abu al-Abbas's men were aboard, all below the age of twenty-five: Majid Yusuf al-Molqi (23), Ahmad Maarouf al-Assadi (23), Ibrahim Fatayer Abdul-Latif (20), and Bassam al-Achkar (17).[3] They were preparing to disembark at the port of Ashdod and to carry out an armed attack against Israeli soldiers and custom officials who defended the harbor.[4] Abu al-Abbas was very excited about it.[5]

At this time, my husband was thirty-seven years old. The *Achille Lauro* Operation was supposed to be the highlight of his life-long military struggle against Israel.[6] In the post 9/11 world, such attacks are generally condemned as "terrorist operations." In 1985 the world was no less quick to condemn the operation. But for us in the PLF, at the height of the Palestinian military struggle for liberation, military and official targets were fair game. We were at war. We were firmly convinced that every spot of land within Israel/Palestine was a legitimate battlefield. We thought of every Israeli as part of the problem. Although the PLF targeted Israeli military and officials rather than civilians, even then civilian casualties sometimes resulted, earning the PLF a spot on the US State Department's list of Foreign Terrorist Organizations. From the perspective of 2014, our actions seem callous or cruel. At the time, we felt that there was no alternative.

Palestinians had been forcibly removed from their land in 1948 and the refugees herded into camps or exiled from the country. A generation later, in 1967, we were still living in camps and still had received no right of return, no compensation, no official apology. At this moment Israel launched the Six Day War, taking control of all remaining Palestinian territory, the land from the Jordan to the Mediterranean. Now, in 1985, another generation had passed. We were still living in camps. And Israel had still not responded to our grievances. Our homeland remained occupied. Three years earlier, the massacre at Sabra and Shatila in Beirut by a Christian militia while these camps were under Israeli control claimed at least 800 - 3,500 victims.

Even many Israeli writers acknowledge that the plight of Palestinians living in camps and Israeli prisons was horrific. Our actions were the desperate cry of a proud people who had lost everything and had no recourse. Our only chance was to attract the attention of fair-minded souls in the international community.

Looking back on the operation in 2012, one of the hijackers, Bassam al-Achkar (who was seventeen at the time) said, "Abu al-Abbas's prime objective was transferring the struggle from the Diaspora, into the heart of occupied Palestine. He wanted to bring arms to our people in the West Bank via the Jordanian border, and to northern Palestine via Lebanon, and to Gaza via Egyptian territory. Our last supply route was via the sea, and this is how the *Achille Lauro* Operation came into being. It all started when Abu al-Abbas stood on the balcony of an apartment in Algiers, overlooking the port. He suddenly noticed how busy the sea traffic was and how painful it would be for Israel if he were to strike at any of its sea entrances.[7]" He summoned an elderly comrade named Abu Ammar who worked aboard a Greek liner and was one of our most prolific intelligence officers in Europe. "I wanted a full report on the occupied ports of Haifa, Jaffa, and Ashdod," he later said to me. "This is Israel's weak spot!"

Tunis. October 7, 1985. 10:00 AM.

Khalil Abdul Rahman ended his call. Between him and the Italian station Rai Uno, I knew that the *Achille Lauro* was more than a tourist cruise ship: it was an operation. I dressed quickly and rushed to the PLF's nearby office, desperate for information. "If Mohammad is behind this and I am the last to know," I told myself, "I am going to show him when he gets back!" Storming out of the house, I noticed the guard Abu Ghazzi and snapped, "When did Abu al-Abbas leave?" Abu Ghazzi, as usual, knew absolutely nothing. "Where did he go?" I asked.

Abu Ghazzi just looked at me with a blank expression on his face. The PLF offices were located in Hammam al-Shatt, twelve miles from the capital, near the PLO's military base and headquarters. It was a modest apartment on the first floor of a colorless building, with no sign post, but everyone in the Tunisian capital, and certainly the Mossad, knew that this was the office of Abu al-Abbas. At the gate I came across Hussein al-Abed, another trusted associate of my husband, who was a prominent member of the Palestinian Workers' Union in Tunisia. We spoke for a few moments, but he, apparently, knew no more than I did. All that we learned was that the ship had tried to dock in Syria, but was denied entry into Syrian waters by President Hafez al-Assad. The Syrians were never too fond of Abu al-Abbas, although he had been raised and educated in Damascus. Abu al-Abbas refused to be a yes-man for the Baathist regime.[8] The captors issued proclamations. "If the Red Cross does not come to our rescue in Syrian waters," they threatened, "we will start killing the passengers, three at a time." Their idea was to force the international community to act. Although they said that they had indeed killed three American passengers and even gave their names, making use of the passports they had collected at the beginning of the siege, the story was baseless.[9] At that point, they thought of heading to Lebanon and disembarking on lifeboats while using the passengers as a shield to protect them from the US Sixth Fleet, rumored to be sailing toward them and preparing for a military takeover of the *Achille Lauro*.[10] Instead of staying in Syrian or Lebanese waters, however, the ship sailed to Egypt and the arms of President Husni Mubarak.

The Cairo government was suffering from an Arab boycott at the time and was completely alienated from the Arab World. It was shunned by the Arab League—and the Palestinians at large—for making peace with Israel in the 1978 Egyptian-Israeli Camp David Accords. Mubarak, who inherited bad blood with the Arabs from his predecessor Anwar al-Sadat, was only four years into office, and he was dying for Arab attention. My guess is that he allowed the *Achille Lauro* into Egyptian waters in order to re-invent himself, and his country, as a credible broker in the Arab-Israeli Conflict. The *Achille Lauro* was a godsend for the Egyptian President, giving him the chance to re-establish contact with the Palestinian leadership and to be seen as solving the crisis using his wide network of friends in the US and Europe.

By noon, Monte Carlo radio had picked up the story, but still, there was absolutely nothing on Tunisian TV. Realizing that the PLF offices were useless, I headed to the headquarters of Fatah, to meet PLO Chairman Yasser Arafat. If Arafat could not help me find Abu al-Abbas and tell me more about the *Achille Lauro*, then no one could. Nothing ever passed in Palestinian politics, after all, without the overt or covert blessing of the PLO Chairman, whom we affectionately called *al-Ikhtiyar* (the Old Man) although Arafat was relatively still young back then, only fifty-seven.

The offices of Fatah were swarming with people. Unlike the modest offices of the PLF, they looked like the headquarters of an international corporation: fax machines, secretaries wearing eyeglasses and long skirts, television sets, and staff members running back and forth. The staff were busy taking notes and talking on the phone, answering to the slightest whim of the highly demanding Arafat. In those days, Arafat had more energy than everyone else in the room put together. The Chairman's bureau chief Ramzi Khoury was there, as I recall. I admired Arafat and so did my entire generation of Palestinians. I held him in high respect and esteem as "godfather" of the Palestinian struggle. When I walked into his private office, Arafat was behind his desk, his black & white checkered *kuffiyeh* neatly draped over his shoulder in the diamond shape of the map of Palestine—dramatic as ever. He looked at me, smiled warmly, and addressed me in his Egyptian dialect (taken from his early years in Gaza) as "*Yakhti*" (My Sister). "*Yakhti*, we are working closely with the Egyptians (on the ship crisis)." Arafat had jumped to the point, sparing me the agony of explanation and too many questions. I politely asked, "Is Abu al-Abbas in Egypt?" Arafat—or Abu Ammar as we called him—was a brilliant politician who only disclosed information on a need-to-know basis. He shook his head, claiming that he did not know, but promised, "We will find out." He was hiding the truth from me. Arafat knew perfectly well the whereabouts of Abu al-Abbas but for security purposes was unwilling to reveal them, even to me.

Arafat & the *Achille Lauro*

Later, Abu al-Abbas told me how he got Arafat's approval and funding for the *Achille Lauro* project. "I always have military operations mapped out in specific detail, ready for implementation," he said. "All they need is political cover, funds, and men to carry them out." When the Israelis attacked Hammam al-Shat, I went to Arafat and said, "I have an operation ready that will shake them. It would be perfect revenge." Abu Ammar nodded, "Go ahead and do it. May God be with you!" As Abu al-Abbas explained later, "He didn't want to go into specifics. He gave his green light, and purposely walked away, leaving me to sort out the details."

Let me explain for a moment the dance that we were doing with the Israelis in those days. We were like boxers trading jabs with Israel, back and forth, back and forth.

We launched the *Achille Lauro* operation (which I believe had been planned or largely planned over the two preceding years) as a response to the Israeli attack on the PLO's seaside headquarters in the Hamman al-Shat district of Tunis which took place six days earlier on October 1, 1985. In this long range mission, which probably involved US knowledge and/or assistance, Israeli fighter jets destroyed the PLO compound and killed, according to some sources, more than 50 Palestinians and 215 Tunisian civilians as well as wounding 100. In the international outcry that followed, President Reagan followed his initial remarks labeling the action as a "legitimate response to terror" by saying that the attack "cannot be condoned."

The Hamman al-Shat attack was, in turn, the Israeli response to the attack seven days earlier on September 25, 1985 by Force 17 fighters from the

PLO who captured an Israeli yacht that was cruising near Larnaca, Cyprus and executed three Israeli tourists. Or were they Mossad agents monitoring Palestinian naval traffic in the Mediterranean? Israel had, after all, been attacking Palestinian shipping in the Eastern Mediterranean.

The Larnaca operation itself was retaliation for the Israeli kidnapping, fourteen days earlier on September 11, of the Force 17 commander Faisal Abu Shara as he sailed between Beirut and Larnaca. Abu Shara was sent to Israel for interrogation and a lengthy prison term.

Most Americans think of their own country in the mid-1980s as being above the fray rather than as participants in this dance of death. (I am thinking of a time that predated the Gulf War in 1991, the War in Afghanistan in 2001, the Iraq War in 2003, and the drone campaigns in Pakistan and Yemen that began in earnest in 2008.) In these years, the US military was less easily associated with unnecessary civilian casualties.

Still, before Americans label the *Achille Lauro* a terrorist incident, and before they condemn Israelis and Palestinians for the primitive cycle of killing and revenge of these years, they should consider an incident on March 8, 1985. In Beirut on this date, a massive car bomb exploded, destroyed a whole block of multi-story apartments, and killed several dozen civilians who had just left a mosque after Friday prayers. The target of the blast was the Hezbollah spiritual leader Imam Hussein Fadlallah, who was not home at the time. The devastation, according to Bob Woodward in his book *Veil,* was the result of a CIA operation financed by the Saudis. Some have speculated that this action was a US response to three Hezbollah attacks on the US facilities in 1983 and 1984. Was the US action terrorism? Was the US, like the Palestinians and Israelis, involved in the barbaric business of seeking revenge for loss of life?

The *pas de deux* of action and response involved twenty or more attacks and counter attacks in 1985 alone. The players were Israel with backing from the US on one side and the PLO with backing from the Soviets on the other. Thrown into the mix was the renegade Abu Nidal and state actors such as Syria and Libya . . . all of whom were enemies to Israel and the US but who also, at various times, opposed Arafat's PLO.

Were all of the participants terrorist groups or terrorist nations? What is the difference between terrorism and an honorable military action? Can we say that the Israeli attack on Hamman al-Shat was a classic military action because it involved long range strike by fighter jets, refueled by a Boeing 707 over the Mediterranean? On the other hand, was the hijacking of a pleasure yacht and the execution of three Israelis tourists in Larnaca terrorism because it involved taking life face-to-face? The three Israelis were given the chance to write out their last thoughts before they were executed. This detail brought home to Israelis the humanity of the victims and solidified the characterization of this action as terrorism. Even if we assume that the three Israelis were tourists and not part of the ongoing Mossad operation to disrupt Palestinian shipping in the area, there is still the point that the Hamman al-Shat attack, whether you call it terrorism or a military action, killed over 200 Tunisian civilians, nearly seventy times more than the death toll in Larnaca. Are some lives worth more than others? Perhaps the distinction between a "terrorist attack" and a "military operation" is in the eye of the beholder.

Israel considered Palestinian operations to be "terrorism" and vice versa. Both sides were engaged in a media battle. Whose definition of terrorism would stick in the public mind? Whose definition would gain international sympathy? Should these incidents make the world think about the unaddressed grievances of Palestinians? Or, were they a police matter that required a brutal response. If the label of "terrorism" could be made to stick on Palestinian actions, then a "throw out the rules" brand of "counter-terrorism" could be justified. This brings us full circle. The US under Reagan was focusing on counter-terrorism rather than attempting to solve the problem at its source by bringing some measure of justice to the Palestinians. Indeed, on March 24, 1985 the *Washington Post* reported that the US had counter-terrorism teams in twelve nations.

It was of utmost importance to the Palestinian cause that it win international support for its perspective on the Israeli-Palestinian conflict. Palestinians needed to make the point that solving the root cause of the problem, injustice toward Palestinians, should be the focus of international concern—not the effort to combat terrorism. And so we come full circle to the *Achille Lauro* affair.

Tunis. October 7, 1985. 2:00 PM.

I was distraught. The Italian TV news told me that the *Achille Lauro* had been hijacked. I deduced that my husband, Abu al-Abbas was involved. The PLF offices of my husband had been a desert of information and Yasser Arafat had been friendly but evasive. Where was my husband? I had been holding back tears since first hearing of the operation earlier in the day. The children were at a boarding school in Tunis. Now, I cried my heart out, certain that no one would hear me in this weak moment. I was still crying when the telephone rang. This time it was my cousin Lutof al-Qaddumi, the son of PLO chief Farouk al-Qaddumi (Abu al-Lutof). An industrialist by profession, Lutof had distanced himself from politics, by choice, but knew the Palestinian scene and its traumas inside out. While his father was visiting the US, Lutof had room at his place. "Come stay with us," he said. "My father wants you to come. It's not safe for you to stay home anymore, all alone." I accepted his suggestion without argument, like a dutiful little girl who had no idea why and no clue where she was going.

The Law of Unintended Consequences

Amman. October 6, 1985.

The day before my world fell apart, Abu al-Abbas was in Amman, Jordan, where he had been attending the annual meeting of the Palestinian Executive Council. He was scheduled to arrive in Tunis on October 6, the night before his men on the *Achille Lauro* were supposed to dock in Israel and display their weapons. In an odd omission, however, he had not reserved his return flight. The four daily flights from Amman to Tunis were all fully booked, due to the high number of Palestinian politicians returning from Amman to Tunis once the conference ended. Instead, Abu al-Abbas flew to Cairo where he planned to catch a flight the following day to Tunis . . . still ahead of the landfall of the *Achille Lauro* at Ashdod and in time to manage the operation. The delay would not matter—unless, of course, something went wrong.

The error in failing to book his flight from Amman was not characteristic of Abu al-Abbas, who paid close attention to the details of any military action. He had been planning the *Achille Lauro* operation for nearly two years. He had a surgeon's eye for perfection, as even his enemies reported. He had sent his men aboard the *Achille Lauro* twice before the operation, which actually cost him a lot of money. He knew its deck, its bunkers, its lifeboats, its staff and their nationalities, its route, and had recorded the exact times—by minute and second—in which IDF guards arrived on duty and were changed at the Israeli port of Ashdod.

Although Abu al-Abbas had done some careful planning for the *Achille Lauro* operation, consider on the other hand, that any physical action taken by a group of people is subject to snafus. The default result of group action is chaos. That's why dance teams practice their moves, revise and perfect their choreography, and work on their timing for day after day. Try some time to cook and serve a meal for ten people. It's easier to do all the work yourself than to work with helpers. Have you ever cooked a main dish? It helps to create the same dish several times. Success depends on very small differences in heat, time, type of oven, and the spices and other ingredients—not to mention the order of composition and the use of substitute ingredients when you suddenly run out of the ingredient you had planned. Constant redo and rework and learning from your mistakes is part of the process of creating a successful dance performance or cooking and serving a meal or creating a main dish. It is the way that real tasks in the real world are accomplished because physical actions, however simple in conception, are extremely complex to implement.

The problem in warfare is that commandos can't easily undertake an action two or three or more times in order to gain experience. That's why major nations invest in training sites in secret locations far away from prying eyes with model buildings, passageways, squares, streets, shops—in order to anticipate the unknowns that will arise when the operation goes live. Training to this degree of expense was well beyond the means of the PLF, especially after the Syrians closed down their training facilities in Homs two years before the *Achille Lauro*. And yet, this type of training in depth was especially important for the type of bold and unorthodox military operations that formed in the mind of Abu al-Abbas.

The primary obstacle that Abu al-Abbas faced, however, was not personnel or training. It was timing. The operation did not move forward at the moment when the training was complete and every detail was in place. Rather, it was implemented based on the political need. After the Israeli airstrike on Hamman al-Shat in Tunis, the PLO wanted to respond within two weeks. That meant that young men and their weapons needed to be dispatched to Italy immediately. Was the missing detail of a flight booking from Amman evidence that, despite the long range planning that Abu al-Abbas had done for the *Achille Lauro* operation, the need to quickly put this operation into action meant that last minute arrangements had been made hastily. Is it possible that this haste contributed to the failure of the operation?

In Cairo, Abu al-Abbas checked into the Hyatt Regency Hotel where he registered using a fake passport. Staying at the same hotel was Hani al-Hasan (Abu Tarek), Arafat's envoy to Germany and a good friend of Abu al-Abbas. Before going to bed, the two men arranged to have breakfast together.

Cairo. October 6, 1985. 8:30 AM.

The next morning when my husband called Abu Tarek for breakfast, the envoy was overwrought. "I cannot make it," he said. "I have just been contacted by Egyptian Intelligence. I have to go there immediately. A cruise ship has just been hijacked in Egyptian waters, and they feel that Palestinian militants are behind it." Abu al-Abbas could not believe what he was hearing—hijacking the *Achille Lauro* had nothing to do with his plan. Something must have gone horribly wrong.

"I am coming with you," he blurted out. The two men rushed out of the hotel while Abu al-Abbas explained. "I think," he said, "I think that this operation is mine!" He later would recall the timidity of the diplomat. "Hani al-Hasan realized that what was happening was very serious," he explained. "He preferred to completely distance himself from it, letting me sort out my own mess."

2
Aboard the *Achille Lauro*

W**HAT ACTUALLY HAPPENED ABOARD THE *ACHILLE LAURO*?** This was a mystery that haunted Abu al-Abbas until his death. Apparently, the four young men aboard the *Achille Lauro,* disguised as wealthy passengers with Latin American passports, had been *forced by events* to hijack the ship.

The Plan
"Their plan," Abu al-Abbas used to say, "was not to take the ship or anybody hostage, certainly not to harm any of the passengers. They had one enemy in sight: Israeli soldiers at the port of Ashdod. That is why I trained them and sent them numerous times aboard the ship, in order to carry out an honorable operation against the Israeli Army. Had I wanted them to hijack the ship, they would have done it from the start. I wanted them to reach Ashdod, not to fight the passengers on board."

There are various theories about how things went wrong. One story held that, while the operatives were fixing their weapons in their rooms, a waiter had burst in. Seeing the weapons, with people speaking Arabic, he raised the alarm and began screaming for help.

Another story cites fumes. Before boarding the ship, the weapons had been hidden in the gas tank of a car parked on Italian territory.[1] As a result, the arms smelled of gasoline, and this aroused suspicion of the housekeeping teams aboard the *Achille Lauro*. First, they thought the smell was coming from leaks within the ship itself. The four young Palestinians, suffering from the same fumes inside their rooms, took out the weapons to dry them with a hairdryer.[2] Bassam al-Achkar claims that he was not there when this was done, having embarked on a stroll around the ship, mingling with passengers.[3] He was the only one of the four militants who could speak a language other than Arabic. The ship's attendants, he adds, had a master-key that they used when cleaning the rooms. Apparently, they used it at that particular moment in order to bring complimentary fruits to the passengers. When they opened the door, they saw three Palestinians perched around a small coffee table, drying hand-grenades, rifles, and pistols.[4] Terrified, the Palestinians had no choice but to take the ship's attendant—and eventually the entire ship—captive.

Another story, promoted by certain Israeli and American writers, says that youths panicked when they discovered that they were being watched by a female Mossad agent, disguised as an Italian security official.[5] She reportedly became suspicious of them since none spoke Spanish even though they were traveling on Latin American passports.[6] In this telling, the fears of the Palestinians were heightened when it was announced that all luggage would be examined before leaving Alexandria, en route to Port Said, the last stop before Ashdod. The trip between Alexandria and Ashdod usually took six hours. The normal way of doing things was to wait until they entered Israeli waters before inspecting the luggage of passengers. The announcement of an inspection prior to entering Israeli waters convinced them that ship authorities were searching for weapons aboard. In this scenario, the inspections triggered the decision of the Palestinians to take the ship hostage: they "arrested" its crew and passengers before they arrested them.

A third tale says that when the ship docked in Alexandria, where most of its passengers went on shore for sightseeing, the Palestinians decided to attack. Of the 774 passengers, only 80 stayed aboard, including the four Palestinians, and to their utter misfortune, two American tourists such as the sixty-nine-year-old wheelchair-bound Leon Klinghoffer and his wife, Marilyn. Rumor had it that President Reagan's daughter had been aboard, but this was never proven and I think was a figment of some journalist's imagination. At noon, ship administrators found out that the radio system was not working, and sent a stewardess to knock on passenger rooms, one at a time, to carry the message that lunch was now being served. The four Palestinians happened to be in one room. When the door-knocking began, they became hysterical. They thought that someone was behind the closed door, with handcuffs in hand, waiting to arrest them. When she entered, they took her hostage and then burst into the lounge, waved their guns, and screamed instructions in Arabic that no one could understand. Everyone aboard was taken hostage.

I think that a combination of all-of-the-above sounds logical, although Abu al-Abbas never bought the story that said, "A waiter burst into the room." He would bite his lips then shout at his men when the operation was over, "Why the hell where you fixing your weapons without having locked the damn door first?"

Dust vs Elegance: A New Explanation

I think that a third factor needs to be taken into consideration, different from all of the above. (I am basing this explanation on a recent interview I conducted with one of the hijackers, Bassam al-Achkar.) Simply, it is that the young men cowered when it was time for them to die. There was no exit strategy, after all. No one was coming to rescue them from Ashdod. Let's not forget that these young men were at the tender ages of sixteen and eighteen. They came from the Palestinian camps of Jordan and Syria and had never seen anything as lavish in their lives as what they experienced aboard the *Achille Lauro*. It was a far cry from the dusty crowded streets of Yarmouk Camp in Damascus, or the Wihdat or Baq'a camps of Jordan. They had received no proper education, were raised in painstakingly small dwellings clustered tightly together, and grew up on the streets.

Suddenly these street boys were sipping champagne at pool parties aboard the *Achille Lauro*, surrounded by beautiful Italian women in bikinis. Before the *Achille Lauro*, they had embraced death, as they never had seen a day of comfort in their lives. After traveling twice aboard the luxury liner, they quickly began to understand that there were indulgences in life that they had previously known nothing about. Life, they learned, could have a sweet meaning to it. Did they come up with an alternate plan? Did they decide to hijack the *Achille Lauro* rather than ride it to their fate in Ashdod?

Myths about the *Achille Lauro*

Of course, the Israeli and American press, along with all books published since then, was filled with mythical stories about what happened aboard the *Achille Lauro*. Most of what was published aimed solely at giving Abu al-Abbas and the cause that he represented a bad name. The Israeli press reported that the four Palestinians were due to enter Israel and attack "a bus full of civilians." That of course, is baseless. In addition, most sources insist that the *Achille Lauro* Operation was a Palestinian response to an air raid on the offices of the PLO in Hammam al-Shatt (known to the West as Operation Wooden Leg), on October 1, 1985. An operation as complex as the *Achille Lauro* certainly needed more than one week to plan, given the six-day difference between the Israeli raid and the ship hijacking. Certainly the implementation of the *Achille Lauro* operation was triggered by the Israeli attack, but its planning had taken place long before the Hammam al-Shatt raid. On this point, the Israelis actually contradict themselves, since they claim that the *Achille Lauro* Operation took eleven months to plan, with Israeli National Security citing November 1984 as the start date for the operation. If it were indeed planned in late 1984, then there is no way it could have been created from scratch in response to the Israeli Army raid on Hammam al-Shatt in October 1985.

On the other hand, there may have been elements of truth to the "spur of the moment" explanation. Bassam al-Achkar, one of the militants aboard the ship whom I referred to above, believes that the *Achille Lauro* operation was at least partly created in response to the Israeli attack. He suggests that the haste with which the final arrangements were made caused the operation to fail.[7]

In another account of what took place aboard the *Achille Lauro*, American writers Janet and John Wallach say:

"The gunmen flipped through the passports [of the passengers left aboard]. Passengers with Jewish sounding names and those who were British were separated from the rest and ordered to the main lounge. Terrified, the passengers could hear the men speaking in Arabic and mentioning the name 'Arafat.'"

This explanation is also hard to digest, for several reasons. One is that Palestinians don't refer to Arafat as "Arafat," as Westerners do. They refer to him, as mentioned above, as either "Abu Ammar" or "al-Ikhtiyar." And why they would mumble his name in the middle of a kidnapping—especially when he officially had nothing to do with the *Achille Lauro*—is beyond me. The story adds that the Palestinians demanded the release of fifty of their countrymen in Israeli jails, including the famous Lebanese prisoner Samir al-Qantar. Wallach adds that the four Palestinian armed men began chanting, "Arafat good. Reagan bad!"

The dramatic story, in their account, goes on:

"The passengers asked for permission to use the bathrooms, but were refused permission . . . . The terrorists ordered the passengers up a flight of stairs to the bow of the ship. Marilyn Klinghoffer could not manage her husband's wheelchair up the steps and sixty-nine-year-old Leon could not climb himself, even with help. She couldn't leave his side. His wife pleaded; he suffered from high blood pressure and was too weak to be left alone. One of the Arabs whacked her feet with the butt of a pistol." The hostages "were asked to stand in the direction of Syria (hinting that the Palestinians were carrying out orders from Damascus). They could see huge cans of petrol placed there deliberately. If anyone fired on the cruise ship, the oil cans would explode; everyone aboard would be dead." The story goes on: "Tormenting the hostages, the terrorists played with live grenades, and shoved them into their captives' hands."

The only truth—very unfortunately—is that Klinghoffer made so much noise that he confused and unnerved four inexperienced young men who had never before held captives and who had not anticipated that hostage control would be a skill required in this mission. Klinghoffer's hysterics created a crisis. And the young men responded without reason—and without reasoning through the consequences: They shot Klinghoffer and then threw him overboard. Abu al-Abbas only found out that Klinghoffer had been killed once the operation ended. Adding to the bad luck, Klinghoffer belonged to an active American Jewish family that was well connected with AIPAC (The American Israel Public Affairs Committee, an extremely effective lobbying group for Israeli and Jewish concerns) in Washington, DC. His murder struck a nerve in American society and obliged the PLO to pay huge sums to the Klinghoffer family over a fifteen year period. This made the *Achille Lauro* operation, according to Abu al-Abbas, "financially and politically disastrous for the Palestinian Cause." Abu al-Abbas did not want to kill Klinghoffer. He understood that the death of Klinghoffer would give Israel cover for the deaths of thousands of Palestinians. And so it was that after the second intifada broke out in September 2000 and more than 3,000 Palestinians were mowed down by the Israeli Army, Western journalists still had nothing to ask Abu al-Abbas except, "Why was Leon Klinghoffer killed in 1985?"

"Sad that you should ask," he would respond. "Gushing rivers of blood are running through my country, and yet the corpse of one man continues to haunt me until this day, fifteen years later." On April 22, 1996, in his capacity as a MP in the Palestinian National Council, Abu al-Abbas said that the *Achille Lauro* Operation was "a mistake that led to other mistakes." When it came to Abu al-Abbas, the Western press never saw past the murder of Leon Klinghoffer. Even when he died in a US prison in 2004, all they could speak about was demise of the man who had been involved in the killing of Klinghoffer. Rather than becoming a heroic milestone in the career of Abu al-Abbas, the *Achille Lauro* Operation would haunt him—along with the death of Kinghoffer—for the remainder of his life.

October 8, 1985. Cairo. About 11:00 AM.

After reaching the headquarters of Egyptian Intelligence in Cairo with Hani al-Hasan, Abu Al-Abbas headed to Alexandria (Abu Tarek refused to join), boarded a rubber boat and sped to intercept the *Achille Lauro*. His aim: to talk his men into surrendering. It must be mentioned that Abu al-Abbas was not doing this at the request of the Egyptians. He did it because he believed it was the right thing to do, now that the operation had diverted from its original objective. The point of the *Achille Lauro* operation, after all, was to gain international attention and sympathy—not to harm tourists.

While his rubber boat cut through the water toward the ocean liner, all that Abu al-Abbas could think about was what went wrong . . . and why. He was furious that two years of planning had come to naught. Tall and dignified, Abu al-Abbas was an Class A military commander who valued honor in any military operation. Mistakes and sloppiness made him furious. With loudspeaker in hand, he addressed his men aboard the ship, by name, one-by-one, ordering them to lay down their arms "immediately." He spoke slowly, making sure to articulate every word and add emphasis to it. "Descend! Leave the ship! It is not our goal to seize the ship!" He even identified himself by his real name, "Abu Khaled" rather than his *nom de guerre*, "Abu al-Abbas." The entire conversation in the middle of the sea was recorded by Egyptian Intelligence and immediately handed over to Mossad and the CIA. On October 16, eight days later, Israel released transcript of Abu al-Abbas's orders to his men aboard the *Achille Lauro*. We only got a copy for our library after reaching Baghdad in the late 1980s. (This recording was confiscated by the invading US Army in 2003, as was everything else we owned.) Abu al-Abbas could be heard shouting, loud and clear, "This is a military order. Don't harm the passengers!" Once certain that they were out of harm's way, the young men gave their weapons to Abu al-Abbas and joined him for what they were promised was going to be a safe trip home.[8]

Abu Ammar Takes the Mic

The immediate effect of the *Achille Lauro* Operation was to torpedo a proposed meeting in London between Palestinian statesmen and Sir Geoffrey Howe, the Foreign Secretary. It had been planned by King Hussein of Jordan and British Prime Minister Margaret Thatcher. Arafat quickly distanced himself from the *Achille Lauro* operation, and ostensibly punished Abu al-Abbas by freezing his membership in the Palestinian Executive Council. Less than three years later, in April 1987, Abu al-Abbas was re-elected to Council with Arafat's full blessing. When speaking to American journalists in the 1990s, however, Arafat told a different story. "We were victims of this terrorism," he said. "The Syrians infiltrated Abu al-Abbas's group. This is an example of Syrian dirty business. They penetrated the Palestine Liberation Front—the Syrian intelligence services. I know everything about it." That of course was Yasser Arafat being Yasser Arafat *par excellence*, distancing himself from a military operation before a Western audience, while laying full claim to it among Palestinians. Arafat would often claim that the attack aimed at undermining him personally, to strengthen Israeli hard-liners wanting to kill him, politically and physically. Not for a moment did American diplomats believe that Arafat had nothing to do with the *Achille Lauro*. One cable said, "He [Arafat] was aware that an operation was being planned even if he didn't know the specific target or how it came out. To say that he had no idea that Abu al-Abbas was planning something is ludicrous."

President Arafat, it must be noted, loved to take credit for any military operation in the 1960s and 1970s, even those that he had nothing to do with. Once his military credentials became well established, he focused on building his reputation as a problem solver, a go-between, and eventually, a peacemaker. Ejected from Lebanon in 1982 and boycotted by the Americans, Arafat was desperately trying to open a back-channel with Washington, DC. Arafat could see that his traditional supporters in Moscow were beginning to step away from their commitments to the Palestinians during what were the autumn years of the Soviet Union. By the mid-1980s, Arafat was already in transition between warrior and the peacemaker. In as much as he wanted the *Achille Lauro* Operation to succeed, he nevertheless could not come out and associate himself with it or with Abu al-Abbas.

When speaking of the *Achille Lauro* after the 1993 Oslo Accords, Arafat said, "I received official thanks from the Italian government [for saving the hostages]. I have a letter from the Prime Minister Bettino Craxi. I saved 400 lives [although the actual number was 774]. The Department of Justice even dropped the request for the arrest and extradition of Abu al-Abbas."

3
Mubarak Gives Us a Ride

Cairo. October 7, 1985. About 5:00 PM.

ONCE THE FOUR PALESTINIANS and my husband were back ashore, they headed to headquarters of Egyptian Intelligence to negotiate an exit plan. The entire world was watching. The Americans were furious, and so were the Israelis, the Italians, the Egyptians, and of course, the Tunisians. The four militants fell asleep, exhausted by the failed operation while Abu al-Abbas handled the negotiations.[1]

Abu al-Abbas insisted that his men would not travel alone back to Tunis, fearing for their lives, and under no condition would he accept handing them over to the Israelis or the Americans. Abu al-Abbas said, "I insisted that the best way forward was to send each young man aboard a separate commercial airplane to Tunis." At the suggestion of President Mubarak, the Egyptians proposed instead to send them back aboard a presidential airplane. Once again, Abu al-Abbas refused. Then, the President of Egypt intervened personally, asking to speak to him. There had been no previous contact between them, and Abu al-Abbas had little affection for Mubarak, a man who had come to power neither through the ballots nor his charisma or any personal attributes. He was, in every sense of the word, a "president by accident" who assumed office when his predecessor Anwar al-Sadat was killed in October 1981. Mubarak managed to stay firmly in control of Egypt for 30 long years thanks to an autocratic regime and a massive network of corruption carried out by his family and associates. As Abu al-Abbas said later, "Egyptian intelligence was infiltrated heavily by US intelligence, with Mubarak's direct approval. When measured by a nationalist yardstick, Mubarak ranked very poorly, especially on his positions toward the Palestinians and his blind adherence to the Egyptian-Israeli peace treaty of 1978."

Mubarak spoke to Abu al-Abbas firmly yet politely, "I give you my word of honor that no one will attack you. Don't worry Abu al-Abbas, you are dealing with Egypt!" Mubarak, as mentioned above, was desperate for an Egyptian comeback in Arab politics. He had been shunned by the Arab League completely since coming to power four years earlier. When recounting the events that transpired at this point, Abu al-Abbas would always smile, amazed that he had been so gullible. Why had he given Mubarak the benefit of the doubt and taken his word of honor seriously?

Cairo. October 10, 1985. About 8:45 AM GMT.

Abu al-Abbas accepted Mubarak's offer, and he boarded the Egyptian presidential plane, Egypt Air 737, with his four associates and his trusted commander Abu al-Izz. It was a gamble, but Abu al-Abbas had no other choice. Aboard was an Egyptian officer sent by Mubarak to accompany the Palestinians. Abu al-Abbas patted him on the back affectionately and joked, "Are you sure that the President does not want to get rid of you?" The officer, with his shining medals and neatly pressed military uniform, did not really appreciate the humor.

"Why is that, Mr. Abu al-Abbas?"

"Because everyone on this airplane might get blown up in the air," he chuckled, "or sink to the bottom of the sea." He sincerely felt that something evil was going to happen to the airplane and everyone aboard, he later confessed to me.

F-14 Tomcats

The airplane took off at 9:15 GMT on October 10. The crew was exceptionally polite, especially the captain and one stewardess, who Abu al-Abbas would befriend and later describe as "bold and impressive." He continued to see her whenever visiting Egypt for the rest of his life, and if anything, this speaks volumes about his charisma. Even those who risked their lives with him—very unwillingly—continued to love and respect him. No sooner had they taken off, however, than four unidentified F-14s met them in the sky, one on each wing and two behind. Abu al-Abbas was the first to catch sight of them. These planes, he soon realized, were part of the 1ˢᵗ Special Forces Operational Detachment Unit – Delta, one of the US Army's counter-terrorism units, popularly known as Delta Force. They had taken off from the *USS Saratoga* stationed off the coast of Albania.[2] Earlier two E-2C electronic surveillance planes (smaller versions of the AWACS aircraft) had already left the *Saratoga* in order to track the Egypt Air flight.[3] President Reagan at the time was traveling from Chicago to Washington and had ordered the confrontation from Air Force One.[4]

Abu al-Abbas rushed into the cockpit and shouted at the captain. "Where are we heading?" he said. "Where are they directing you?" Abu al-Abbas wore his sidearm—he never went anywhere without it—and the captain could see it in the holster on his hip. "If they are ordering you to head to Israel, I will not let you land! You will listen to me, not to them!" The captain was sweating. He had no clue to what was happening. He nevertheless answered calmly, "They are ordering me to go west."

"Can this airplane cross the Atlantic?" Abu al-Abbas asked.

The captain replied, "Relax. We don't have enough fuel to do that. We would need to stop in Europe first." To Abu al-Abbas, this meant that they were most likely headed to Israel. Abu al-Abbas concluded that Mubarak had arranged for the Americans to hijack the airplane and to arrest or kill the Palestinians on board. And the airplane *was* hijacked.. The fighter escorts forced the plane to land at Sigonella, a NATO military base in Sicily near Catania at 11:45 GMT. Abu al-Abbas could hear instructions in English from the Americans to ground control, words which echoed through the presidential plane. "You have to let this airplane land!" the Americans demanded.

"We don't have clearance to do so!" the Italians replied.

"We are the Delta Force," the Americans warned. "We order you to let them land safely!" After the plane descended and came to rest on the tarmac, Abu al-Abbas looked out the airplane windows and saw Carabinieri with assault weapons, immediately surrounded the airplane while a ring of US troops, armed to the teeth, stood behind them. Parked nearby was a US C-141 transport plane, which Abu al-Abbas reasoned was ready to take the Palestinians to the US.

The Americans and the Italians were NATO members and allies, but for three long unbearable hours, the Italian military police prevented the Americans from boarding the aircraft. Finally, Prime Minister Craxi sent an envoy to the airplane, carrying a message: "The Prime Minister wants to talk to you. You have to disembark to the terminal to speak with him." Abu al-Abbas feared that this was a trap, so he sent one of his men, Abu al-Izz, down the airplane staircase. To his surprise, Abu al-Izz found that US troops had moved beneath the airplane. Each troop had his finger on the trigger. One American soldier approached and Abu al-Izz, fearing for his life, punched the soldier and then rushed back up the staircase.

"Comrade Abu al-Abbas," he said, "you cannot go down. The US Army is all over the place!"

Abu al-Abbas then calmly sent word to the Italians, "My agenda for today does not have a scheduled meeting with Prime Minister Craxi. I am sorry. I won't be able to speak with him."

Craxi, however, did not give up. He sent a telephone with hundreds of feet of cord dangling from it. He came on the line and told Abu al-Abbas, "You have to trust us. What we are doing is for your own good. We won't let anybody harm you, and we are coordinating every single move with Chairman Arafat." Still, Abu al-Abbas declined to leave the aircraft.

Cairo. October 11, 1985. 3:00 AM GMT.

Finally, early in the morning, President Reagan (apparently at Craxi's request) ordered US troops to stand down and allow the Italians to take custody of the Palestinian hijackers while Abu al-Abbas, Abu al-Izz, the Egyptian officers, the pilot, and stewardess stayed aboard.[5]

The four hijackers were arrested and kept in Sicily for a few days, while Abu al-Abbas flew to Rome's military airport, where the Egyptian officers disembarked at the request of the Egyptian Ambassador Farouk Husni. That trip, also, was accompanied by the US F-14 jet fighters.

On October 12, Abu al-Abbas was scheduled to land at Rome's civilian airport, Leonardo da Vinci, and then head to Yugoslavia on a civilian aircraft. As the Egyptian plane prepared to take off for the hop to da Vinci, the captain picked up the radio and told the Americans at ground control, "This time if you follow me, I will fly at such low elevation that I will crash into one of the many buildings of Rome!"

Abu al-Abbas beamed at the pilot's bravado. He felt that he had inspired the pilot, transforming him for a moment from civilian commander of Husni Mubarak's airplane into a swaggering Palestinian commando (*fedayee* or *fedayeen*, plural)—or something close. Abu al-Abbas finally made it to Belgrade Airport, where he noticed a throng of reporters with cameras waiting at the terminal. In the main lounge, he found the Palestinian Ambassador Nimer Hammad waiting for him, flanked by Yugoslav intelligence. "Who was on the plane?" he asked Hammad, "He must have been very important that so many reporters are here to see him." He did not imagine, not for a moment, that he was the star of the flight, and that the reporters were there to see the man who had sparked off an international crisis involving the US, Italy, Egypt, and Israel.

The Ambassador smiled, "Abu al-Abbas, are you not aware of the international crisis you have created? Let's get in the car, and I will explain." When they got to Hammad's house, they turned on the radio to hear coverage of Abu al-Abbas's adventure. He stood there silent, shocked by the way simple events had been amplified. As it turned out, this incident had repercussions that rippled through Palestinian and Arab politics and became a factor in the international arena for years to come. For Abu al-Abbas—his life had reached a turning point.

Just what had transpired in Italy? The Craxi government refused requests to extradite Abu al-Abbas claiming that in his capacity as a PLO official he merited diplomatic immunity. On October 11, 1985 Marilyn Klinghoffer, with three other former hostages from the *Achille Lauro*, identified the four hijackers in a police line-up in Sicily. On October 16, Israel's military intelligence chief, Major General Ehud Barak, revealed the transcripts of intercepted radio communications between Abu al-Abbas and the hijackers.[6] The four Palestinians were charged with hijacking, kidnapping, murder, and illegal possession of firearms and explosives. Also charged and already in custody were Mohammad Khalaf and Mohammad Issa Abbas, (a relative of Abu al-Abbas), for their roles in bringing the arms and explosives from Tunis to the hijackers in Genoa. Those in custody were convicted of the arms and explosives charges on November 18, 1985, and sentenced to jail terms ranging from four to nine years. Mohammad Issa Abbas received the harshest sentence—nine years—for delivering Abu al-Abbas's instructions to the four hijackers. On November 27, 1985 the Klinghoffer family filed two lawsuits, one in the State Supreme Court in Manhattan, suing the PLO for $1.5 billion, and another in the Federal District Court in Manhattan suing Chandris-Italy Inc, the Port of Genoa, and Club ABC Tours Inc., for "compensatory and punitive damages."[7]

Saved by Italian Prime Minister Bettino Craxi

The Italian Prime Minister Craxi ought to be recognized for refusing to extradite Abu al-Abbas and for standing up to the Americans. It was the first such show of defiance by the Italian government toward the US since World War II. According to US sources, Craxi initially had given Reagan permission to detain the Palestinians but later reneged on the deal, probably under pressure from Arafat, who was a good friend of Italy. During his tenure in government, a total of 26-months, Craxi had worked hard on fostering good relations with the Arab world and his primary instrument was to support the PLO. Craxi would later claim that he ordered the Italians to surround the airplane to protect it from the Americans. This move was supposedly dictated both by security concerns about terrorists targeting Italy if the United States had had it their way and by the Italian tradition of diplomacy with the Arab world.

Although the Americans demanded that the Italian authorities extradite Abu al- Abbas, Craxi stood firm on the grounds that the crime had been perpetrated on an Italian vessel which was Italian territory. Thus, in Craxi's argument, the Italian Republic had sole jurisdiction. Craxi is the one who enabled Abu al-Abbas to leave unharmed and head for Yugoslavia. This episode earned Craxi an article in *The Economist* titled "Europe's strongman" and a standing ovation in the Italian Senate. Apparently, Craxi was telephoned by Reagan during the operation, not before it, informing him of the US's decision to land the airplane at Sigonella and to apprehend the occupants. It was more of a dictate, than a consultation. Craxi said no, claiming that such an unauthorized landing violated the US-Italian accord regulating use of the NATO base. Craxi paid a price, however. His stand-off with the US brought down his government on October 18, eight days later, after his defense minister Giovanni Spandolini, withdrew his Republican Party from the governing coalition government because of the *Achille Lauro*. From that point, Craxi would lead an interim government and eventually win parliamentary approval on November 8, 1985 to form a new government. Ironically the Craxi government, which had tried so hard to placate the PLO and Arab governments in its handling of the *Achille Lauro* affair, faced another Palestinian attack upon Italian soil on December 27, 1985 when gunmen of the Abu Nidal faction, a staunch opponent of both Abu Ammar and Abu al-Abbas, coordinated attacks at the El-Al counters in both the Rome and Vienna airports, murdering 18 travelers and wounding 60. Abu al-Abbas was nothing like Abu Nidal. He could not abide terrorism, military attacks that targeted civilians. Such violence, Abu al-Abbas knew, did his country and his cause a great disservice.

Persona Non Grata

The events of the Delta Force Operation, which has become a de facto Part II to the *Achille Lauro* saga, had a pronounced effect across the Arab world. Mubarak's back-stabbing triggered anti-American demonstrations in Egypt and added to popular outcry against the Egyptian President. Tunisian President Habib Bourguiba had been shocked by the Israeli bombing raid on Tunis which preceded the *Achille Lauro*. After the hijacking of the Italian cruise liner, he found himself at odds with the Egyptians for their complicity in taking control of Abu al-Abbas's airplane.

The *Achille Lauro* incident and its aftermath stoked a sense of betrayal by Arabs who reeled at the actions of Mubarak. They had seldom seen a more blatant example of an Arab leader serving Israeli interests by bowing down to American wishes. For his part, Abu al-Abbas was now *persona non grata* in Tunisia. He fled to Yugoslavia and shortly thereafter to Iraq where he lived until his death in 2004.

4
Abu al-Abbas: A Rebel with a Cause

Tiret Haifa Northern Mediterranean Coast. Palestine. 1948.

"PACK WHAT YOU CAN CARRY," Abu Ismail al-Abbas said to his young wife Latifa, "we won't be too long." Palestinians had been asked to leave their homes for what was supposedly a quick stay in Syria or Jordan. Latifa, a mother of two who was pregnant with her son Mohammad (Abu al-Abbas), complied willingly. Like thousands of other Palestinian women, she packed a few belongings and followed her husband's instructions. They took along their land registry papers, IDs, and the keys to their home in Palestine. We'll be back "in a matter of weeks," they thought. Some Palestinian families even left the radio on, as though they would return in a few hours.

On May 14, 1948 Zionists announced creation of the State of Israel. The Palestine War of 1948 was about to start. After 400 years of stability under the Ottoman Turks and thirty years of British rule, Palestinians were suddenly experiencing turbulence like no time in their recent history.

Abu Ismail lived with his small family in Tiret Haifa, a small village on the north shore of Palestine. Like most residents, he had a small farm where he harvested olives, lemons, and other fruits for which Palestinian orchards were famous. Like most residents of their village, they had little cash income. Yet they lived a decent and dignified life.

Abu Ismail reassured Latifa. "In no time," he said, "the invading Arab Armies will defeat the Zionist forces and expel them from Palestine. Then we can return to return to Tiret Haifa." This is what the Arab League told them, and it was echoed by Arab leaders of all stripes and colors. A few years earlier, these same Arab leaders had liberated Syria and Lebanon from the French and Iraq from the British. Surely, they could not go wrong on Palestine. Abu Ismail, a simple yet stubborn and courageous man, believed the radio when broadcasts told of Arab armies preparing to throw the Jews "into the sea." The people of Tiret Haifa were known in Palestine as hot-tempered warriors who would fight anything that crosses their path "including, the sea itself." Little did Abu Ismail realize that in a matter of weeks no less than 760,000 Palestinians would either flee their homeland or get expelled from it by the very same Israelis they were supposed to be on the verge of defeating.

1948: The *Nakba*

In the Arab world, we remember the 1948 war as *al-Nakba*, the Catastrophe. The Arabic term was coined by American University of Beirut President Constantine Zureik, one of the philosophers of modern Arab nationalism. In Hebrew, the Israelis refer to it as *Milkhemet Ha'atzma'ut* (War of Independence). The history, of course, has been beaten to death by Palestinian scholars, but the injustice done to the Palestinians cannot be stressed enough since it laid the foundation for the political consciousness of all Palestinians born in the post-1948 era—including Abu al-Abbas and me. We grew up and grew old listening to stories that were all too true. We bequeathed to our children and grandchildren the etched facts and precise details of the 1948 *Nakba* as it was handed down to us from our fathers and forefathers.

In late November 1947, the United Nations General Assembly adopted a resolution recommending the partition of Palestine, based on UN General Assembly Resolution 181. The Palestinian Arabs would receive an enclave in Jaffa, and the Jews would get 56% of the territory of Palestine. The Arab League, with due right, said, "No" to the Partition Plan and ordered the Arab armies into Palestine on May 15. "According to Article 73b of the UN Charter," the Arab League argued, "the UN should develop self-government of the peoples in a territory under its administration."

The Arab armies involved in combat ranged from 10,000 in the Egyptian Army to a mere 1,000 in the Lebanese Army. Units from Iraq and Syria joined the war, as did a volunteer army of Arab guerrillas known as the Army of Deliverance, commanded by a Syrian named Fawzi al-Qawiqji. It included fighters from Yemen, Saudi Arabia, and Syria. Of course they were joined by Palestinian commandos led politically by Haj Amin al-Husseini, the ex-Mufti of Jerusalem, and militarily by the legendary Palestinian leader, Abdul Qader al-Husseini.

By May 29, the UN declared a truce in Palestine, which came into effect on June 11 and lasted for twenty-eight days. The ceasefire was overseen by UN mediator Folke Bernadotte, who was eventually murdered by the Stern Gang, an Israeli militia commanded by Yitzhak Shamir who later became the Prime Minister of Israel. Bernadotte's UN mandate, written off by the General Assembly, had been to "assure the safety of the holy places, to safeguard

PFLP poster commemorating the Nakba.

well-being of the population, and to promote a peaceful adjustment of the future situation of Palestine."

The first truce collapsed rather quickly, since neither side was willing to respect it. Both the Israelis and the Arabs used it to improve their fighting positions, which in itself, was a direct violation of the ceasefire. The newly created Israeli Defense Forces (IDF) acquired arms from Czechoslovakia and increased its manpower from 30,000 to 65,000 during the truce. Ironically, sixteen years later, Abu al-Abbas trained with Czech weapons—the same weapons that were used to destroy his family home in 1948. The Israeli Army, during the truce, was able to increase its arms supply to more than 25,000 rifles, 5,000 machine guns, and more than fifty million bullets. The truce finally fell apart when the Israeli Army invaded the Palestinian cities of Ramla and Lodd, expelling no less than 60,000 Palestinians from their homes. Ramla was vital for the Israelis, because it was close to the fighting lines of the Egyptian Army, whereas Lodd was on verge of occupation by the Jordanian Army, which had taken over its police station. On July 16, 1948, Nazareth was occupied by the Israelis, and by the time the second truce came into effect in the evening of July 18, the whole lower Galilee from Haifa Bay to the Sea of Galilee had been captured by the Israelis.

In late October, the Israeli Army occupied the entire upper Galilee, which had been originally allocated to the Arabs by the UN Partition Plan. By October 30, the Israelis had captured all of Galilee and advanced 8 km into Lebanon, driving the Lebanese Army back to the Litani River. On December 22, they drove the remaining Egyptian forces out of Palestine, securing the entire Negev and forcing King Farouk to accept a cease-fire on February 24, 1949. Other ceasefires followed: Lebanon on March 23, Jordan on April 3, and Syria on July 20. Israel was given seventy-eight percent of Mandatory Palestine, eighteen percent more than the UN Partition Plan had given the Jews. The Gaza Strip and West Bank were given to Egypt and Jordan respectively, leaving the Palestinians with practically nothing. Once a proud people, they were reduced to refugees living in need, pain, and poverty.

Although the right of return of the Palestinian refugees was recognized by UN Resolution 194 in December 1948, it did not happen. Eighty-five percent of the Palestinian population, a total of 1.8 million in 1947-1948, had been forced to abandon their homes, fleeing to the West Bank and Gaza, while one third (fifteen percent) fled to Syria, Lebanon, and Jordan. They set up base in what quickly mushroomed into fifty-eight refugee camps, ten of which came into being after the 1967 war. Citizenship or legal residency in host countries like Lebanon, for example, was denied because the absorption of Palestinians would upset a delicate confessional balance. Most of the Palestinian refugees who fled to Syria in 1948, were from northern Palestine, mainly from Safad, Haifa, and Jaffa. My husband's family was one of them. They moved first to Lebanon and then settled in Afrin (also "Ifrin"), a Kurdish town in northern Syria near the Turkish border that is 1,000 km from Tiret Haifa. Abu al-Abbas was born in a Palestinian refugee camp in December 1948, seven months after the loss of Palestine. By then, his father Abu Ismail and his mother Latifa were certain that this was going to be their new home—that they were not returning to Tiret Haifa, anytime soon. In 1951, they moved east to the Neirab Refugee camp near the northern merchant city of Aleppo. When Abu al-Abbas was eleven, his mother grew sick and died. His father never remarried.

"She probably died from the horrible health and sanitary conditions in the camps," Abu al-Abbas would later recall. Her death had a dramatic effect on his childhood and continued to torment him well into his adult years. "My mother was like my homeland. I never distinguished between the two. It is so difficult to lose a mother, and a homeland, and spend a lifetime looking for both." Abu al-Abbas considered his mother's death as yet another manifestation of his helplessness and statelessness. It prompted him to leave his family and rely on himself, acting much older than his years. He had only one old black & white photograph of his mother, Latifa al-Abbas, and it was eaten away at the corners by the passage of time. She looked like typical women from the Palestinian countryside: pale, poor, and proud. He carried that single photograph with him from the Palestinian camps in Syria and Lebanon to Tunis and then to Iraq. He made sure that it survived the Lebanese Civil War and the Iraq-Iran War of the 1980s. It too was "confiscated" by the US Army after they stormed our house in Baghdad in April 2003.

1951: Life in the Camps

Neirab. Near Aleppo, Syria. 1951.

Neirab was the largest official camp operated in Syria by the United Nations Relief and Works Agency (UNRWA). It was established two years after the loss of Palestine, in 1950, and was located 13 km east of Aleppo, near the present Aleppo Airport. It occupied forty acres in and around an army barracks once used by the Allies during World War II. The Abbas family found shelter in these barracks, as Abu al-Abbas later recalled: "We divided them into 'rooms' with sheets and later with plywood and hollow bricks to provide some privacy and accommodation for our growing families. Most young men worked as day laborers or street vendors. I spent my childhood painting fences and walls for small sums of money. The poor construction of the barracks resulted in soaring temperatures in summer and freezing conditions in the exceptionally harsh Syrian winters. Water leakage and rodent infestation remained a problem for the refugees, and I will never forget the hardships we went through during those cold winters. The quality of life was also affected by the lack of privacy. The camp's dusty and dirty streets—often no wider than the span of a child's arms—were the only place for children to play." When he was old enough to attend school, Abu al-Abbas studied at the UNRWA (United Nations Relief and Works Agency) administered schools inside the Neirab camp.

Yarmouk Camp. Damascus. 1962.

At fourteen years of age, Abu al-Abbas moved to Damascus with his family. Here they found space in the Yarmouk Refugee Camp on the city's south side. Yarmouk, now the largest camp in Syria, was not much better than Neirab, although Damascus itself was certainly more attractive for the fourteen-year-old boy. Yarmouk, located 8 km from central Damascus with stone buildings constructed in 1957, resembled the urban quarter of a traditional Arab city. As Abu al-Abbas recalled, "The refugees of Yarmouk were of a higher social caliber than Neirab—namely doctors, engineers, and civil servants. Damascus at the time was filled with attractions to any young man who could afford them: cinemas, cafes, and restaurants. I could afford none since my father was completely incapable of providing a comfortable life for his children."

Education was free in Syria, however, which enabled Abu al-Abbas to enroll at the public Kawakbi High School and, after graduation, to enroll in Dar al-Mouallimeen, a pre-college institute that trained students to become elementary and high schoolteachers. Like other students at Dar al-Mouallimeen, Abu al-Abbas attended class and also visited nearby secondary schools where he gained experience as a student teacher. To help his father support the family, Abu al-Abbas performed odd jobs. He ran errands for shopkeepers, painted the block walls with cemented glass shards on top that surrounded the courtyards of the wealthy, watched children, and in general made himself useful in exchange for a few coins. While Abu al-Abbas attended class and while he worked at menial jobs, he thought . . . about Palestine. As a poor kid from Yarmouk, Abu al-Abbas could see that he needed a day job to support his interest in politics.

Odd jobs were a precarious way to earn a living. And so the project of political activism on behalf of Palestine came to depend, in his teenage mind, on the profession of schoolteacher.

1963: Revolt of the Schoolteachers

Damascus. March 8, 1963. The 8 March Revolution.

A military coup d'état took place in Syria that brought several generals and two schoolteachers, Michel Aflaq and Salah al-Bitar, to the seat of power in Damascus. Bitar became the Prime Minister of Syria while Aflaq held onto his position as chief ideologue of the ruling Baath Party. Bitar and Aflaq represented educators, university students, and the under-privileged urban and rural poor of Syria. Schoolteachers flooded the government bureaucracy and rose to become cabinet ministers and CEOs of state-run industries.

The example of Bitar and Aflaq suggested to Abu al-Abbas that a teacher could develop an ideology, an organization, and could use that organization to create change. Aflaq in particular stood out. He was a Christian who gave thrilling public speeches that rallied Damascus crowds composed largely of Muslims. A man who was short of stature, he rose above his background and limitations. He made history.

Damascus. 1964. Abu al-Abbas joins the PLO.

In two years living in Yarmouk, Abu al-Abbas developed a political consciousness. He joined the PLO at age sixteen in 1964, soon after its founding, and became one of the PLO's youngest members. Later, he recalled his "basic training" with Czech-made weapons.[1] Abu al-Abbas would maintain his loyalty to the PLO for forty years until his death in 2004. (The PLO was an umbrella group, and most PLO members had an additional affinity to a Palestinian faction that gave allegiance to the PLO and, in return, received PLO funding.) Here Abu al-Abbas came into contact with more seasoned Palestinian resisters. Ahmed Jibril, for example, was a decade older and had served as a captain in the Syrian Army. He was trained and he was deadly.[2]

Damascus University. 1965.

At seventeen, Abu al-Abbas enrolled in Damascus University where he studied Arabic literature and continued his focus on teaching as a career. Teaching was a respectable profession in Arab society. It promised to lift the young man from the deadening chores of laboring and craft work, to keep his mind alive, and to earn him a steady and decent income. The teaching profession held special promise for a young man who was developing a taste for politics. Aside from any help that teaching might give to a future political career, this vocation promised to give Abu al-Abbas the social and professional elevation that he badly needed to progress in life. The value of education and the importance of educators were a verity among Palestinians, who were deprived of everything under the sun after 1948. With no money, property, or position in society, they reached for education. A good sound education, they reasoned, would be their salvation. For Abu al-Abbas, education was the first task in his lifelong struggle to improve his livelihood, provide for his family, and to nurture his cause.

Abu al-Abbas.

The Palestinian Underground

His years in the university gave Abu al-Abbas a taste for free-wheeling intellectual exchange among like-minded thinkers. On campus, he rubbed shoulders with students of all types and was most engaged by other Palestinians students who had been raised in the camps and shared his sense of the grievance over 1948. The authorities kept tight wraps on the campus itself. In the evenings after class, however, Abu al-Abbas and his Palestinian friends traveled to the outskirts of the Syrian capital where they met secretly in the smoky crowded rooms of what they thought of as the Palestinian Underground. Abu al-Abbas and his young friends evaluated the events of 1948 and the years that followed, analyzed reports of current day injustice, and retold stories of *fedayeen* commando raids into Palestine. They responded to events with inflammatory poetry and military strategies to liberate Palestine. Most of these plans never got past the drawing board.

Even though Abu al-Abbas told me that he had received military training with Czech weapons upon joining the PLO, he and his young comrades had no weapons of their own and no access to weapons. They did not have an organization. They were not connected. They were young guys from the local camp, poor kids with anger and edge and a sense of the possible. At this stage they were thinkers with big dreams and out sized ambitions, even while military opportunities were developing all around them.

Abu al-Abbas and his young co-conspirators spent a lot of time in smoky rooms at the edge of Damascus where one question continued to claim their attention: Who would lead them?

When it came to leaders, whom could the Palestinian youth trust? The early hope of the region's Palestinians was the young charismatic Egyptian President Gamal Abdul Nasser, who was only thirty years old in 1948, too young to be tainted by that defeat. Four years later in July 1952, Nasser staged a coup d'état in Cairo that toppled the flamboyant King Farouk. Nasser pledged to right the wrongs and injustices committed against the Arabs and Palestinians during and after the war of 1948. Palestinians listened and believed.

Three years later, however, Palestinians began to doubt. In February 1955 the Israelis launched Operation Black Arrow. Responding to the death of an Israeli civilian at the hands of an Arab infiltrator, they sent 150 paratroopers into Egyptian-controlled Gaza, attacked an Egyptian army base and ambushed an Egyptian convoy. Nearly forty Egyptian soldiers were killed. The Israelis claimed a military victory while the Egyptians marked the event as a public humiliation. The UN Security Council condemned the raid. How did Arab regimes respond? The Arab League also issued a condemnation. Nasser closed the Gulf of Aqaba to Israeli ships and planes. Then, nothing.

As a freshman and sophomore at the university, Abu al-Abbas questioned the potency of Arab Arms and the ability and sincerity of Arab national leaders. His doubt was fed by the absence of a single step of progress toward reclaiming Palestine in the years since 1948 and by the Sharon raid of 1955. Twelve years later in 1967, when nineteen-year-old Abu al-Abbas was a junior at Damascus University, the Six Day War with Israel dropped on his dreams like a giant anvil. The promises, the emphatic gestures, the florid rhetoric were stripped away. Abu al-Abbas and his young compatriots could see that even Nasser was helpless against Israeli arms. "Palestine," they concluded, "can only be liberated by the Palestinians themselves."

Who else gave models of leadership? There were two Palestinians who were about a decade younger than Nasser and were a generation older than Abu al-Abbas and his friends. They had experienced the expulsion of 1948—not as children whose first memories were ones of exile and who heard the tale from their parents—but directly, with their own eyes, as impressionable young adults. In the years that followed they developed ideas—and organizations—of resistance nearby at the American University of Beirut.

Wadih Haddad (also Wadie Haddad or Abu Hani) was a Palestinian from the northern town of Safad. His family home was destroyed in 1948 and his family moved to Lebanon where he studied medicine at AUB. Here he got to know a man his age, a fellow Palestinian refugee and med school student named George Habash. He also met an older intellectual, history professor Constantine Zureik who had been born in Damascus. All three men were Christians, but in those days one's politics was more important than one's faith. As the decade following *Nakba* progressed, Arab nationalist sentiment in and around AUB came into focus. By the early 1950s a coherent if informal student group had coalesced around the goal of uniting the Arab world and liberating Palestine. In 1958, a decade after *Nakba* and five years after the Sharon raid, Haddad and Habash gave a name to their group and, in so doing, created something more than rhetoric—they started an organization: the Arab Nationalist Movement (ANM). A decade later, after the disappointment of the 1967 Six Day War, they brought together the ANM and two other groups: Heroes of the Return and Ahmed Jibril's Palestine Liberation Front. On December 11, 1967 they announced the formation of an umbrella organization: the Popular Front for the Liberation of Palestine (PFLP). The PFLP, at this point, saw itself as an ally to the PLO. In the year following, the PFLP established its headquarters in Damascus and began training commandos in bases that included as-Salt, Jordan. According to several sources, Abu al-Abbas joined the PFLP in 1967 at age seventeen.

Damascus University. 1968.

In 1968, Abu al-Abbas was a senior at the University of Damascus. He and his friends cultivated attitude and edge fed by bitterness over 1948, the Sharon raid of 1955, and the humiliation of the Six Day War of 1967. They had been failed by Arab Armies. In their view, Arab governments had proven to be impotent, corrupt, and complacent. If they waited for Arab national leaders to liberate Palestine, they could see, they would wait forever. Enlightened by the teachings of Constantine Zureik and inspired by the actions of fellow Palestinians such as Wadih Haddad and George Habash, Abu al-Abbas and his comrades were beginning to look closer to home for answers. Haddad and Habash were in Beirut, not Damascus. They were more than twenty years older than Abu al-Abbas and his crew. It is plausible, as some sources report, that Abu al-Abbas joined the PFLP-GC in 1968 while he was still at the University of Damascus—just a few months after its founding, presumably because he found it more action-oriented than the PFLP.

Although Haddad and Habash were older, they were far closer to Abu al-Abbas and his friends than were Arab national leaders. These two figures gave young Palestinian men like Abu al-Abbas the notion that they could develop leadership from within their own ranks—and could create organizations that, at least in theory, were capable of taking action.

1968: Working as a Schoolteacher

al-Midan neighborhood of Damascus. September, 1968.

After graduating with a BA degree in Arabic literature, Abu al-Abbas took a job at the al-Arabi School in al-Midan, a conservative section in the west end of town. He had realized his dream of a teaching career. Now he could support himself financially and take a step toward recognition and status. At this point, Abu al-Abbas became something more than a refugee living at the margins of society. He could now spend his days reading aloud from his favorite Arabic poets—and get paid for this pleasure.

If poetry was one of the passions of Abu al-Abbas, teaching certainly was not. He quickly realized that he was not cut out for a life of classrooms and students. Unlike other teachers, he did not spend long evenings and weekends mentoring students, correcting exams, and preparing lesson plans. He was almost always late for class and would show up with wrinkled clothes. His eyes had black streaks underneath from too much smoking and no sleep. After school, he spent long nights with his young Palestinian friends, debating politics and cursing Arab weakness.

At one point, the director of the al-Arabi school complained to the Department of Education using Abu al-Abbas's formal name. "This young Palestinian teacher, Mohammad al-Abbas," the director said, "is a detriment to the school. I want him gone!" The director worried that this young teacher's behavior would erode the school's standards and encourage other teachers to take similar liberties. One elderly principal working at another institution under the Department of Education offered to help. "Send this scalawag to my school," he said. "*I* will teach him discipline!"

Ultimately, the al-Arabi School terminated the tenure of Abu al-Abbas and sent him to a new school that gave its teachers less latitude. Abu al-Abbas was instructed to show up for work promptly at 7:30 AM in time for the flag raising ceremony in the school courtyard and the start of class at 8:00 AM. On his first day, however, Abu al-Abbas showed up at 11:30 AM. The school director was furious at the attitude and audacity of this Palestinian who was, after all, just a step out of the camps. Why did this young man feel that the rules that applied to everyone else did not apply to him? He summoned Abu al-Abbas. "Explain yourself," he said.

"Do you know why I was late?" Abu al-Abbas replied, "I was late because I was working for Palestine!"

Abu al-Abbas believed—until the last day of his life—that the mere mention of Palestine should be enough to arouse the nostalgic and patriotic sympathy of any Arab. A mention of Palestine, he felt, should send shivers down the spines of Arabs. And, usually it did. Palestine was Abu al-Abbas's hall pass. By 1968 the utter lack of progress toward a Palestinian solution had fueled an equally severe emotional attachment to this cause. Palestine united Arabs from the Gulf and from North Africa and from Syria, Arabs with black hair and brown skin as well as those—like me—with blonde hair and blue eyes, Arabs who were Muslims as well as those that were Druze, or Christian, or Alawite, or secular. Palestine became a touchstone.

Across the Arab world, Palestine became a banner that lifted the thinking of Arabs. It inspired a tangible Arab nationalism. In Damascus, Abu al-Abbas found that the ideal of Palestine could lift him in the regard of other Arabs, enhance his career, and give him entre to the highest levels of society. He had spent years studying and student teaching to assume his intended career of schoolteacher. Now, Abu al-Abbas sensed that his connection to Palestine could lift him much higher.

Back at his new school, on the first day of work: Abu al-Abbas stood before the director of the school while the older man tried to figure out what to make of this new teacher and his unusual excuse for tardiness. Then, Abu al-Abbas opened the package under his arm and shoved at the school director a bundle of manifestos. Abu al-Abbas and his comrades had composed these documents in flowery and high-toned Arabic and had formatted them so that the most catchy phrases were displayed magazine style, in big bold letters. The text was filled with contemporary stories of injustice at home in Palestine and urged the restoration of Palestine to Palestinians. The director was taken aback, but not moved. He drove home the message that Abu al-Abbas, at this point, was not the charismatic leader of a transcendent cause. He was just a guy who had showed up late to work. "Your excuse," he intoned, "is not accepted."

Abu al-Abbas telephoned men in positions of power—Palestinians and anyone else who would take his calls—all over Damascus, demanding their assistance to save his job. He urged them to respect his ideas and his work with other young Palestinians. Was Abu al-Abbas really asking for help with his job? Yes and No. The problem with his job was one that he had manufactured. The crisis with his school director was largely a pretext that enabled Abu al-Abbas to demand that highly placed Damascenes recognize the urgency of Palestinian suffering . . . and to honor his own position as an agent of Palestinian redemption—a tactic that he would use frequently over his career. "I am something more than an unknown schoolteacher from a ramshackle refugee camp," he was saying. "I am the voice of the Palestinian Underground."

5
Rifaat al-Nimer & Our Family

1918. WWI ended. The Ottoman Empire collapsed. My father was born.

MOST WOMEN ARE ENCHANTED BY THEIR FATHERS, no doubt, but mine was exceptional. Rifaat al-Nimer (Abu Rami) was one of a kind. He had talent and strong character. He based his life on honor and good sense. He dedicated his life to the Palestinian Cause. He was generous, tough, reliable, and immutable.

Rifaat's Early Life
Rifaat al-Nimer haled from a prominent and powerful Palestinian family in Nablus, located in the northern West Bank, approximately 73 km north of Jerusalem and an equal distance west of Amman. The Nimers had acquired land, power, soldiers, and money during the final years of the Ottoman Empire. Their family mansion in Nablus was a gathering point for the city's notables and intelligentsia. Wealthy residents came to the Nimer mansion to cultivate political connections that they hoped to translate into civil service positions in the Ottoman bureaucracy or lucrative business opportunities for their private enterprises. The poor, for their part, came to the Nimer mansion each day seeking financial assistance which the Nimers generously provided whenever possible. The Nimers were agents of the Ottoman regime. They offered protection and services to locals in exchange for loyalty to the Ottoman sultan, and played this role with high effectiveness until the curtain fell on the Ottoman Empire in 1918.

Made of stone with high ceilings and walls, the Nimer mansion was graced by large gardens sprouting a wide variety of fruits and vegetables as well as a fountain. It had large salons and guest houses, furnished with three stables for horses. Although protégés of the Ottomans in the years leading up to World War I, the Nimers (along with the prominent Touqan family) had actually resisted the Ottomans two centuries earlier, in 1657. After World War I, the Ottoman Empire collapsed and the fortunes of the Nimer family went into decline.

If my father's life had followed the arc of history, from his birth in 1918 he would have presided over the impoverishment of his clan. Rifaat al-Nimer, however, proved resourceful at adapting the diminished family assets to a new era. The system of lands and government connections that had ensured the prosperity of an earlier generation under the Ottomans was disrupted by WWI when the British took control. Although their political influence was diminished, the Nimer family continued to hold land and to preserve their social standing through the 1948 war. In the Six Day War of 1967, Israel seized Nablus and replaced Jordan as the administering government authority—a move that further distanced the family from its earlier prosperity. As his family's tangible sources of wealth eroded, Rifaat compensated by developing the financial skills to make the best of the family assets that remained and to find trustworthy partners for his business ventures. A nimble man, Rifaat mastered the art of managing abstract wealth. It was a new world where education, talent, and trustworthiness had become essential skills that replaced name, position, and inherited wealth as the key to success.

Rifaat al-Nimer holding his first child, a daughter whom he named Reem.

In 1928 when Rifaat was ten years old, his father Sudki al-Nimer died. From this age, Rifaat was cared for by his older brother Rashed. Rifaat studied at state-schools in Nablus that were run by the British during the years of the Mandate. Among his schoolteachers were the prominent Palestinian nationalists Wasfi Kamal and Akram Zueiter (Palestine's future Ambassador to the Arab League). Another teacher was the Druze notable Farid Zayn al-Din, who became Syria's ambassador to the US in the 1950s.

In 1936, shortly before the outbreak of the first Palestinian uprising against the British, my father cofounded the Palestinian Students' Union and was elected President. From his base in Nablus, Rifaat avidly supported the revolt of Haj Amin al-Husseini, the Mufti of Jerusalem, helping smuggle arms, money, and food to the rebels. For his efforts, the British tossed him and his uncle, Abdul Rahman al-Haj Mohammad (Abu Kamel) into a dungeon in Nablus. Detention would leave a mark on Rifaat's record that closed many doors. On the other hand, it would open other doors wide. In prison, Rifaat met leading figures in the Palestinian underground, such as Izzat Darwaza, Rashed Abu Ghazaleh, Abdul Hameed Shouman, and his own schoolteacher, Akram Zueiter. He stayed in jail for three months and, upon release, learned that he had been expelled from school. Rifaat's brother sent him to complete his education in Souq al-Gharb, a Lebanese village in Mount Lebanon. He was looked after by his uncle Abu Kamel, who by then, had taken political asylum in Damascus and traveled frequently to Beirut.

Upon completing high school, Rifaat went to the King Fouad I University (later renamed Cairo University). His brother wanted him to study medicine, although his schoolteachers had tried talking him into engineering, given his excellent command of mathematics. The young rebel said no to both, and majored in Arabic literature instead. Among his university professors was Taha Hussein, the "dean" of Arabic literature, a towering figure who had immense influence on Rifaat al-Nimer. Hussein used to affectionately call young Rifaat, "the rebel Palestinian." In college, my father cofounded and chaired the Arab Students' Union. Upon graduation, he returned to Nablus searching for a job. He had no other choice: family wealth was in sharp and constant decline and the family lands could not generate enough cash to support Rifaat and his siblings. Employment in the British-administered state service was off-limits to Rifaat, because of his prison record under the Mandate regime. He was finally offered a banking job in Nablus by Abdul Hameed Shouman, who knew Rifaat from their prison days in Nablus and had founded the Arab Bank in Jerusalem in July 1930 with a startup capital of fifteen thousand Palestinian Pounds.

Rifaat's First Banking Job

The year was 1937. The Arab Bank was expanding and had just opened a branch in Baghdad. Rifaat took a position here and grew in stature as the Arab Bank flourished. In 1942, Rifaat married a woman from Nablus who belonged to the powerful and aristocratic Masri family. By 1943, the Arab Bank had become one of the leading financial institutions in the Middle East with branches in Damascus, Baghdad, Amman and Beirut. In 1947, Rifaat was promoted to Assistant Manager of the Amman branch of the Arab Bank. While he worked in the Jordanian capital he was only an hour or two by car from his family home in Nablus, so he was able to better stay in touch with family and to participate in overseeing the family lands. By this point, on the eve of the 1948 war, Rifaat's prospects had begun to improve thanks to his well-paying job and his advantageous marriage.

Rifaat's posting in Amman also enabled him to resume his participation in the Palestinian underground. The international border was close by and Palestinians from British controlled territory were frequent visitors to Amman. Rifaat worked days in his bank job and met at night with secret Palestinian societies.

When the 1948 war erupted, the family was divided between Nablus and Amman. While the hostilities lasted, Rifaat's political activity likewise was cut off.

My Mother

1922. Rabiha al-Masri is born in Nablus.

My mother, Rabiha al-Masri, was raised in the grace of Nablus aristocracy by a well known land-owning family. She studied at a Jerusalem branch of The Friends School. The Friends School was a highly regarded private school serving both male and female students. It was operated by the Quakers who began their efforts in Palestine in 1869. Their school placed special emphasis on the education of women to enable them to "develop their potential and realize their opportunity to be equal members of their community."[1]

When Rabiha and Rifaat married in 1942 she was twenty years old and he was twenty-four. She joined him in Baghdad and then followed him to Amman in 1947. I was their first child, born in 1952 in Nablus. Rami, my younger brother, was born in Nablus in 1956 and my sister Rana was born in Beirut in 1961.

Rabiha was an intelligent and independent woman from a proud family. In accord with Arab tradition, she kept her family name. And in her marriage, she never hesitated to speak her mind to her husband and family. On the other hand, Rabiha did not chafe at the role of wife and mother. In the chaos of the years following the 1948 war, she followed her husband from Nablus and Amman to Saudi Arabia and then to Beirut with children in tow. She did not fret about the lack of opportunity to create a career independent of her husband. Rabiha was a pillar of support to Rifaat. She came to her role naturally, and with dignity.

While Rifaat Bey traveled to banking conferences on all four corners of the globe, Rabiha kept their house running like clockwork and kept their children clean, clothed, and fed. She was a warm and nurturing mother, one who was always available and always willing to listen. My memories of childhood are fond ones. I remember in particular a traditional Palestinian dish our mother served us. *Msakhan* was a type of pizza where spiced chicken was spread on flatbread, wrapped with onions, seasoned with cumin and sumach, cooked with olive oil, and garnished with pine nuts. Rabiha made sure that my siblings and I got the best formal and cultural education. In addition to

Rabiha and Reem, 1954.

Reem dancing in restaurant, 1956.

Rifaat and Rabiha watch Reem dancing in the sand, 1955.

In the long, hot summers Rifaat and Rabiha took their family from Nablus to the Syrian mountains where they ate afternoon meals in open air cafes with rivers flowing past and spent evenings in restaurants with live music. Many of the men in the audience wore ties and the women—a few were covered but most wore bare sleeves and flowing skirts. They also traveled to the seashore where they laid carpets on the sand and sat in the shade of tented awnings. Other times, they cruised in excursion boats, sitting beneath canvas canopies for shelter against the sun.

Rifaat, Rabiha, and Reem (above) on the water, 1957.

our school work, we learned to dance ballet and play the piano. Growing up as a child in British Mandate Palestine, Rabiha had received a high quality education—and she saw to it that our education was just as rigorous as hers. We children worked hard at our studies during the school year and then looked forward to summers with our family. In the hottest days of July and August, we traveled to mountain resorts such as Bludan and Zabadani in Syria, where the cool air was a welcome relief. We enjoyed casual meals in open air cafes with family friends. The sunlight was bright and warm and cafes filtered the light with canvas awnings and grape-covered arbors that dappled our table tops with shade.

At times, Rifaat found himself under great pressure in his work. Without Rabiha's assistance and support, Rifaat might have frayed or cracked. She gave him the power to move forward when times were tough. She stood in his shadow, confident of her own abilities and her importance. She was a loving wife and a caring friend. She set a rather high standard as mother to their children. She was the example of motherhood that I modeled when faced with raising my own young children.

Our Family after the 1948 War

After the war, Jordan took the place of Britain as governor of the West Bank. During the Mandate years, the British had tossed Rifaat into prison and eventually the Jordanians got the same idea. In 1957, they ordered a warrant for Rifaat's arrest, forcing him to flee to Riyadh, Saudi Arabia with his wife and their two young children. I was just a toddler, too young to remember anything about life in Saudi Arabia. Rifaat took a job as assistant manager of Riyadh Bank offered to him by Ali Shaath, the father of Palestinian Foreign Minister Nabil Shaath. Over the next four years, Rifaat worked for several different banks in Saudi Arabia and also continued his political activities. He became an earnest supporter of Egyptian President Gamal Abdul Nasser. (I was startled when, in 1970, my implacable father cried tears of grief when he heard of Nasser's death.)

Among other things, Nasser was a fierce critic of the House of Saud. Ultimately, after three or four years in the Kingdom, Rifaat was declared persona non grata by the Saudi authorities due to his support for Nasser. By 1960, Beirut was emerging as the banking hub of the Arab world. Rifaat moved to Beirut in 1961 to set up Bank al-Ittihad al-Arabi, his first lending institution, with funding from Arab investors. Our family moved with him to an apartment in Ras Beirut, a prominent neighborhood that included Hamra Street, a commercial center with a number of banks. I grew up here from nine years of age and—despite stints in West Africa, Tunisia, and Iraq—I have thought of Beirut as home ever since.

Along with Kuwaiti investors, Rifaat bought shares in the Beirut Bank for Commerce. Then, he was named the bank's CEO. Despite the outbreak of the Lebanese Civil War three years later in 1975, Rifaat refused to leave Beirut. He continued to live and work in Beirut even though, in 1982, the invading Israelis stormed the bank offices in an attempt to arrest him.

Rifaat's Career in Banking

Rifaat al-Nimer was a pioneer in banking and finance. Recall that, at the time of his birth, finance in the Levant was in Ottoman, British or French institutions. During the course of Rifaat's life, Arabs and Persians fed a thirsty world with their oil. After World War II, they took control of their wealth from Western businesses and governments. The region was floating in cash. And, by now, an entire financial industry grew up within the ranks of Middle Easterners. Beirut emerged as the banking capital of the Arab world, and Rifaat was one of several who played a significant role.

Beirut. 1964. Rifaat Joins the PLO.

Rifaat was a banker, and yet he also received some stripes due to his politics. The British had imprisoned him, the Jordanians chased him from the country waving a warrant for his arrest, and the Saudis had expelled him. Still, Rifaat persisted. In 1964, he joined the newly formed Palestine Liberation Organization (PLO) and supported the rise of its first chairman, Ahmad al-Shuqayri. From May 28 through June 2, 1964, Rifaat and nearly four hundred representatives from Jordan, Syria, Lebanon, Gaza, Egypt, Kuwait, Libya, and Iraq attended the First Palestinian National Council in East Jerusalem. He wore a badge carrying the map of Palestine inscribed with a variation on a familiar phrase from the US Civil Rights anthem (which was in the news at the time): "We Shall Return." The conference announced establishment of the PLO as the representative of the Palestinians in the West Bank, Gaza, Israel, and the Diaspora. Shuqayri announced formation of the Palestinian National Fund in September 1964 and appointed Rifaat as its Deputy President.

Rifaat had high hopes for Shuqayri, a seasoned Palestinian notable and statesmen who wore neatly pressed suits and looked more like a businessman than the leader of a revolution. After the 1967 Six Day war, Shuqari left office in deference to a leader who seemed better fitted to lead an armed rebellion.

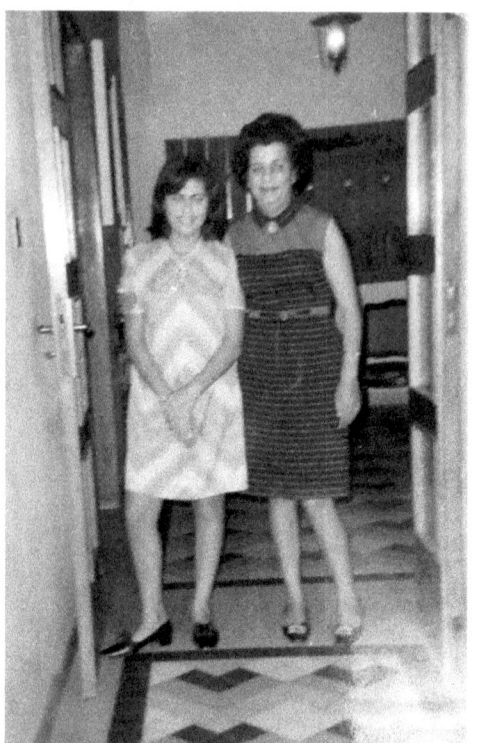
Reem and Rabiha in their Ras Beirut home, 1966.

Yasser Arafat always wore a gun on his hip. He looked the part of a revolutionary commander. Arafat bridled at fiscal restraints, whereas my father's career was all about financial probity. Arafat wanted to spend money at will, without reporting to the Fund. My father, on the other hand, wanted transparency and accountability. In Rifaat's world, everything needed to balance. Arafat, it must be remembered, used money as an instrument of control. He bought loyalty, certainly, but his ability to spend with utterly no oversight allowed him to refine the art of manipulation to a precise and sophisticated tool. Funds from Arafat molded everyone and everything in the world of the PLO. Arafat was not personally corrupt, but he was a grand corrupter. He ruled by dishing out financial rewards to his allies and buying off his enemies for nearly fifty years.

Rifaat may not have had enemies on the scale of the PLO chairman, but neither was his life smooth sailing. Once, in the mid-1970s, Rifaat refused to cash a check made out to the Palestinian commando leader Zuheir Muhsen, although it was signed by Arafat himself. Arafat telephoned him to complain, but Rifaat refused to budge, telling Abu Ammar that the expense drew on an account that was "currently unnecessary." When the money never came through to Zuheir Muhsen, Arafat was furious. It wasn't only Arafat who was upset with Rifaat al-Nimer. So were the Syrians, who in 1976, sent their tanks rumbling into the middle of the Lebanese Civil War. Although he was a frequent visitor to Damascus, Rifaat al-Nimer never became a yes-man for the Syrians who occasionally retaliated. On one trip into Syria, Lebanese police, at the urging of Syrian officials, detained Rifaat at a police station in Shtura, a town near the border. He was only released after Imam Musa al-Sadr, founder of the Amal Movement, intervened on his behalf with Lebanese authorities and with the PLO Chairman.

1968: Sweet Sixteen

I turned sixteen on September 9, 1968. I had no idea that, in this month, Abu al-Abbas was in Damascus where he slept at night in the oldest part of the Yarmouk refugee camp and, during the day, was making an ill-fated attempt to succeed as a schoolteacher. What was Abu al-Abbas doing in his spare time? In the evenings, in crowded smoky rooms, he and his young friends dreamed of joining the Palestinian resistance. For my part, I was staying in well appointed rooms in Ras Beirut, the most expensive part of town at the time. I was a Palestinian and a communist. Still, my father had money and I loved to have fun.

Beirut. 1968. I am sixteen. I get an Alpha Romeo.

I spent my teenage years in comfort and privilege thanks to the warmth and grace of Rifaat al-Nimer and my mother Rabiha al-Masri. Money was never an issue. Could it be that our wealth, in itself, fed my emerging political consciousness? My father was eager to satisfy my teenage indulgences. I recall that my first car, for example, was a mustard-color Alfa Romeo convertible. It's funny when one thinks of it: a young communist driving an Alfa Romeo! In the late 1960s, fancy cars were abundant in Beirut. On a typical outing, I would drive down the coast just a bit—3 or 4 kilometers from AUB—to the Raouche district with its distinctive Sea Rocks a hundred meters off shore. I would cruise along the Mediterranean in my shiny new car with impertinent Beatles tunes filling the air. Of course I played that wild parody, *Back in the USSR*, which turned western self-worship on its head and therefore jived with my emerging political sensibility. I wore Charlestons: designer bell bottom jeans. My tops featured designer logos and I was smoking a Marlboro (which I found incredibly cool) while my long blonde hair flew in the breeze. When I stopped for the view or for cold drinks at a roadside stand, young men would whistle and shout compliments while the older men just stared and kept their thoughts to themselves. I was young and I enjoyed the attention.

At the time, there were only two other sports cars in Beirut. One was driven by a member of the powerful As'ad family. The other by Walid Jumblatt, the son of veteran Lebanese leader Kamal Jumblatt. Being the crazy young girl that I was, I challenged the other two to races in al-Ramleh al-Bayda, which translates as "the white sand," and refers to the beautiful white sand beach another kilometer down the coast from the Raouche Sea Rocks. Now a posh neighborhood of Beirut, at the time the al-Ramleh al-Bayda district was nearly void of buildings and had large paved spaces that begged us to indulge our racing madness. One day the director of Beirut Police spotted us and told my father. Rifaat

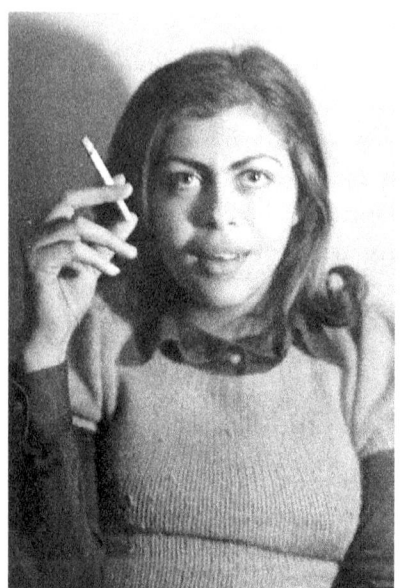

Reem with a Marlboro, 1968

Bey confiscated the car, and sold it in punishment. Now, if I wanted to go somewhere, I had to ride in the back of my father's shiny black Cadillac. Still, there were some great places close to home in Ras Beirut. I met my friends at upscale restaurants such as Faisal, a famous establishment on Bliss Street near AUB where we ate pasta and escalope. My favorite, however, was a burger place called Wimpy on Rue Hamra where communists congregated and history was made several times over. Wimpy was a UK Chain based on the rotund, hamburger-loving hyper intellectual character J. Wellington Wimpy from the comic strip *Popeye*. (Sad to say, Wimpy on Rue Hamra is now Vero Moda clothing store.) Any restaurant in Ras Beirut, of course, cost ten times as much as eateries in working class neighborhoods that served traditional fare.

I grew up at private boarding schools in Palestine, Lebanon, and Egypt. When I was at home, my mother taught me the proper way of eating, dancing, reading, and making polite talk at social gatherings. Through her I learned to appreciate Arab classic singers like Um Kalthoum and Mohammad Abdul Wahab, while sophisticated classical music—Beethoven and Bach—came through my boarding schools with their Western curricula where I played the standards: Bach's *Minuet in G,* Beethoven's *Für Elise,* and then the middle movement of the *Moonlight Sonata.* Table manners? Absolutely. I moved through a room with perfect posture, thanks to my training in ballet. My mother raised her

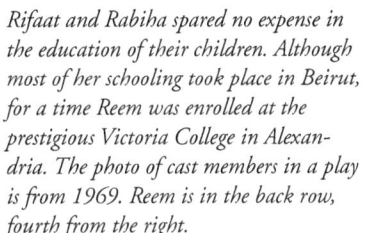

Rifaat and Rabiha spared no expense in the education of their children. Although most of her schooling took place in Beirut, for a time Reem was enrolled at the prestigious Victoria College in Alexandria. The photo of cast members in a play is from 1969. Reem is in the back row, fourth from the right.

children to be refined, polite, poised. When we were children, she instilled in us the confidence we would need as adults to move in Lebanese high society.

Rabiha and Rifaat spared no expense in my education. Although my principle schooling took place in Beirut, for a time I was enrolled at the prestigious Victoria College in Alexandria. It was there on El-Iqbal Street that world famous celebrities studied: Simeon Saxe-Coburg-Gotha the King of Bulgaria; King Hussein of Jordan; Egyptian actor Omar Sharif; and the Palestinian scholar Edward Said. One of my earliest memories in Egypt was when Gamal Abdul Nasser was sailing into Alexandria with Soviet Premier Nikita Khrushchev. As schoolchildren, we were asked to carry flowers and wait at the port to greet the two leaders, waving Egyptian and Soviet Flags. I was a fan of Nasser, having grown up in a Palestinian home that adored him.

When I spotted the handsome and charismatic President, I broke out of the crowd. Completely ignoring all rules set up by the school mistress, I ran toward him shouting: "Abdul Nasser!" A young child, I did not even call him, "Mr. President." When his bodyguards tried to prevent me, Nasser signaled them to stand back. He motioned me to him, patted me on the head, and kissed me on the cheek. The image of the tall and towering Egyptian President remains vividly imprinted in my mind until today. The next day, the school director telephoned my father to complain, saying that I had broken the rules. Rifaat al-Nimer listened respectfully. His daughter was a rebel as he could see. Yet she shared her love for Nasser and was chafing not at him but at a system that stood between her and her dream: nationhood for Palestine. Later, Rifaat laughed off the incident, dismissing it as childhood passion for iconic figures. From that day, the rebel in me began to grow until I was willing to break every rule and defy every order to get what I wanted. Where Palestine was concerned, I was convinced that what I wanted was the right thing.

6
Operation Gamal Abdul Nasser

While I was enjoying my sheltered, carefree teenage years in Beirut, Abu al-Abbas was in Damascus, scrounging for odd jobs to finance his education and to help support his younger brother. As I've mentioned, he joined the PLO at age 14 in 1964, and three years later—during his first year in college—he joined the PFLP. During college his extracurricular activities consisted of late nights in smoky rooms as he and his comrades in the Palestinian Underground plotted strategy. In 1968 as a senior at the University of Damascus, he joined the Popular Front for the Liberation of Palestine - General Command (PFLP-GC). After graduation, in the fall of 1968, he spent a few months intentionally failing at his profession of schoolteacher and then made a risky leap to an altogether different field: professional activist on behalf of Palestine.

In Damascus, the PFLP-GC was the premier Palestinian resistance organization. Abu al-Abbas worked within this organization until 1977 when the PFLP-GC with Syrian backing sent troops into Lebanon to attack the PLO. At this point, Abu al-Abbas broke with the PFLP-GC and took charge of his own organization, a re-creation of the Palestine Liberation Front (*Jabhat al-Tahrir al-Filistiniyyah*), which he referred to as the "PLF" or the "Front." In the Western media, the PLF became synonymous with "terrorism" because of its connection to Abu al-Abbas. In reality, however, the PLF was anything but a terrorist organization. It was the embodiment of everything that Abu al-Abbas fought for during his life: The liberation of Palestine; the establishment of a Palestinian State with its capital in Jerusalem; Palestinian refugees granted the sacred right of return.

1961 - 1966: The Palestine Liberation Front (PLF)
The roots of the PLF trace back to firebrand Arab communism and Marxist thought, popular in the Middle East in the 1960s. It was founded in 1961 by two like-minded Palestinian communists, Ahmed Jibril and Shafiq al-Hout. Later the PLF was brought under the umbrella of the Palestine Liberation Organization (PLO), which from February 1969 until November 2004 was headed by Arafat himself.

Ahmed Jibril was also known by his *nom de guerre* Abu Jihad (not to be confused with another Abu Jihad, Khalil al-Wazir, an associate of Yasser

Arafat's). Jibril was ten years older than Abu al-Abbas. Although they had similar objectives, the two men never got along. Abu al-Abbas disliked Jibril and so did Arafat. Both saw him as a pawn for the Baathist regime in Damascus where he has been based since 1948. In their view, he was willing to sell out his own countrymen to win favors in Damascus.

After the *Nakba* in 1948, Jibril's family fled to Damascus where Ahmed Jibril was raised from ten years of age. He joined the Syrian Army in the late 1950s, rising to the rank of captain. During the short-lived Syrian union with Egypt, Jibril was expelled from the army due to his communist sympathies. President Nasser did not approve of communists in the military.

PFLP 10th anniversary poster, 1977.

If Abu al-Abbas did not admire Jibril, he did think highly of Jibril's partner, the PLF cofounder Shafiq al-Hout who seemed to Abu al-Abbas to be far more principled and worldly. Educated at the prestigious American University of Beirut, al-Hout had gone into a teaching career in Kuwait which brought him into early contact with Arafat and the current president of Palestine, Mahmud Abbas. He was more focused and balanced than Jibril. He also had a cleaner financial and political record. Over the years, his hands were never stained with Palestinian blood and, through his writings, he contributed more to the ideology of the Palestinian Cause than Ahmed Jibril had ever done—despite the latter's ostensible commitment to Arab nationalism and leftist Marxist thought.

In 1966 under the joint command of Jabril and Hout, the PLF launched its first military operation, an attack on an Israeli settlement in the upper Galilee that killed two Israelis. Another operation followed shortly before the Arab-Israeli War of 1967. Then came an attack on a cinema in Haifa, where the Israelis took a PLF commando prisoner. Samir Darwish was the first PLF troop to land in an Israeli jail. By 1967, the PLF had become a magnet for aspiring young men committed to the Palestinian Revolution.

After the June 1967 Six Day War, Jibril and Hout merged the PLF with Heroes of the Return (*Abtal al-Awda*) and the Arab Nationalist Movement (ANM) to create the Popular Front for the Liberation of Palestine (PFLP). The Arab Nationalist Movement was headed by the enigmatic George Habash, who was based in Beirut in those days. Like al-Hout, Habash was an AUB graduate. In these years, George Habash was a figure of immense stature among Palestinians. He was to the Palestinians what Nehru was to India or Charles de Gaulle to France. Most observers, thought that Jibril was fortunate and would benefit from his association with Habash. By the end of 1967, however, it became clear that Jibril and Habash differed on the question of Syrian involvement. Jibril wanted a closer alignment with Syria. George Habash, however, felt that the Palestinian Cause would be jeopardized if it became totally dependent on Syria. The Syrians could not be trusted, Habash argued, even though the Syrian leadership had close relations with the Soviet Union and the Soviets had taken a public stance against Israel and its American and British backers. As a result of this disagreement between Jabril and Habash, in early 1968 Jibril broke away to form the Popular Front for the Liberation of Palestine - General Command (PFLP-GC). The new organization, which ripped off Habash's party name and many of his commandos, became a Syrian-backed and Syrian-funded military organization based in Damascus.

1977: Abu al-Abbas Revives the PLF

The al-Fakhani neighborhood of Beirut. April 24, 1977.

In 1976, Ahmed Jibril deployed PFLP-GC commandos to Lebanon in support of Syrian troops opposed to the PLO. Abu al-Abbas was shocked and disgusted at this move. The time was right, he felt, to assert himself. Abu al-Abbas broke away from the PFLP-GC for a new - old organization, a re-invented Palestine Liberation Front (PLF) under the leadership of Talaat Yacoub. Like Abu al-Abbas, Yacoub had worked as a schoolteacher. [1]

Ahmed Jibril did not brook dissension among his subordinates and declared open war against his former associate. In August 1977, Jibril bombed the PLF headquarters located in the al-Fakhani section of Beirut: 200 Palestinians were killed in cold blood. Abu al-Abbas was outside the building at the moment of the blast. He never forgave Ahmed Jibril. "The man is mad," Abu al-Abbas told me. (In 2012 during the Syrian Revolt, I watched TV reports of Jibril's forces pounding Palestinian civilians in the Yarmouk Refugee Camp of Damascus because they had stood with the Syrian rebels. I recalled Abu al-Abbas and how right he had been in his assessment of Ahmed Jibril, thirty years earlier.)

After Abu al-Abbas became secretary-general of the PLF, he brought his own men aboard. At his urging, for example, Comrades Omar Shibli and Abu Ahmed Halab were voted into the PLF's Central Committee. Abu al-Abbas also amended the PLF charter, adding "socialism" to its doctrine to remain on good terms with the Soviet Union, which was aggressively involved in Palestinian politics and had an excellent working relationship with Arafat and the PLO. The PLF also established a media arm that featured a periodical called *Ila al-Amam (Forward)*. Abu al-Abbas became the mouthpiece for the PLF, since he was the one who could best articulate the group's vision for liberation. From this point, Abu al-Abbas had no other life: Palestine became his one and only obsession, more important than power, safety, money, health, and family.

The PLF under Abu al-Abbas launched its own operations. In 1978, the year that Israel invaded south Lebanon in Operation Litani River, three *fedayeen* from the PLF traveled through Jordan, entered the occupied town of al-Himma in the Southern part of the Golan, and engaged Israeli security forces near a resort packed with Israelis. It was an Class A operation, and all of its members returned to home base, unharmed by the Israeli Army. Another operation followed the assassination of Lebanese philosopher Kamal Jumblatt, an ally of the Palestinian resistance, and carried his name. It was a paragliding operation, for which Abu al-Abbas became famous, where two commandos landed in Galilee and engaged in fierce battle with Israeli soldiers, resulting in the death of Ghassan al-Kakhi and the arrest of Jumaa Khalaf Yusuf and Abdul Halim Mohammad al-Hafez. The most famous of all the PLF operations code named by Abu al-Abbas as the Gamal Abdul Nasser Operation. It involved an attack on the Israeli settlement of Nahariya on April 22, 1979.

1979: Operation Gamal Abdul Nasser

Operation Nasser was planned by Abu al-Abbas and his military commander, Said Yusuf, in response to the Egyptian-Israeli peace agreement signed by Nasser's successor, Anwar al-Sadat in 1978. Four commandos, carefully handpicked by Abu al-Abbas, carried out the operation. Three where from Syria: Abdul Majid Aslan (from Hama), Mohammad Ali (from Suwaida), Ahmed al-Abras (from Latakia). The leader was Samir al-Qantar (also transliterated "al-Kuntar") from Mount Lebanon, a young militant, only sixteen-years-old (who would later become the "dean" of Lebanese prisoners in Israeli jails).

So popular was the PLF under Abu al-Abbas's command that young men from different Arab countries flocked to join in the 1970s, pretty much as they had joined Fatah after the 1968 Karameh Battle. Abu al-Abbas was careful to make room in the PLF for Arabs from varied backgrounds. The organization

Israeli navy hits back after raid

Newspaper report of the Abdul Nasser Operation, 1979.

was never 100% Palestinian. Abu al-Abbas claimed that all Arabs supported the liberation for Palestine.

Operation Nasser saw the four young men launch a small rubber boat with a fifty-five horsepower outboard motor and a speed of 88 km/hour from Tyre in southern Lebanon at dusk. By midnight, they had penetrated 10 km into Israeli waters and ran their boats onto the beach in Nahariya. Their goal was to attack the Israeli security forces and to trigger attract worldwide attention for the Palestinian Cause.

The story of what happened varies from one source to another, with Western writers often saying that the PLF commandos knocked on the door of a private home, calling out in Arabic via the intercom to frighten the inhabitants into calling the police. When the police showed up, one of them (Eliyahu Shachar) fired at the Palestinians (or were they "warning shots" as the Israeli security services insisted?) and was killed by return fire. Samir al-Qantar says that he personally fired thirty bullets during this incident. The Palestinians then entered an apartment at 61 Jabotinsky Street, planning to abduct several Israelis and take them back to Lebanon where Abu al-Abbas would then swap them for Palestinian prisoners in Israeli jails. One apartment was occupied by Charles Shapiro, an Israeli immigrant from South Africa, who shot the Front commander Abdul Majid Aslan dead with his pistol. The three remaining militants then broke into the apartment of the Haran family. They took thirty-one-year-old Danny Haran hostage along with his daughter, Einat, and dragged them down to the beach, where a shootout ensued with Israeli police and Israeli soldiers from the elite Golani

Special Forces. The gunfire disabled the boats that were waiting by the shore, prompting al-Qantar to shoot Danny and his daughter. He was arrested, along with al-Abras, while his comrades were shot dead. In response to the operation, the next day Israeli gunboats shelled the Naher el-Bared refugee camp located north of Beirut 16 km from Tripoli, and according to Western press reports killed three civilians in an hour-long bombardment.[2]

Samir al-Qantar and Ahmed al-Abras were convicted of the murder of four Israelis by an Israeli court in 1980. They were sentenced to four life sentences and an additional forty-seven years for injuries inflicted on Israeli troops. In May 1985, al-Abras was released in a prisoner exchange deal between Israeli Prime Minister Shimon Peres and the PFLP-GC. Israel released 1,150 Palestinian (including Hamas founder Ahmed Yassin) and Arab prisoners in exchange for three Israelis captured during the Lebanon War. Samir al-Qantar, however, spent nearly thirty years in prison before he too was set free on July 16, 2008 as a result of a swap between Israel and Hezbollah Secretary-General Hasan Nasrallah.

7
My Life in Politics

Beirut. 1970. I join Fatah.

THE STORY OF MY LIFE WAS one of extreme and often painful contradictions. I grew from a leftist teenager who liked to have fun in the 1960s into a committed leftist revolutionary in the 1970s. To phrase this transformation in the language of food, I went from eating Wimpy burgers and escalope in classy Ras Beirut establishments with printed menus, plate glass windows, and tables on the street where the elite could see and be seen—to al-Fakhani and the camps where I savored dense, working class fare in nameless, drab hole-in-the-wall places with poor light, crowded with folk who did not pose by the windows—these places scarcely had windows—and did not talk that much but concentrated on nourishing themselves. These places were steaming hot and filled with the aroma of falafel and *mujaddara*, lentils and borghol or cracked wheat.

1970: Flirting with Fatah

I began my political career at the age of eighteen in 1970. While still a high school student in Beirut, I enrolled in Yasser Arafat's Fatah movement, which he had founded about a decade earlier. My "patron" in Fatah was Shadia Helou, a young Palestinian woman only a few years older who studied at the American University of Beirut (AUB). The main thrust of Fatah was simple: Palestine would only be liberated by the Palestinians themselves. Based on the track record of Arab nations since 1948, the strategy of relying on Arab nations to restore Palestine was futile. The notion that Arab leaders had power or even the desire to exercise what power they had was a horrible illusion. To members of Fatah, every spot of land in the world was a battlefield for the Palestinians, and every Israeli was an enemy. Fatah's message resonated with me, with Abu al-Abbas, and with an entire generation of Palestinians who grew up in the 1950s and 1960s.

Fatah had been founded in 1959 by members of the Palestinian Diaspora, specifically young men working in the Arab Gulf: Arafat, Salah Khalaf (Abu Iyad), Khalil al-Wazir (Abu Jihad), and Mahmud Abbas (Abu Mazen).

The 1959 edition of the group's journal, *Filastinuna Nida al-Hayat* (Our Palestine is the Call of Life) explained that Fatah was motivated by occupation, injustice, and the plight of Palestinian refugees across the Arab World. Of course there were many cells in the Palestinian underground and an enormous amount of dialogue and debate. What brought Fatah to public notice and caused it to intersect with Palestinian politics was the fiasco of the Six Day War with Israel in June 1967. After this catastrophe, Fatah joined the PLO, receiving 33 of 105 seats in the Organization's Executive Committee. By the time I had joined, Arafat had become Chairman of the PLO in addition to his capacity as head of Fatah.

Flashback:

Jordan. March, 1968. The Battle of Karameh.

Eight months after the Six Day War, in March 1968, the Israel Defense Forces (IDF) invaded Jordan with the objective of destroying Palestinian training camps at Karameh. The PLO, with supporting Jordanian forces, withdrew most troops from Karameh in advance of the attack and focused on counter attacking the IDF once the battle began. Although the Israelis claimed a tactical victory following the battle, the myth of Israeli invincibility that the IDF had claimed after the Six Day War was pierced. Fatah and other Palestinian groups with Jordanian support had attacked the Israeli Army in full force. Under the weight of Israeli arms, Fatah held its ground—which was a surprise to the Israeli military. Karameh was the only military victory achieved by Palestinians—ever—and the event has been bathed in glory among Palestinians ever since. The Battle of Karameh did for Arafat what the Suez Canal War did for Nasser. It elevated him to heroic standing throughout the Arab World. Following Karameh, thousands of young men flocked to join Fatah in Amman, Beirut, and Damascus.

Beginning in September 1970, Fatah fighters fled Jordan and quickly resumed their attacks on Israel—this time using Lebanon as their base. Several times I visited Fatah military camps in southern Lebanon where I donned fatigues, did calisthenics, crawled on the ground with a rifle under my chin, and learned to fire a rifle at a target. I also helped provide first aid to wounded Palestinian fighters. I was part of the crew that transported the wounded from border villages to Beirut hospitals. When not traveling back and forth to the border with Israel, I was in Beirut where I helped out as a walking talking PR person for the Palestinian cause. When not chatting with the public and helping to raise funds, I was visiting hospitals to lift the spirits of the injured and dying.

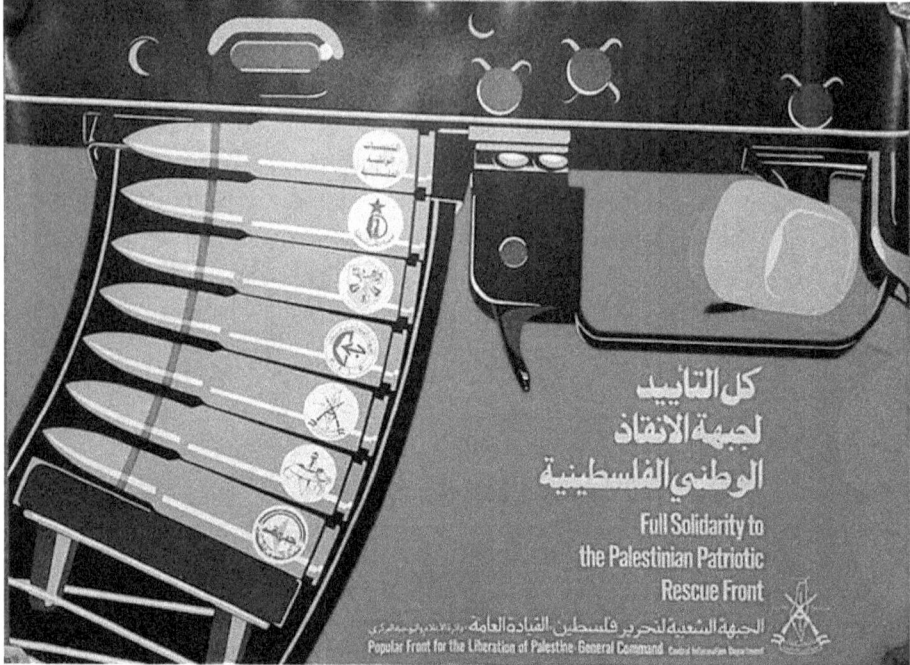

A poster by the Popular Front for the Liberation of Palestine (PFLP) displays the logos of Palestinian groups on the bullets in the magazine of an AK-47. Below left: The PFLP logo. Below right: the PFLP-GC logo. The PFLP, more than all other Palestinian factions, used poster art in its media efforts.

Facts on Palestinian Factions

Fatah was created in 1959 by Palestinian professionals (including Yasser Arafat) who were working in the Arab Gulf. In 1961, Ahmed Jibril and Shafiq al-Hout formed the Palestine Liberation Front (PLF). In 1964, at the first Arab League summit in Cairo, the Palestine Liberation Organization (PLO) was created. It evolved into an umbrella that centralized fundraising for several Palestinian groups, the largest of which was Fatah, headed by Arafat.

In 1967, following the disaster of the June Six Day War against Israel, Jibril and al-Hout merged their PLF with the Arab Nationalist Movement headed by George Habash and other groups to form the Popular Front for the Liberation of Palestine or PFLP.

In 1968 Ahmed Jibril broke away from the PFLP to found the Popular Front for the Liberation of Palestine - General Command or PFLP-GC. He accused Habash of being "all talk and no action." Unlike Habash, Jibril was willing to accept Syrian arms and training.

In 1969, Arafat became head of the Executive Committee of the PLO, a post that he held until his death in 2004. In 1976, the PFLP-GC attacked PLO forces in Lebanon during the civil war. The attack inspired Abu al-Abbas to break away. The following year, with Talaat Yacoub, he re-established the PLF.

In 1977, Ahmed Jibril retaliated against Abu al-Abbas and Talaat Yacoub: Jibril's PFLP-GC forces with Syrian backing bombed the PLF offices in Beirut, killing 200. In 1981 the PLF split, with Talaat Yacoub heading a faction that accepted Syrian support.

The PLO logo (above left) and the PLF logo (above right).

Fatah logo.

In 1982, after PLO forces departed Beirut, leaving the US and Israel in charge of security, the residents of the Sabra and Shatila refugee camps were massacred by a Phalangist militia. The death toll: at least 800 - 3,500.

In 1983, Abu al-Abbas refused Syria's efforts to turn him against Arafat. As a result, the PLF lost their offices and training facilities in Syria. In 1984, Arafat rewarded the loyalty of Abu al-Abbas by elevating him to membership in the PLO's Executive Committee.

In 1985, after the *Achille Lauro* operation went bad, Talaat Yacoub denounced the PLF faction led by Abu al-Abbas that launched the *Achille Lauro* attack. Abu al-Abbas, in response, slammed the Yacoub faction for its ties to Syria.

1971: The PFLP

Beirut. 1971. I leave Fatah for the PFLP.

In 1971 I stopped paying my dues to Fatah and embraced the Popular Front for the Liberation of Palestine (PFLP) that was headed by my father's friend, George Habash. I knew PFLP figures well—they were always at our house and spent hours on end with my father. They considered me the PFLP's "daughter" and I considered myself a legitimate child. As revolutionary young people, we were taken away—completely enchanted—by the PFLP's Marxist-Leninist rhetoric. My attachment to the PFLP was emotional and intellectual, however, and I never enrolled as an official member.

Arafat, unlike the PFLP cadres, was an Islamist at heart. As a young man, he had flirted with the Egyptian Muslim Brotherhood. The Islamist approach clearly contradicted our secular and revolutionary views. By then, I was beginning to view the capitalist world in which I had been raised as regressive, backward, and ultimately wrong. I wanted a classless society with an equal distribution of wealth. I wanted to bring down pro-Western regimes in the Arab World and dabbled with hard core communism, socialism, and Marxism.

I was a Palestinian, and yet my orientation and my developing ideology were international. Beirut was, after all, an international city. To entertain its large Christian population, Beirut received Western media—the same sports, news and celebrities that Europeans and Americans saw on TV and heard on radio. Beirut was a favored tourist destination for Europeans.

Our American University was founded by American missionaries in the 1860s and was witness to the long-standing involvement of Americans in our town. I was a communist, and I did not approve of capitalist Western governments, however strong their cultural presence in Beirut.

The Soviets were run by an older generation that may not have kept up with the times, but they were backing the Palestinians politically and financially—and for me and my generation that was enough. In my room at home in Beirut, I had two posters pinned on the walls: Mao Zedong and Che Guevara.

Flashback:

Bolivia. October 9, 1967. Che is executed in the village of La Higuera.

Che had been executed just three years earlier in 1967 in Bolivia by soldiers trained and equipped by the US—and his death suggests the tension between a pure communism of the type that my friends and I admired and the pragmatic operating rules that governed the day-to-day actions of national governments of any ideology. What was Che even doing in Bolivia? Che Guevara was part of the ruling clique in Castro's Cuba until, in 1965, he began criticizing the Soviet Union as an "accomplice of imperial exploitation," among other things.

In response, Castro removed Che from his position of influence, and the next anyone knew he was out of the country and standing in front of a rightist firing squad. Che Guevara spoke the clear cutting truth. In a world where *Realpolitik* ruled the day in the East as well as the West, Che's words and Che's being made it impossible for him to live. He became a martyr for a pure communism that did not exist in any government in the world, certainly not in the Soviet Union.

We thanked the Soviet Union for its support. We would have been dead without it. Yet that did not mean we were oblivious to its shortcomings.[1]

Before I could bring myself to become a registered member of the PFLP, I found myself criticizing the group among my friends. The PFLP was the work of an older generation that was out of touch. They did not possess our international outlook and our political consciousness. When the Jordanians disbanded PFLP training camps in 1971 and expelled the PFLP militias, we were underwhelmed by the response of PFLP leaders.

1972: The PRFLP

We accused the leaders of the PFLP of being too willing to play by the rules. Wasn't the first rule of being a revolutionary, after all, to break the rules? That is exactly what we did.

Beirut. 1972. I leave the PFLP for the PRFLP.

About a year after I began my dalliance with the PFLP, my friends and I joined a break-away faction. There were about 150 of us. In 1972, we established the Popular Revolutionary Front for the Liberation of Palestine (PRFLP) headed by one of our colleagues, Abu Ali Irbid. Our organization was short-lived and achieved nothing substantial. Still, it was progress. We succeeded in bringing a younger group of like-minded rebels into one room and one organization. We were the future.

The idealism of the PRFLP was palpable and seemed utterly compelling at the time. We established a base in the all-Palestinian al-Fakhani neighborhood of Beirut and were poised to make great things happen. In these days, I was no longer spending time in Ras Beirut at high society restaurants like Faisal or even the dear burger joint Wimpy. Instead, I would meet for quick meals or extended conversations with friends in small downscale places in Fakhani. Looking back, it surprises me to realize how brief was the life of the PRFLP. It had no real achievements. It was, simply, a debating society. It brought young Palestinian and

Poster photo of Che Guevara by Alberto Korda.

Lebanese intellectuals into a political salon where we would explore the dire conditions of the Arab World.

Mohammad & Ali

At one PRFLP forum I met the man who would become my first husband, Mohammad al-Ghadban. A twenty-four-year-old man from Quweiqat, a village in the suburbs of Acre, he was half Palestinian and half Lebanese from his mother's side. Mohammad was handsome, a dashing embodiment of our shared Palestinian ideals. He definitely made my heart flutter. Like all women whose marriages ultimately dissolve, however, I now wonder how I failed to see a more balanced picture of this man who was so appealing at the time.

Mohammad had begun his university studies and read widely on his own, but never took the trouble to complete the requirements for a degree. By then I was studying at an elite women's college, The Beirut University College (BUC) which is now known as the Lebanese American University (LAU).

Mohammad was the middle son and to a degree was overshadowed by both siblings. His older brother was based in Africa where he was financially successful and was able to support the family from abroad. His younger brother Ali was a political natural and the bright star of our group. He was one of several who founded the PRFLP. Ali was my friend—we locked minds and hearts: spirit, soul, revolution. We called him *Che*, in reference to Che Guevara. Intellectually, Che Guevara was associated with the concept of a new revolutionary man . . . as the prerequisite to creating a revolution. My father's friend George Habash who lead the PFLP tipped his hat to Guevara when spoke of the "new breed of man" on whom our hopes rested. To me and to my friends in the movement, Ali al-Ghadban was this man.[2]

Ali was a local guy who was not widely known beyond our group. But to us, he was a role model and a towering inspirational figure: his flame burned more brightly. He transcended his class and seemed to travel deeper, farther, higher. The challenge he posed to the status quo was profound. He was a sacrificial figure. Like Che himself, Ali was too beautiful to live.

Mohammad was far more willing to accept the limitations of his class than either of his brothers. Mohammad attended university, yet he seemed to sense that a university degree in his hands would not mean the same thing as it would if he came from a wealthy family—hence his lack of motivation to complete his degree. Mohammad was not bitter about the limitations that his background placed on him. Rather, I think he felt that he was just being realistic. He did not want to waste time and effort reaching farther than was possible. He did not want to bite off more than he could chew. You could say that Mohammad lacked drive. He seemed poor, in a financial sense—although he had the same finances as his brother Ali and no one would ever have described Ali with this adjective. Perhaps it was just that Mohammad had an instinct for survival. He was satisfied with the simple pleasures of ordinary life.

Mohammad and I agreed on our politics: we were both fully committed to an independent Palestine. But in temperament we were opposites. He was timid, whereas I was full of life. He was hesitant, while I threw caution to the winds. People remarked that I was a "tiger." (And this is the literal meaning in Arabic of my family name "Nimer.") I felt as though I was spending my life walking in and out of the hangman's noose. Mohammad, on the other hand, stood at arm's length from trouble and lived a life of comparative peace and tranquility. I don't recall a single moment in our participation in the RFLP where he spoke out or took any manner of action. When it came to planning RFLP events, Ali and I would do all the planning while Mohammad sat in the corner.

What drew me to Mohammad? For one thing, he was incredibly handsome. If his brother Ali had the heart of Che, it was Mohammad who had Che's looks. Mohammad was highly intelligent, widely read, and a very good writer. I could not help but notice, however, that in those days he never lent his talents to our cause. He was a resource for us, but not one that could be focused or directed toward a tangible goal.

1973: The Egyptian Students' Movement

Cairo. 1973. I participate in the Egyptian Students' Movement.

I was also briefly evolved with the Egyptian student movement. On October 6, 1973 Sadat's Egyptian army had crossed the Suez and thrust into the Sinai Peninsula in the October War (the Yom Kippur War). They were blocked by Israeli forces for three days, as if accepting a stalemate, only to advance again later—after it was too late for the Syrians on the Golan Front. Although the Syrians had made stunning advances they were nevertheless routed by an Israeli counter attack. We felt that continued Egyptian fighting in the Sinai would have increased the chances of the Syrians on the Golan Heights. In October and November, I joined protests against President Anwar al-Sadat's behind-the-scenes talks with the Americans which eventually led to an Egyptian-Israeli peace agreement in 1978.

Our revolutionary spirit dictated that we liberate Palestine and topple Sadat simultaneously. My meetings and demonstrations in Cairo got me into trouble with Egyptian authorities, and at one point I was arrested at Cairo Airport. I had to call up my cousin Nabila (Um Lutof), the wife of Palestinian leader Farouk al-Qaddumi, to bail me out. I spent one night in jail and was questioned curtly by the officer on duty who grew more and more angry with my non-response responses. Finally, he threw his hands in the air. "Take her," he said to Um Lutof, "and tell her never to come back to Egypt!"

During my visits to Egypt, I met Sami Abu Yaghi, a student of medicine at Cairo University and roommate to Tawfiq Qabbani, another student at the Faculty of Medicine who was the son of legendary Syrian poet Nizar Qabbani. Sami was a Jordanian who hailed from a very prosperous family. Briefly, I juggled two romances: the impoverished Mohammad in Beirut and the wealthy Sami in Cairo. My relationship with Sami, tender as it was, nevertheless was sending me in a direction that lacked the challenge that I was after in life. He was too decent. He was just like the people in my family, just like the friends I had developed in my stints at expensive private schools. In Cairo, Sami liked to attend the Cairo Opera. When he visited me in Beirut, Sami's idea of a good time was to attend a lecture at AUB. My instinct and my pleasure, in contrast, was to spend the night talking politics in a shabby bar, smoking the night away. Sami once sent me a letter. "I've completed my medical studies in Cairo," he said, "and I am preparing to travel to the US to take an internship, as required to gain experience in my specialty. Before I travel abroad, I'd like to visit Beirut to ask for your hand in marriage."

No thanks. Instead, I cut off all communications—which broke Sami's heart. He slid into depression and canceled his travel plans to the US. Ultimately, he traveled instead to London for his internship. He then married a woman from Venezuela and established a successful practice in her country, where he resides today, over forty years later.

1974: Mohammad and I Decide to Marry

I was young, so was Mohammad. We had been seeing each other for about a year. Now that Sami was out of the picture, we fell in love. Yes, there was lust involved. But more than that, I felt that Mohammad could give me a life of commitment. I wanted my life to be significant. I wanted to participate in the making of history. Yes, I was also looking for the thrill that came from taking risks. I wanted adventure. My feelings for Mohammad, of course, were colored by the working relationship I had developed with his brother Ali. Mohammad had the face I loved, Ali had the soul. The three of us together, as they say, were greater than the sum of our parts.

In February 1974, Mohammad and I decided to get married. My parents saw Mohammad as a poor boy from the slums of Beirut who lacked initiative—not a suitable match at all. It would have been more accurate to say that Mohammad's family was an honorable one from a rural village in south Lebanon where the economy was slow and cash was hard to find, but my family was not listening at the moment. When I approached my mother with my bold decision, she went insane, completely drowning the idea. "Your father," she said, "will never approve!"

Although I was an impulsive and daring girl, I nevertheless grasped the need for a winning strategy. Also, finance: I had pulled out a pencil and calculated that we could survive for a year or two if needed on various bits of family money that had come my way over the years. Rather than approaching my father directly, I did it through his bureau chief Akram Istanbuli, a trusted family friend. When he returned with my father's veto, it made me all the more adamant. "I must get married," I told him. The decision to marry was a good fit with the revolutionary persona that I was developing. Shouldn't a good revolutionary break away from her life of stability, privilege, and comfort to live with a poor man in the Palestinian underground? So it was that I began to plan this stunt and to arrange financing. I accounted for every detail, from A to Z.

Beirut. March, 1974. Mohammad and I elope.

Inspired by black & white Arabic movies, in a scene I had probably seen somewhere, I left a note that read, "Mother: You have decided to stand in the way of my happiness and prevent me from marrying the man I love because he is poor and because you are a bourgeoisie family. I have therefore decided to pursue my happiness and marry him without your consent."

Mohammad and I escaped my family and fled to East Germany. We chose this country because my father's connections in Syria, Jordan, Iraq, and Lebanon were too strong. He or his friends would catch us. We wanted to go as far away as possible. Why Ost Deutschland? It had a strong relationship with Palestinians at the time. More than this: no other country would give Mohammad a visa, since he only had a Palestinian-Lebanese document. Travel for Palestinians from Lebanon and other countries was, and still is, a nightmare. They would wait for months for a visa approval, which often never comes, and are treated cruelly at airports around the world. I did not have the same problem since I traveled on a Jordanian passport.

When I departed with Mohammad, my father was stained with embarrassment. Rifaat was a pillar of the community, the gold standard of probity, and an unyielding bulwark in the city that banked the oil wealth of sheikhs. Some of the wealthiest individuals in Beirut and in the region turned to him to handle their most precious financial assets. His wisdom and judgment were legendary. What did it say that his daughter could not accept his guidance? And what did it mean that he was unable to control the women in his own family?

My father lost standing, just a bit, within Beirut society and within the banking community. And there were also repercussions within the conservative Nimer family. His older brother Rashed, who had raised my father as a child, learned of my marriage and then, suddenly, suffered a stroke and died. I was forever blamed by the family for his death. According to Nimer family tradition, it was unheard of that a man would marry someone from outside our social caste—don't even mention for a woman to do so. And for a woman of the family to elope? Well, it was just not done.

Mohammad Is Kidnapped

Mohammad and I stayed in East Berlin for several weeks. When we felt that we had made our point, we returned to Lebanon, got legally married, and addressed our mission. How to liberate Palestine? And, at this moment the problem for Palestine, as we saw it, was not so much the Israelis as it was the backward and regressive regimes in Arab countries that forever sold out Palestinian interests. Mohammad and I traveled south to Tyre and then 10 km more to Qana, a sleepy village in southern Lebanon—his mother's mountain village—and rarely ventured into Beirut. We lived in an old and simple Arabic home with a spacious courtyard—a far cry from the European style apartments of Ras Beirut where my family lived. Qana was located 12 km north of the border with Israel. It later came to international notice after the Israelis committed massacres here in 1996 and 2006. In 1974, however, it had nothing but elderly people, small huts, and a society that went to bed by 8:00 PM. There were no cafes, no social clubs, and scarcely any cars on the roads.

Qana, Lebanon. April, 1974. Mohammad is abducted.

Mohammad and I had made it back from Europe, but now we were worried about my powerful family. The prospect of being "captured" by my parents haunted us day and night. One day in April, shortly after our return from East Germany, Mohammad was indeed abducted on the street in Qana by Palestinian commandos working for Fatah.

Frantic at being busted, I asked around, only to discover that Mohammad had been taken by Fatah's strongman, Abu Iyad—a good friend of my father. I got on the telephone, called Abu Iyad's office, and received an appointment. I traveled to Beirut and stormed into his office in Fakhani. He stood to greet me—tall and proud—surrounded by a group of men. Among them were his two bodyguards, who I later got to know better, Atef Bsisso and Amin al-Hindi (the future governor of Gaza). Abu Iyad's first instinct was to embrace "baby Reem," given that he had known me as a child. He imagined that a young girl with pigtails would walk in and he would take her hand and lead her back home. Instead, he found a storming young woman shouting at him. "What have you done?" I said. "You kidnapped my husband! You are working for regressive powers in society! Are you not claiming to be a revolutionary uncle Abu Iyad? Why then have you abandoned all that you stand for in committing such a crime?"

Here was the Fatah founder, one of the champions of the Karameh Battle, a man whose military prowess kept Moshe Dayan and Menachem Begin awake at night. Now, he was being dressed down by a twenty-three year old woman who looked even younger. Instead of kicking me out, as I expected, Abu Iyad patiently listened to my temper tantrum without saying a word. After I made my point and stomped out as rudely as I had walked in, he called my father to tell him what happened. "To blazes with him and with her," said Rifaat al-Nimer. "Let him go. I don't want to hear of them again in my entire life!" Hours later, Mohammad was released from captivity and returned to his home in Qana.

Now that we had obtained a ceasefire with my family, Mohammad and I returned to Beirut, got in touch with his brother Ali, and resumed our lives of resistance. Ali, Mohammad, and I were a team. Although you could say that Mohammad was a silent partner, the three of us worked well together. Certainly it was difficult to be estranged from my family. It would have been good if Mohammad could have found a job. Yet, when Ali and Mohammad and I were together, my partnership in activism with Ali was effective and satisfying—and my marriage to Mohammad was working just fine.

As 1974 unfolded, Ali and Mohammad and I could feel a slow winding toward—we did not know what. Beirut was the money capital of the Arab world. It was a safe zone. Everyone needed Beirut and no one dared to break it. Mohammad and I were happy with the life we were making together. We felt strangely confident, secure, and we decided to start a family. In July, we conceived our first child.

8
Dark Skies

In the summer of 1974, storm clouds were gathering that would unleash the Lebanese Civil War the following spring.

Causes of the Civil War, Briefly

To simplify, the causes of the Lebanese Civil war which began in April, 1975 can be traced directly to the French Mandate in the Levant. At this time, Lebanon was ruled by a government that gave the balance of power to Christians. Yet the French had enlarged the Ottoman borders to include the fertile Bekaa Valley, a Muslim enclave. Now, a solid majority of Lebanese were Muslim.

On top of this imbalance were the ripple effects from the war of 1948. Palestinians had been driven from their land into neighboring countries, especially Jordan. After World War I, King Abdullah and his Hashemite clan had been granted control of the newly created Emirate of Transjordan. Now, half a century later, the PLO commanded armed troops that used Jordan as a base for launching operations into Israel. Especially after the PLO showed its mettle in the battle of Karameh, a question floated in the air: Was Jordan to be ruled by Arafat and the PLO or by King Hussein and the Hashemites? The war between Abdullah's grandson King Hussein and the Palestinians began in September 1970 when the Jordanian army attacked Palestinian forces in Amman and other locations across the country.

The Syrians invaded Jordan from the north in support of the Palestinians. However, the Syrians never committed their air force to the battle. Two months after their retreat, a coup d'état in Syria brought Hafez al-Assad to sole power.

Hafez al-Assad was not about to let a Palestinian army cross his border, let alone take control of Jordan. As a result of Jordanian military action and Syrian indecisiveness, the Palestinians were expelled into the only nearby country too weak to oppose them: Lebanon. Afterward, certain Palestinian factions honored Syria for its military intervention, and remained pro-Assad until the curtain fell. Others, however, felt as though Syrian troops had raised their hopes only to abandon them to death and exile when things got rough.

Arab leaders met in Cairo on 27 September and forced King Hussein to accept a cease fire. The next day, however, Egyptian president Nasser died of a heart attack. The Palestinians had lost their protector, Hussein resumed military action, and the leaders of the other Arab nations did nothing. By July 1971, Hussein had regained complete control of the country and had expelled all armed Palestinians to Lebanon.

Over the following two or three years, Palestinian troops took control of south Lebanon and used it as a base for attacks on Israel. Palestinian troops also were garrisoned in Beirut. The PLO felt that it was acting, simply, to oppose the Israeli occupation of their land. Lebanese Muslims, Arab nationalists, and political left-wingers under the umbrella of the Lebanese National Movement made common cause with the Palestinians, whose arms gave them political clout. Only now could they make gains against the Christian block that the French had left in power. For their part, the Maronite Christians who ran the country and dominated the national army regarded Palestinian troops as occupiers, or close to it. The Christian position was simply untenable. A rebalancing needed to take place. But Maronite leaders felt that the threat to their political dominance was a threat to their existence. What to do if fighting broke out? Well, they had a hunch that Israel would come to their aid.

For its part, Syria was pursuing its own interests. Syrians still believed in their hearts that Lebanon was a province of Syria—and frequently cited the Ottoman organization of these lands as authority. Syrian intelligence seemed to be on every block. The Syrian elite were forbidden from conspicuous consumption at home, lest the socialist ideals of the Baath Party be undercut by the indulgent life styles of Baath officials. In Beirut, however, it was "anything goes." The Syrian elite personally made enormous amounts of money by controlling the smuggling routes into Syria, and the larger Syrian economy depended on Beirut as its link to the world. The Syrian government officially praised the Palestinian cause. Still, Syria was ultimately allied—not to any specific party or movement—but to its de facto position as a big brother who exerted authority over this ostensibly independent nation. The Syrian aim was to keep Lebanon within its sphere of influence.

1974: The Arab Communist Organization

Beirut. August, 1974. I leave the PRFLP for the ACO.

Now that I was pregnant with our first child, Mohammad and I turned to a different sort of conception on the political front. In August we walked out on the short-lived PRFLP and, in August 1974, participated in the creation of yet another group: the Arab Communist Organization (ACO) with a twelve member core committee. The PLO was fighting a low intensity guerrilla war against Israel, so there was no particular need for a new group to strike directly against the ultimate foe. On the other hand, the PLO had made deals with Syria and other Arab regimes—deals that let these regimes off the hook. Rather than confronting Israel, these regimes stepped back from all military action and, to satisfy Palestinians, they let the PLO engage in skirmishes with the Israeli Defense Forces—with no real hope of success.

The ACO wanted to punish Arab nations for accepting and institutionalizing the military stalemate with Israel. We wanted to strike at what we thought of as pro-Western regimes in Saudi Arabia, Egypt, Lebanon, and Syria. These regimes stood by in the fall of 1970 when King Hussein violated the ceasefire he had agreed to, resumed combat, and over the next ten months killed or removed all PLO fighters in Jordan. Had it not been for the scheming and denial of these regimes, we preached, then Palestine would have been liberated years earlier. The Syrian government, in particular, was guilty as hell.

Unlike the polemical PFLP or the poetic PRFLP, the ACO focused on practical things: buying arms, training commandos, and taking what we argued was rightfully ours—by force. The Organization's chief was Mohammad's brother Ali al-Ghadban (our Che) and I was one of his aides. As our first order of business, we created secret cells inside the countries that we targeted, starting with Syria. To finance our activities, we decided to copy Robin Hood. We planned to rob the rich and—not to feed the poor exactly but to "liberate the poor from tyranny and oppression," as we phrased it in those days. How to finance our actions? Well, my father was a banker. We certainly knew where the money was.

Law-breaking contradicted the principles I had been taught from early childhood. Our family's livelihood was banking. We were at the top of the social order, at least as high as Palestinians could get in Lebanon. More than any other institutions, banks could not exist without laws that were respected and obeyed. We were the farthest possible thing from criminals. At this time in my life, however, I was in thrall to the revolutionary persona I had created. I saw no other way to make money for our resistance and so I supported this tactic. We felt that we had advanced beyond our debating society days with the PRFLP. Now we had a plan, and we were going to act.

1975: My First Child

Beirut. April, 1975. I give birth. The Lebanese Civil War begins.

The first attacks and counter attacks of the Lebanese Civil War made news in our region. But Mohammad and I devoted more thought to our work with the ACO and to our growing family. In April, 1975 I gave birth to our first child, a boy whom we named Louai. Over the months that followed, I took leave from nursing my baby to help Ali plan our first action. Mohammad, per usual, did nothing. I joined Ali on visits to Syria to enlarge our members and to map out potential targets for our attacks.

We noted, among other things, American firms taking part in the annual Damascus International Fair. The cell we founded in the Syrian capital was based in a building inhabited by Fihmi al-Yusufi who was, at the time, Speaker of the Syrian Parliament. We reasoned that Syrian authorities would never search for us in a building occupied by one of the regime's top officials and his security detail. Ultimately, we decided to blow up the Syrian Ministry of Defense located in Umayyad Square—the heart of the Syrian capital. To raise enough money to purchase the explosives, we robbed two banks, one in Sidon and another in Tyre. In deference to my father, estranged though he was, we selected banks other than his own. For each heist, Ali put on a ski-mask and walked into the bank, with gun in hand. In the meantime, I stood at the gates, covering my face and carrying a rifle similar to the one I had learned to use at the camps of Fatah. When Ali ran out the doors of the bank with the money, I drove us to safety—testimony to my wild driving skills. In the evenings I returned to Beirut to care for my baby.

As an office worker, I had helped Fatah do fundraising. With the ACO, we did fundraising as well—but our approach did not require much office work or accounting. In total, we raised—or should I say stole—a total of 120,000 Lebanese Liras. This was the one secret I never confessed to my father, who died at the age of eighty-nine in 2007 without ever knowing that his precious daughter had become a bank robber. When I eloped, it was a horrific embarrassment for Rifaat. My status as an outlaw, if it had become public, would have ruined him.

Damascus. July, 1975. The ACO strikes.

Several members of our group set up our explosives at the gates of the Syrian Defense Ministry in July while Mohammad and I held our breath in Beirut. At last we heard: The charges had exploded per our plan, the building had been damaged, and the Syrians had gotten a message. We toasted our victory. Exactly what message did the Syrians receive? Did we change the Syrian policy toward Palestine? While these larger questions floated in the air, Syrian authorities immediately began hunting for members of the Arab Communist Organization. They quickly arrested anyone with the slightest link to us under warrants signed by Syria's President Hafez al-Assad. In Arabic, Assad means "lion." We were now feeling the lion's teeth.

Ali Is Executed

My friend Ali was abducted in Lebanon by agents of the Syrian *mukhabarat* and taken back to Damascus. On the night he arrived, he was given a mock trial. The next day—Saturday July 29, 1975—he was hanged in public, along with his comrades. President Assad let them twist in the wind in Marjeh Square—the city center since Ottoman times—the place where the Ottomans and after them the French had hung independence activists. Ali was only 25, recently married, and left behind a young widow and an unborn son. Among other comrades who were hanged alongside Ali were Mohammad Giath Sheeha, a student at the Faculty of Engineering at the University of Damascus, Walid Udan, Mohammad Kheir Nayef, and Ali Hourani. Three of our female Lebanese comrades, Youmna, Lucy, and Leila (all code names) were saved from death by Abu Iyad, who whisked them out of the lion's mouth and gave them sanctuary at secret locations controlled by Fatah. For our part, Syrian dailies published our mug shots beneath a headline that read, "WANTED!"

At this point Mohammad and I were *persona non grata* with Abu Iyad (Salah Khalaf), so we did not receive the protections that he extended to our associates. We had to arrange our own hiding places. One Lebanese lawyer, an ally of the Arab Communist Organization, approached us with the keys to his home in Sidon. "You can stay here," he said, "until the danger has passed." From Sidon, we moved to another hideout in the Yaacobian Building in central Beirut, overlooking the seaside.

I had been raised in comfort and luxury. I had enjoyed every advantage. Now, life was difficult. I was caring for a four-month-old baby. I feared for our safety and wondered about the future I was creating for my child. My father was a powerful man. I was sorely tempted to call him, to apologize, and to collapse in his comfort zone. Yet I did not break. For that matter, the more difficult the challenges became, the more I seemed to take strength from our plight. Yes, I could have married Sami with my family's blessing and become a doctor's wife and spent time at clubs overlooking the Mediterranean. But I had chosen Mohammad for the promise of a life that had meaning as well as risk. On this count, Mohammad had clearly delivered—but wait. Was Mohammad leading me into a life of urgency, commitment, and risk? Or was I the one leading Mohammad?

My husband was so afraid that he never ventured outside our new Beirut apartment. I can only imagine his resentment. As a young man from a modest background, he had not been eager to overturn his personal status quo. Unlike his brother Ali, he had a sense that the poor always lose when conflict erupts. Mohammad knew that money did not grow on trees. He valued stability, continuity, and a life where you could take a breath in the morning without looking over your shoulder. What did Mohammad think of me, deep down? I was the rich kid, spoiled by an indulgent father, fighting my father for control of my life, searching for meaning and refusing to be enticed from my burning vision of freedom for Palestine. And now, after Ali and I had cooked up our Syrian foray, Mohammad was paying the price. He and I were tied together by the blood of his brother, the warrant for our arrest, and by our young child. Why is it that young fathers always feel the impulse to flee when faced with the need and dependency of a new child? Yes, Mohammad was fearful. He was living a life created in my dreams, and he can be forgiven for wondering at times if my dreams had been delusions. He had never asked for this.

I did the shopping and cared for the baby and also attended what remained of our secret meetings with Palestinian comrades. One day armed men dressed in the military uniform of al-Saiqa, the pro-Syrian militia, showed up on our street corner. The moment I saw them, I knew that we were being watched. I hurried upstairs to pack a bag, grabbed the baby in my arms, then ran out the back door. Mohammad followed, frantically. A block away, I flagged down a cab.

Although we were staying a jump ahead of the authorities, Mohammad and I were feeling no thrill at our life of commitment. We were wanted by Syrian intelligence. Also, the cease fire with my family was not especially firm. At any moment, we expected someone to grab us at the instructions of my father. And what of our child? Instead of growing up surrounded by loving grandparents, he had to be carried from one rude hiding place to another.

His life, unlike my own as a child, was not one of comfort and stability. We were depressed. Our world had imploded. Our Che was gone. Deprived of a friend, a brother, and an inspiration, we found that our life together no longer worked.

A Desperate Proposal

We returned to Mohammad's mother's village, and at this point, he suggested that I could stay with his family in Qana while he joined his brother's business in Africa. Although living apart, we could remain married. Or, if it made more sense in the face of my family's objections, we could legally divorce. I listened, then countered with a proposal that we escape together—to the east, through Damascus. I had a friend who promised to provide us with fake Lebanese IDs. Again, it was crazy to go to the very same city where there was a bounty on our heads. But we were in Lebanon and had no other choice. Lebanon is surrounded by the sea, by Syria, and by Israel. We could not go to Israel, obviously, and I now wonder why we never thought of traveling to Cyprus by sea—it certainly would have been easier and less risky than Damascus.

Still, the Syrian capital was the last place that the Syrian *mukhabarat* would be looking for us. We left our young son in Qana, in the care of his grandparents. Then, thanks to the new IDs which were Class A fakes, we easily passed through the border checkpoint and into Syria. We drove directly to Jobar, a small town 2 km northeast of the capital Damascus that is known for its 2,000 year old synagogue, a site for Jewish pilgrims over the centuries.

We stayed at the home of a Palestinian Bedouin from the Negev Desert. He wore traditional costume and had a big gold tooth that gleamed at us whenever he smiled. Chickens walked in and out of the courtyard, and a rooster woke us up every morning. We lived in an alcove separated from the rest of the household by a miserable blanket. At night, his children would peak around the blanket to watch the two strangers who had landed from another planet to share their living space, their food, and their animals. Our life in Jobar wasn't very comfortable, but it was safe. It gave me time to reflect on the point that Mohammad and I had eloped without any of the elements required for a successful marriage. We did not have a place to live. Mohammad did not have a job. The two of us were socially, and mentally, incompatible. We shared our political goals, but our styles in politics were very different. I was a doer and Mohammad was an observer. Now, of course, we were suffering the consequences of my approach. Yes, my friends and I had gotten something done. We had pulled off a military action. But we had been victimized by the law of unintended consequences—a law that asserted itself, as well, a decade later on the *Achille Lauro*. Military actions—any actions in the physical world—are easy to conceive but extremely difficult to implement. How naïve we had been! We had no idea that the Syrian response would be instantaneous and deadly. We were good at late night debate. I had proven, as an educated woman, that I could wrap bandages on the Fatah wounded and could make a fundraising pitch to a small audience. Mohammad could listen and study the dialogue and events around us, and when asked he could brilliantly parse what he had seen and heard. Beyond these things, we were clearly out of our depth.

I Will Take You to Mezzeh!

A month after we took refuge with the Palestinian Bedouin, our new host presented two Palestinian-Iraqi passports. "Take them; they will get you out of Syria." They were real documents, authenticated by the Iraqi government, probably stolen from two Iraqis traveling to Syria.

At this time, the Baath regimes in Damascus and in Baghdad were at daggers' points. Each considered themselves the true father of pan Arab nationalism. Iraqi President Ahmed Hasan al-Bakr would welcome with open arms two dissidents who had struck at the heart of Hafez al-Assad's authority. A bomb at the Defense Ministry in downtown Damascus? This was music to Iraqi ears. We would be safe in Iraq. At this time, Iraq was swarming with Syrian dissidents including founder of the Syrian Baath Michel Aflaq and Syria's ex-President Amin al-Hafez. We would easily "melt in" with this crowd of Arab fugitives.

Mohammad reserved two seats for us in a taxi cab headed to Baghdad. We treated each other as total strangers, so as not to arouse suspicion. I got in the back seat next to another passenger, and he sat in the front, next to the driver. We did not even look at each other during the long journey from Damascus to the Iraqi capital. Our route took us along a narrow road through the Syrian Desert, guided by the moonlight rather than proper street lamps. When reaching the Tanf – Alwaleed border crossing, the officer on duty stamped Mohammad's fake passport without ado, then looked at mine and said: "I want to see her." The woman in the photograph, about ten years my senior, was obviously poor. She had different facial expressions, sulking eyes, a bony face, and darker hair. The Syrian officer immediately realized that the passport was either fake or stolen. "What is a woman doing all alone," he asked himself, "Why is she traveling alone through the Syrian and Iraqi desert, in such times. Where are her children? Where is her brother, uncle, or husband? Something smells fishy."

I descended from the taxi as Mohammad fidgeted and struggled to keep a plain face on his panic. Marching slowly into the officer's corner, I put on a poker face. "Is this you, Mariam?" Mariam was the name of the woman in the passport. I nodded. "Yes Sir." He looked at me from top to bottom, cracking a wicked smile. The remains of my family's wardrobe were still with me. I was wearing designer jeans and a Channel branded sweatshirt. "Tell me who you are," he shouted, angrily banging his fist on the counter. I did not even blink, "I am Mariam, sir." I had memorized the information in the travel document. I gave him Miriam's date of birth, family name, date of issue, and date of expiry. "It cannot be you," he remarked, flipping through the passport. "This woman is much older than you!" When I insisted, he threatened: "I will take you to Mezzeh young girl, if you don't tell me who you are!" He was referring of course to the notorious prison in Mezzeh on the outskirts of the Syrian capital, famed for holding political dissidents of all stripes and colors. Mezzeh was never a temporary stay: those who went to Mezzeh spent a lifetime behind bars. "They will pluck out your hair and cut your tongue," he barked.

Again, I insisted that I was Mariam, investing in the incredible courage that God puts in human beings during moments of utter danger. He gave a long sigh then surprised me by adding, "Listen. I don't know who you are, and I don't know why you are traveling on a passport that is not yours. But, something inside of me tells me that I should let you pass." He stamped my passport and let me through. As I rode away into the night, I reflected that this official had thrown up his hands in dismay—just as the officer on duty in Cairo had done in 1973. Now, just a few minutes beyond the grasp of Hafez al-Assad, I had the feeling that history was once again working in my favor. I have carried that feeling with me ever since.

Safe in Baghdad

Baghdad. September, 1975. Mohammad and I take jobs in a hotel.

Baghdad, which later became a second home for Abu al-Abbas and me, was painfully large and scary when we first got there. It was my first trip to the Iraqi capital. I was only twenty-two, away from my family, away from my baby, and pregnant with my second son, Reef. I was emotionally drained, penniless, and physically tired from the nomadic life I was living. We stayed at a commercial lower-end district of the Iraqi capital, in a cheap hotel on Al-Rasheed Street. We were surrounded by street peddlers and vagabonds—certainly not the honorific, cultured, and wealthy Baghdad one reads about in history books. Our savings could last for no more than two weeks. I tried talking Mohammad into going to the Iraqi government and telling them, "My wife and I are the founders of the glorious Arab Communist Organization! We are the ones who carried out the heroic attack in Damascus!"

"They will give us a pension," I told him, "and keep us as guests of honor of the Iraqi government. They might give us a car, or even grant us an audience with Ahmed Hasan al-Bakr."

Mohammad, of course, would never hear of it, fearing that if the Iraqis discovered our true identity, they would extradite us to Lebanon. As a woman, I could not approach the Iraqis on my own. My father had lived in Baghdad in the 1940s, and he surely still had friends who could have helped us, if we asked. But I refused to make a single call.

We decided to find jobs with the idea that we were going to settle permanently in Baghdad. We ended up working at a five star hotel called *al-Qasr al-Abbasi* (The Abbasid Palace) that was run by a wealthy Iraqi family and faced Kahramana square, located just across the Euphrates from what would later become the Green Zone. Remember Firdos square where Saddam's statue was toppled in 2003? If you walk south for five minutes on al-Sadoon Street, the next square you reach is Kahramana, a famous spot located at the crossroads between the two sections of Karrada. In the 1960s the central fountain was refurbished with a statue of a woman pouring water into open jugs and the pool below. The woman depicts Kahramana (or Qahramana), a figure from pre-Islamic times who used her wit to defeat a gang of thieves who threatened her father's caravanserai. (The Abbasid Palace was closed in 2004 due to violence following the 2003 US invasion. More recently, Japanese tourists—who favor this location for taking "I was here" pictures—have restored the damage done to the sculpture and fountain in the recent war.)

The hotel was busy with tourists and businessmen. Mohammad, thanks to his good looks, was hired as a receptionist. For my part, I was sent to the Operator Room. This was my first paid employment as an adult—the Fatah gig I took at nineteen had been pro bono. I spent long hours in a stuffy, windowless room where I connected our guests with domestic and international phone calls. I was hired by my new name "Mariam!" When bumping into me during work, even Mohammad would call me "Mariam."

I Meet Abu al-Abbas

One day during work, Mohammad contacted me from the reception. "Reem," he said, "A senior Palestinian delegation is coming here. They are important guests of the Iraqi government. They are staying at this hotel." The delegation, he added, was headed by Mohammad al-Abbas [ie. Abu al-Abbas] one of the leaders of the PLO. I had heard the name Abu al-Abbas once too often since the late 1960s. When working in the Beirut underground, Mohammad's brother Ali had told me plenty of stories about Abu al-Abbas. "You will love him Reem," said Ali. "He is unlike the rest. He doesn't care for the prestige of high position or pose for accolades as do Abu Iyad or Abu Ammar (Arafat). He is a true embodiment of our revolution!"

Abu al-Abbas had been a ranking member of the Popular Front for the Liberation of Palestine – General Command (PFLP-GC), led by the pro-Syrian Ahmed Jibril. The latter's pro-Syrian views prompted Abu al-Abbas to defect, re-establishing the Palestine Liberation Front (PLF) with Talaat Yacoub in April 1977. More than once, Mohammad's brother Ali had taken me to meet Abu al-Abbas at his headquarters in Beirut. But every single time we missed him. Now, months after Ali's death, I finally got a chance to meet this iconic Palestinian rebel.

When Mohammad told me that the Palestinian delegation had checked in, I abused my position at the Operator Room and called up his room number #201. "Excuse me," I stuttered, "I want to speak to Abu al-Abbas." A rough yet polite voice replied: "The Comrade is in a meeting. Who is it?" I tried to wiggle out of giving my name, but he insisted, saying that Abu al-Abbas cannot call back unless he knows my full name. "Reem Rifaat al-Nimer," I said. I hadn't used my real name in months, and it was good to feel that one way or another, it would ring a bell. Clearly, I said to myself, Abu al-Abbas would either know my father, or recall my role in the Arab Communist Organization. As it turned out, he knew both, in addition of course, to remembering the young crazy teenager driving a mustard colored Alfa Romeo around Beirut—a scene that remained imprinted in his mind. Minutes later, the switchboard light turned on: Abu al-Abbas was on the line! "Reem!" he shouted, as if he had known me for ages. "What are you doing here?" I explained that I was working at the Operator Office and did not want to bore him to death with my story—at least, not over the telephone. "Come up immediately," he commanded.

I smoothed the wrinkles out of my uniform, took a quick look at the mirror to see if my hair was in proper shape, and walked confidently into Abu al-Abbas's room. In those days, he was just twenty-seven and still an incredibly handsome young man. "I cannot believe that this is the young girl that has rattled Beirut and challenged the Nimer family!" He was smiling, with a flattering sparkle in his eyes. He suddenly looked around, seeing that I was alone, and asked: "Where is your husband? Where is the brother of *Che*?" Abu al-Abbas, apparently knew perfectly well who we were, why we were in Baghdad—our entire saga. Mohammad followed quickly, and Abu al-Abbas hugged both of us passionately. We told him of our dramatic exodus from Lebanon, and he roared with laughter.

Abu al-Abbas was kindness itself on that first encounter, treating me like a father. By no means was it love at first sight. He asked whether we needed any assistance, financial or political. No longer able to put on a brave face, I nodded, trying to hold back my tears. He gave us money, and asked if we wanted to stay at this hotel or move anywhere else in Baghdad. We had decided that it was time to move, yet again. So we asked if he could help us travel to Abidjan, the former capital of Ivory Coast, where Mohammad's brother was based. Abu al-Abbas nodded affirmatively. Thanks to his excellent relations with the al-Bakr regime, Abu al-Abbas was able to get us authentic Iraqi passports. Mohammad and I had stayed in Baghdad for two months total. Now, we were free.

9
Our Time in West Africa

Abidjan, Ivory Coast. July, 1976. Our family is together in Africa.

AFTER MY FIRST MEETING WITH Abu al-Abbas in Baghdad in 1975, Mohammad traveled directly to West Africa. I returned to Lebanon on my new Iraqi passport to give birth to my second child and to pick up my eldest son from relatives. Then, in July, the three of us joined my husband in the city of Abidjan, Ivory Coast. Second only to Paris, Abidjan was the largest French speaking city in the world.

The exclusive neighborhoods in Abidjan were occupied by the local elite as well as by wealthy foreigners. We rented a modest house with a single floor in the section of town where Europeans and Arabs stayed. Many of our neighbors were Lebanese. When I went to market or Mohammad drank tea in a café, we rubbed shoulders with Lebanese—who were quick to let us know how things were going back home. We spent a month getting settled and then tried to figure out how to support ourselves.

1976: Finding Work in a New City

Mohammad's brother owned a chain of supermarkets and seemed to be doing well. What made things difficult was that the job Mohammad had hoped to take with his brother turned out not to be a consistent source of income. Mohammad's brother ran a lean operation and did not need another full time manager—especially one who knew nothing about business in general or the food business in particular. Mohammad was a concept guy. But it turned out that running supermarkets required a person who thrives on busywork. Although he took paid work when it became available to him and his brother helped us financially whenever he could, the pickings were slim. For my part: Like Mohammad, I had not completed college. With two young children to care for and no family or friends in this city to make connections for me, I was in a position to take a job.

These were rather boring, uneventful years, especially compared to what I had lived through in Lebanon, Syria, and Iraq. My life here was domestic, not professional or, for that matter, political. I began to think about food—something more subtle than the pasta and Wimpy burgers on Rue Hamra of my teenage years; something more elaborate than the hearty working class falafel sandwiches and lentil soups I ate in the camps and in al-Fakhani. I began to see food as an art that embodied and gave definition to home and family.

Now, a continent away from my parents and struggling to create a family of my own, I began my first tentative culinary experiments—efforts that I have continued through the years. I tried in different ways to mix Arab and African cuisine. One point I remember well: local cooks used peanuts to thicken their sauce. I began to think of food as a way of concentrating and distilling culture. I thought of the Arabic-African stews I created—my beginner's efforts—as a fusion. And I could see an equally delicious fusion of people and cultures every time I walked down the street. Abidjan was a city where traders from all over the Mediterranean and Europe had made port going back centuries. They left trading communities behind.

And so I found a city filled with expats: French lived alongside Arabs, North Africans, and West Africans—along with a few of everyone else. You could also say that I was creating another sort of fusion in my own life. In Lebanon my politics had been heartfelt, willful, emphatic—and had taken over my life. Now my politics receded into the background and was fused with practical domestic concerns and the profound pull of motherhood.

These days the walls of our little house were bare: no more posters of revolutionary icons or any other type of decoration. I no longer worshiped international political rock stars. Yet the lack of decoration said something more. The bare walls reminded me that these were temporary lodgings. I did not want to put down roots. Palestine was still my spiritual home and Beirut was my home town. Bare walls reminded me of who I was, where I came from—and pointed to the inevitability of return.

I was twenty-four years old now and I was busy at home. While changing diapers, cleaning house, and chopping up vegetables for our meals, I had plenty of time to think back on my life.

In my sports car days in Beirut I had been the teenage child of a wealthy family and possessed a political consciousness that was superficial but gradually growing deeper. Politics had become more serious to me by the time I was nineteen, in 1970, when I joined Fatah. At this point, I was a flaming young revolutionary wanting to liberate Palestine from the Israelis and the Arab world from tyranny.

Over the next five years my dedication to Palestinian liberation continued to burn strong, yet my naïveté fell away little by little. I saw from the inside the tensions between different factions within the PLO. I saw the clashes of ego and personality that seemed to overshadow the goal of aiding those who suffered and giving justice to the dispossessed. I also began to see that there were generational differences. The generation that was in its twenties in 1948 and saw the expulsion of Palestinians with adult eyes had a different orientation than activists such as Abu al-Abbas, who had been born in a refugee camp.

I was only four years younger than Abu al-Abbas but my political development had come later in my life. He joined the PLO at age fourteen and I was eighteen when I joined Fatah. Abu al-Abbas grew up in Yarmouk and Damascus which were bereft of western chains—no Wimpy burgers here—and had a dreary East bloc feel about it. I grew up in Beirut, a city far more alive to international business and more exposed to European media and culture. It felt as though Ali, Mohammad, and our friends in Beirut were from a different decade than Abu al-Abbas. We were part of the New Left that made egalitarian thinking a fashion statement among the youth of the world. I was sixteen in 1968 and watched on the news when Paris was brought to a halt by days of barricades and protests. Ten million workers demonstrated that idealism could challenge a national government. Yet, conversely, it showed that ultimately the state would prevail.

Two years later in Jordan in 1970: Black September. My idealism was battered and ultimately toughened by the specter of the Jordanian government expelling Palestinian freedom fighters while other Arab governments said nothing. As I mentioned, the PFLP-GC had split off from the PFLP in 1968. Their backing for Damascus only increased after Black September. On the face of it, Syria had earned kudos from Palestinians for its commitment of troops to assist Palestinian commandos in Black September. Yet, I had sensed that something sinister was behind the Syrian sponsorship of the PFLP-GC. Then our Che was hung by Hafez al-Assad, a man who often professed his support for our cause in public speeches. Then, we were on the run. And now, we were living in another world entirely.

Abidjan, Ivory Coast. August, 1977. News from Beirut.

Mohammad and I were living more than 3,000 miles from Beirut. Yet we still heard the news and we still discussed events that involved Palestine. In 1976 we learned that Ahmed Jibril (Abu Jihad) of the PFLP-GC had followed the direction of his Syrian masters and had attacked the PLF in Lebanon. We followed reports that our friend Abu al-Abbas re-constituted the Popular Liberation Front (PLF) in April, 1977. Originally, the PLF had been Jibril's group and now, we learned, there were tensions between the two. We were not entirely surprised when we heard, in August 1977, that Ahmed Jibril's

PFLP-GC had bombed the PLF office building in the al-Fakhani section of Beirut (2 km south east of Ras Beirut near an area called Mazraa). Two hundred had been killed when the building collapsed. Was Abu al-Abbas dead? What of his wife and child? Later we heard that all three had survived.

In Abidjan, I realized that everything we experience lives in us forever. I still had a love for Palestine, only now it was a cruel love. The realities of men and nations had toughened me and, yes, made a certain part of me cynical. I needed a break from that whole scene. I needed to find a life for myself apart from politics, and Abidjan gave me what I needed.

1978: A Gift from My Uncle

Abidjan, Ivory Coast. 1978. Rabiha al-Masri, my mother, visits us.

During my time in exile in Africa, I grew into a traditional housewife utterly occupied with challenge of raising two children in poverty. Part of my transformation was due to wisdom that came with age and pain that came with the hardships of life. The most memorable experience I had during these years in Africa, apart from the seemingly endless rationing of money, was a thaw in relations with my family—at least my mother's side of the family. Rabiha al-Masri visited our new home in Abidjan in order to finally meet her two grandsons, Louai and Reef. Apart from the hugs of pain and anguish, she carried with her financial help from her brother, Sabih al-Masri, a renowned banker in his own right who now serves as CEO of the Arab Bank. Sabih sent me $10,000 (the equivalent of $38,000 in 2014 dollars), which is more than Mohammad and I ever could have hoped for. The defiant young woman in me was still present. Yet she stepped aside for a few moments as the impoverished one gladly accepted the money.

These funds enabled us to move to a better house in Abidjan and to meet our expenses for the next couple of years. We viewed these funds as God-sent. Although we had always thought of ourselves as secular and as communists, now we had the sense that a higher power was caring for us. Later in 1978, we decided to relocate to Morocco in North Africa and then to Las Palmas, the island off the Moroccan coast administered by Spain.

Washington. September 17, 1978. The Camp David Accords are signed.

In this year, the Camp David agreement between Egyptian President Anwar al-Sadat and Israeli Prime Minister Menachem Begin moved Egypt and Israel from a state of war to a cold peace. Egypt received concessions from

Israel, yet Palestinians felt that they had been stabbed in the back by Sadat. After Camp David, Fatah attacks across the Lebanese border continued with renewed vigor. I followed these events. I discussed them with Mohammad. I cared. But I was no longer a participant. I was far away, struggling to work out the fate of our family. We moved from Las Palmas to Greece.

By 1980 we had been on the run or in exile for five years. We were tired. The Lebanese Civil War which started in April, 1975 was now at its zenith. Even so, we were homesick. We reasoned that it was crazy to remain outside of Lebanon since the main reason why we had left in the first place was to escape my parent's wrath. Of course, there were also the Syrian *mukhabarat* and the Syrian militias who wanted to arrest us, drag us to Damascus, and throw us into jail. Had the Lebanese Civil War distracted Hafez al-Assad?

1980: Return to Beirut

We had left Baghdad for Abidjan at the end of 1975. By 1980, I was a different person. What is it that changes people suddenly and profoundly? You hear about the Stockholm Syndrome—people taken captive who are deeply traumatized by fear for their lives. These people suddenly change their political beliefs to jive with those of their captors. Well, what do you call it when you and your husband, carrying a small child, are running for your lives, passing through checkpoints with false papers, trusting your fate to the whim of the uniformed official at the next checkpoint—and all with the hangman's noose in the background? What do you call it when you have two children and no money and still have a warrant out for your arrest and live in exile 3,200 miles from home in West Africa? All these things put me in a frame of mind where my most prominent willful construction, my persona as a rebel, could be swept away. The transformation in my outlook was prepared by the stress of circumstances. Yet it was motherhood that changed me utterly.

When you have a child, you learn quickly that this child is the most important thing in your life. Children scream when they are hungry, sick, cold, or when they just detect a trace of uncertainty in their parents. Children capture your attention—and hold it fiercely. It is their will to live. My kids, at times, seemed an impossible challenge. How to raise them in ad hoc circumstances as my mother had raised us in a settled home? I did not have relatives to help with child rearing. And none of my husband's efforts at sharing the burden ever seemed to be enough. Children demand a mother's full attention. When I left Beirut on the run in 1975, I was a revolutionary. When I returned in 1980, I was a mother.

Ras Beirut. Rue Hamra. 1980. I reconcile with my father.

After we returned to Beirut, the first thing I did was to go to our family home, walk into my father's bedroom, and break into tears. I kissed his hand and apologizing from the bottom of my heart. "Please forgive me *baba*," I sobbed. I was his first child and his favorite. Even so, he was a proud Arab. He too was crying but hid his tears lest he show weakness.

The arrest warrant issued by Hafez al-Assad was still valid, and my father feared that the Syrians, who by now were in control of most of the country, would come after me. I took that risk, however. Didn't the Syrian Army have better things to do in Lebanon, like combating the Israelis and Arafat? Would they really bother to run after a young woman from a disbanded communist party—a woman who, nowadays, was nothing more than a mother of two young children?

Divorce

At the time of our return to Beirut in 1980, Mohammad and I were weary of our marriage. In Greece, he had been seeing other women. I suppose that my pride was hurt, but I understand that this was his way of asking once again if we could go our separate ways. I was no longer the young teenager seeking a Guevara-like rebel, willing to give up everything and everyone for him. He was no longer the dashing warrior of the Palestinian underground. Mohammad and I had lost our groove. It was time. With the blessing of my family, I filed for divorce.

Mohammad and I had held things together for five years while we were on the run and living in penniless exile. Before we left Lebanon, Mohammad had suggested divorce. He was acknowledging that—without Ali—Mohammad and I just did not click.

Flashback to 1975:

From the time I met Mohammad, I thought of our relationship as a political statement. It was the expression of the rejectionist persona I was creating for myself. I was asserting my identity as a woman and as a political being apart from my family. There was a certain element of rebellion from Arab tradition as well. Was it my right, as a woman, to choose my own husband? Or, would that choice be made for me by father and family? This question, which was beginning to split daughters from fathers in all Arab societies, was not as severe for our cosmopolitan family in the modern city of Beirut as it often was in more remote towns and villages. I never for a moment thought that my father would send my brother to commit an honor killing, for example. Still, my feminine independence was far from the norm. I did not have the support of society and, like all who tread new ground, I was feeling the tension.

Yet, I also felt that I was making a statement. What would my example be if I folded, left my husband, and allowed myself to be pulled back under the wing of my father?

Not so obvious, but probably more to the point: in 1975, I was still grieving for Ali. My marriage to Mohammad was my last link to our dear Che. And Ali was the one individual who saw me and understood me as a political being. I could not give up on my marriage to Mohammad and I could not give up on my memory of Ali because I could not give up on myself.

My Life in Ras Beirut

Ras Beirut. 1980. My new life.

I rented an apartment for myself and my two children in tony Ras Beirut not too far from our family home in the seven-story Nimer Building that my father had built at the corner of Rue Sadat and Rue Hamra. Ras Beirut was situated on the bluff above the Mediterranean, a brief walk from the corniche where lovers dallied, kids kicked soccer balls, grandmothers pushed strollers, students made early morning jogs, and the under class fished with long poles and swam from the rocks as the gentle surging swells kissed the seawall. We were not too far from the American University of Beirut campus which perched on the steep hillside above the corniche and looked out on the Mediterranean as if were viewing history. AUB had emerged from the ferment and promise of an independent Arab culture under Ottoman rule. In the early 1800s Protestant printing presses came to Beirut from France and soon were cranking out inspiring cultural and political literature in addition to religious publications. A number of religious schools emerged. In the 1860s, AUB became one of them.

The intellectual component of the Palestinian resistance was shaped at AUB by prominent students such as Wadih Haddad and George Habash as well as professors such as Constantine Zureik. AUB students, many of them internationals, filled the many small eateries on level ground facing the university: *shish tawouk, shawarma,* and *falafel.* A few blocks away, Hamra Street featured fine dining, gold plated banks, and high end retailers.

Beirut. 1980. I enroll at BUC.

In 1980, after my divorce, I resumed my studies at Beirut University College (now the Lebanese American University). BUC was located in Ras Beirut above Hamra Street, a two minute walk from our family home. Upon graduation, I was hired by the Beirut Bank of Commerce where my father was the general manager—my second job after leaving home as an adult. Since the Civil War had intensified, the bank had left its headquarters on Banks' Street and moved a ten minute walk west to the corner of Hamra and Sadat Streets. It took space in the ground floor of the Nimer Building. After work, it was easy for me to visit my family upstairs before walking home to my apartment nearby.

As an employee of the Beirut Bank of Commerce, I was not favored. My father treated me just like the others. I had to request an appointment in advance through his secretary, if I wanted to see him at the bank. He made sure that I addressed him properly as "Mr. Nimer," and I was especially careful about showing up for work on time, since Rifaat Bey was very religious about punctuality. Rifaat probably leaned too far in his efforts to be even-handed. He was often more harsh when dealing with me than with other employees.

1981: The PLF Flies into Israel

Beirut. March 7, 1981. Abu al-Abbas launches two air attacks.

Under the command of Abu al-Abbas, whose primary office was in the al-Fakhani district of Beirut, the PLF trained several hundred commandos in Syria and deployed them in operations against Israeli targets. These operations were innovative, if not always effective. In March of 1981, for example, PLF flew hang-gliders over the Israeli border aiming to drop hand grenades on IDF positions near Haifa. The attack failed for lack of the proper thermal currents.[1] On April 16, PLF commandos flew a hot air balloon into Israel with the aim of kidnapping Israeli security officials. The plan might have succeeded except that the balloon made an easy target for Israeli guns and was quickly shot down.[2]

Abu al-Abbas Meets My Family

After returning to Beirut, I renewed my acquaintance with Abu al-Abbas. He was married to Samia Costandi, a university professor, and they had two sons, Khaled (4 years) and Omar (1 year old). His marriage was shaky. Abu al-Abbas remembered me from Baghdad five years earlier. He would often visit the Nimer family home. I suppose that he came to see me, yet he seemed more interested in my father. The older banker who had kept his politics on the side saw something of himself in the younger man. Abu al-Abbas had left his day job as a schoolteacher to become a military commander. At a certain level, I think my father felt that he might have followed a similar path. Why not? Well, Rifaat was older and the profession of

PLF poster (above): "Operation Martyr Kamal Nasser: They entered the homeland to inspire the revolution." (To the right) PLF poster: "Heroes of the Kamal Jumblatt Operation."

Palestinian commando was not especially developed or well-funded in his day. Also, Rifaat always had commitments to his extended family in Nablus and in the region. He needed to be the responsible one who held down a 9 to 5 job, who married, raised a family, maintained a sober Palestinian face in local Arab society—and preserved a position where he could protect the Palestinian cause as well as his own extended family. Ottoman rule was long gone, but you could still sense the "patron" in the way that Rifaat defined his life and his responsibilities. Rifaat had become a pillar of the community. In temperament and instinct, however, he was not far from Mohammad al-Abbas.

Beirut. 1982. Abu al-Abbas and his wife divorce.

Samia was a woman whom I respected and liked. We came from similar educational backgrounds. When Abu al-Abbas told me that he wanted to divorce, rather than encourage him I advised him to give his marriage a second chance. I knew that he was starting to develop feelings for me, and I did not want to be the source of a family rupture. For that matter, I often played the go-between. But my efforts were in vain.

1982: Dating Abu al-Abbas

Once Abu al-Abbas and Samia had gone their separate ways, I noticed that Abu al-Abbas was visiting the Nimers more frequently. Before long, we were dating. Our commitment to the Palestinian Cause, my obvious admiration for him, his affection for my father, and the fact that we both knew a lot about troubled marriages created a special bond between Abu al-Abbas and me. He respected the spirit of my social rebellion and the sacrifices I had made. It was one thing to step out of line if you came from a refugee camp as he had done. It was another thing entirely to give up a life of privilege.

Reem al-Nimer.

I was equally impressed with Abu al-Abbas. How had a poor boy without connections, a kid from the freezing Neirab camp near Aleppo and the slums of Yarmouk in Damascus gained so much knowledge, wisdom, and self-assurance? Still, Abu al-Abbas seemed unmarked by his struggles to rise. He was not angry, aggressive, or arrogant. He had confidence in his own abilities, and he had an open mind and heart. He showed what Palestinians in exile can make of themselves if given just a faint glimmer of daylight. I was proud of him.

10
The Lebanese Civil War: 1975 - 1982

THE MULTI-FACETED CONFLICT KNOWN as the Lebanese Civil War was a nightmare, not only for Abu al-Abbas and me, but for all those who lived it. It began in April 1975 and lasted fifteen years until 1990. An estimated 18,000 people were killed in 1975 alone. Before the war was over, 120,000 people had died. Of these victims, only 675 or one half of one percent, were Israelis.

1975 - 1978: Background & Early Years

After the *Nakba* of 1948, Lebanon became home to 110,000 Palestinian refugees. This community was the popular base that supported the PLO in the late 1960s. The number of PLO followers and sympathizers increased dramatically after the expulsion of Palestinian commandos from Jordan in September 1970. Five years later, the 300,000 Palestinians in Lebanon (who were primarily Muslim) tipped the confessional and sectarian balance in favor of Lebanese Muslims and against Christian Maronites. The PLO became an unofficial state-within-a-state, especially in south Lebanon where it maintained bases used to launch operations against Israel. To a lesser extent, the same was true in Beirut where the PLO was almost in full control of the city, with political and military headquarters in the al-Fakhani district. Lebanese Christians grumbled, claiming that the Palestinian Cause was not theirs to fight, whereas Lebanese Muslims, like Rashid Karami, Saeb Salam, Nabih Berri, and Kamal Jumblatt, all endorsed the Palestinian Struggle.

An amusing anecdote is that Arafat used to hold his meetings with Lebanese leaders, and everyone else, well into the middle of the night. Abu al-Abbas was used to that and always showed up on time for talks that often would last until 3:00 AM. They would drink strong black Arabic coffee to remain alert to the PLO Chairman. Kamal Jumblatt, however, hated the late night meetings. Running a very strict Gandhian lifestyle, and diet, the Druze leader would go to sleep early in the evening and wake up long before first light. He never consumed too much food, steered clear from chemically inflicted nutrition, and did not favor coffee as an aid to wakefulness. He would always grumble at being called up in the middle of the night for a meeting with the PLO Chairman, arguing that they were not only a nuisance, but also, extremely unhealthy. Once, he walked into Arafat's office, rubbing his eyes to wake up, and snapped: "Abu Ammar, is this a revolution we are running here, or a cabaret!"

The Lebanese Phalange of Pierre Gemayel was hardly as sympathetic to the whims and habits of the PLO Chairman. They hated him, and longed for the day that he was killed or at least expelled from Beirut. They had similar views toward Abu al-Abbas and his comrades in the Palestinian struggle: Abu Iyad; Abu Jihad; and Abu Hasan Salameh (associated with the Munich Olympics action in 1972). In 1975, Christian militias launched an all-out war against Palestinians in different parts of Lebanon, trying to expel them from the country that they considered rightfully theirs—and only theirs.

Gemayel was a man who thought of himself as purely Lebanese and had no affiliation whatsoever with Arabism. He was more at ease speaking French than Arabic. He did not have the slightest hesitation about getting into bed with the Americans and the Israelis if that would end Palestinian influence in Lebanon.

1978: Israel Invades Lebanon

The Lebanese Civil War was marked by two Israeli invasions, one in 1978 and another in 1982. Each incursion was framed as a response to a Palestinian action.

March 11, 1978. Ahmed Jabril launches a commando raid.

In an action that the Israelis later called the Coastal Road Massacre, eleven troops under the direction of Ahmed Jibril landed rubber Zodiac boats on the beach north of Tel Aviv. After a day of wild gun fights and grenade throwing, they had killed more than three dozen people, most of them civilians. Included in the casualties was an American nature photographer.

South Lebanon. March 14, 1978. Israel launches Operation Litani.

Using the events of March 11 as a pretext, the Israelis invaded south Lebanon as far as the Litani River and then withdrew seven days later. The PLO forces moved north ahead of the advance and for the most part did not engage the Israelis. One to two thousand Lebanese and Palestinians died and another 100,000 to 250,000 were internally displaced. The Israelis suffered twenty casualties. They succeeded in establishing a security zone along the border. They populated this zone primarily with Christian inhabitants who enrolled in the South Lebanese Army headed by the notorious general,

The cover of a PFLP publication a year before the Israeli invasion..

Antoine Lahad. On March 19, 1978, the UN formed a peacekeeping force called the UN Interim Force in Lebanon (UNIFIL). The Israelis had come and gone and now a UN force policed the border. These arrangements sounded as though the Israelis had created a stable situation that would be the basis for peace. The Israelis, however, were not done.

Later in 1978, Israeli Likud Prime Minister Menachem Begin, referring to the Palestinian forces in Lebanon, declared that Tel Aviv would not allow the "genocide" of Lebanese Christians at the hands of "Palestinian terrorists." After Alexander Haig became US Secretary of State, he told Begin that Israel could not make another invasion of Lebanon unless it had a "pretext."

London. June 3, 1982. Abu Nidal tries to kill the Israeli ambassador.

Four years later, Israel found its pretext in the attempted assassination of Ambassador Shlomo Argov in London. The man who tried to kill him was a member of the Fatah Revolutionary Council, headed by the notorious Sabri al-Banna (known by his *nom de guerre*, Abu Nidal).

Abu Nidal was unaffiliated with either Arafat or Abu al-Abbas, yet both of them paid the price for Abu Nidal's madness. For years, people falsely associated my husband with Abu Nidal—which caused him great distress. Abu Nidal was a serial killer who would have been a plain criminal if there had not been Arab governments willing to use him against their enemies. He was a classic terrorist who Patrick Seale correctly described as "a gun for hire." He offered his services to whomever paid the most, be it the Syrians, the Libyans, the Iraqis, or even the Israelis themselves. He had as much Palestinian blood on his hands as the Israelis, having carried out target assassinations of leading PLO figures during the 1980s and early 1990s. Abu Nidal killed people with no regard to their status as civilians or children, and his goal, certainly, was not the liberation of Palestine. He never blinked before pulling the trigger, whereas Abu al-Abbas planned his operations with the goal of avoiding harm to women, children, and other civilians.

Abu al-Abbas was a sincere human being who did what he believed was absolutely necessary for the weakening and eventual defeat of Israel. True, he firmly believed that every Israeli was an enemy and every spot on earth a battlefield for the Palestinians, but he never targeted an Arab or a fellow Palestinian. And his stated policy was never to target civilians, including Israelis. The fact that both Abu al-Abbas and Abu Nidal were sponsored at different stages in their careers by Saddam Hussein added to the connection between the two men in the public mind. So was the fact that both died in Iraq in 2004. People continued to make the link, ignoring—perhaps on purpose—that Abu Nidal had been sentenced to death by a PLO court for treason against the Palestinian Cause and, after this finding, had become a sworn enemy of both Arafat and my husband.

In his memoirs, Ariel Sharon said that Abu Nidal's attack on Israeli ambassador Argov was "merely the spark that lit the fuse." When debating the invasion in the upper echelons of power in Tel Aviv, the Israeli government was reportedly reminded that Abu Nidal was behind Argov's assassination, and not Arafat. Rafael Eitan, the Israeli Army Chief, famously said: "Abu Nidal *Abu Schmidal*, they are all the same!" He added that they were going to use the assassination attempt to "screw" the PLO. The specific party responsible for the assassination attempt did not really matter to the Israelis. The assassination attempt was used and abused to justify war against the PLO and Lebanon—a war in which thousands of civilians perished.

1982: A Second Israeli Invasion

The PLO immediately distanced itself from the London attack. Arafat, who at the time was on a visit to Saudi Arabia, went as far as to say that he was willing to suspend cross-border shelling, if the Israelis would halt their invasion. Both he and Abu al-Abbas were horrified by the potential death toll among civilians that such a large invasion could cause. Also, they realized that it would turn Lebanese public opinion against them and play out nicely in favor of people like Pierre Gemayel and Antoine Lahad. The Israelis refused to listen.

Legends of the resistance left to right: Abu Jihad (Khalil al-Wazir), Abu al-Abbas (behind), Abu Iyad (Salah Khalaf), Talaat Yacoub, Yasser Arafat, and George Habash.

Lebanese - Israeli Border. June 4, 1982. The Israelis invade Lebanon.

Israel authorized a large scale invasion headed by Defense Minister Sharon. In total, 78,000 troops were allocated by Israel for the 1982 war in addition to more than 1,200 tanks.

We later found out that Sharon received sensitive information and logistic assistance from none other than the Lebanese Phalange's charismatic young leader, Bashir Gemayel, who actually escorted him into Beirut. The Israeli Army publicly said that its only objective was to push the PLO forces back forty kilometers to the north. They actually went much further, engaging in fierce battles with the Palestinians, Lebanese, and Syrians at Beaufort Castle in Nabatieh, and Jezzine. Then they pushed through toward their ultimate destination: Beirut.

Life in Beirut under Israeli Guns

Beirut. June 13, 1982. The Israelis encircle Beirut.

The Israelis call the 1982 invasion Operation Peace for Galilee. We call it "the invasion and occupation of Beirut." Seven days after Israeli troops crossed the southern Lebanese border, they occupied positions on the heights outside Beirut and began to shell the city. Abu al-Abbas and I lived through the entire episode in bunkers, not knowing what the future had in store for us. The summer of 1982 was like none other: jet fighters strafing and bombing residential districts; artillery rounds landing on their targets and also landing, it seemed, at random; debris from destroyed buildings lying in the streets; blood and body parts. The Siege of Beirut has permanently distorted the psychology of every Palestinian and Lebanese who survived it. And it had a profound effect on my life and on the life of Abu al-Abbas. I still wake at night, reliving images from those days. Today, I recall these images when seeing the carnage in contemporary Libya, Iraq, and Syria. Our lives were never the same after Beirut, 1982.

Fast Forward:

On December 27, 2013, while editing this book, I was at home in the modern downtown area of Beirut with my son Reef, my grandson, and our dog. An enormous bomb exploded in the street outside my house, sending shards of glass into my apartment and killing our dog. Just a few seconds before the blast, my infant grandson had been sitting near a plate glass window. My family and I survived, but we became refugees in our own city for two months. The bomb assassinated Mohamad B. Chatah, who had served as Lebanon's ambassador to the United States and was a government minister allied with Saad Hariri. When I felt the explosion, I thought for a moment that it was 1982 once again.

It wasn't pleasant to love a Palestinian commando who was wanted by the Israeli Army in the midst of the Lebanese Civil War. When Abu al-Abbas left the house, there was no telling if he would return in one piece. And he did not make things any easier. For him, the idea of a good night out was walking through war-torn Beirut, donning night-vision goggles when the power was cut for the nightly blackouts. After the Israelis invaded the city, my association with Abu al-Abbas was even more dangerous and heart wrenching—for the Israeli Army wanted him DEAD or ALIVE. When Abu al-Abbas's offices in the al-Fakhani section of west Beirut (about 2 km south of Ras Beirut near Mazraa) were targeted by Israeli jets, I grabbed a cab and rushed there like a madwoman, pushing aside the debris and rubble, screaming out his name "Mohammad, Mohammad"—almost certain that he had been killed. I then saw him in a nearby spot that had avoided destruction. He was covered with dust from the explosion, giving a press interview to the British journalist Faris Glubb, the son of the famous British figure John Bagot Glubb. (Nicknamed Glubb Pasha, he trained the Jordanian military from 1939 until 1956.) From this moment, I learned patience, tolerance, and fatalism from Abu al-Abbas. This was the first lesson in our relationship.

Back and Forth to Homs

From 1980 until the fall of 1982 Abu al-Abbas and I lived in Beirut. During this period, Abu al-Abbas maintained his PLF administrative offices in the al-Fakhani district as part of a compound that included the Fatah offices of Yasser Arafat. But where could PLF commandos train? They needed space away from the war zone. And this point led Abu al-Abbas to accept the hospitality of Hafez al-Assad next door in Syria.

Syria, of course, was not only next door—it also was deeply enmeshed in Lebanon. Syrian troops played a major role in the Lebanese Civil War and they essentially enforced peace after the war came to an official close in 1990. Syrian government troops and pro-Syrian militias were a fact of life. And Syrian intelligence, well, it was omnipresent. For Palestinians in Lebanon and especially for the Palestinian leadership in the al-Fakhani section of Beirut, daily life included a persistent sideshow: Syria. Men like Arafat and Abu al-Abbas, whose goal was to fight Israel, found themselves more immediately engaged—not with Israel but with Syria. Every day Abu al-Abbas and his fellow Palestinian leaders were chatting with Syrians on the phone or deciding not to take their calls; they were either meeting with Syrians or avoiding them; they were doing the bidding of Syria or undercutting Syria.

In 1980, Hafez al-Assad invited Abu al-Abbas to open a PLF facility in Homs. And so Abu al-Abbas would frequently travel from Beirut 70 km over the mountain to Damascus—a drive of three hours. Both his mother and father were gone, so he would see his brothers and sister. They were still living in the older and poorer section of Yarmouk, but by now the family was living in their own apartment. Abu al-Abbas stayed in the Ruk al-Din neighborhood on the north side of town where he had rented an apartment in a concrete building with rebar sticking in the air (in case the builder decided to add a floor later). His local staff in Damascus worked out of a couple of other nearby apartments that they used as offices. Abu al-Abbas sometimes would meet with Syrian officials in Damascus and consult with the dozen or so PLF aides who stayed in town and then return to Beirut. More often, however, he would travel from Damascus north on the Aleppo highway for a couple of hours to Homs where his PLF offices and training facilities held a staff of 200. At times, he would stay in Homs to oversee training operations.

It was in Homs that Abu al-Abbas got to know Ghazi Kanaan, a Syrian colonel who had fought the Israelis on the Golan. He was a capable and controversial figure whom the Syrian novelist Colette Khoury described as "handsome, with a striking resemblance to Jacques Chirac." In 1981 - 1982, Kanaan was based in Homs as the intelligence chief for central Syria. Hafez al-Assad was not a man who welcomed foreign armies onto his soil. At the end of Black September in 1970, his door was closed to most Palestinian commandos who were fleeing Jordan. For about two years, however, Assad did consent to hosting PLF training facilities in Homs. Here, Palestinian fighters were kept under close watch by Ghazi Kanaan and his men.

Abu al-Abbas liked Ghazi. The two worked well together. And Ghazi performed a favor that was particularly important to me: in 1981, at the request of Abu al-Abbas, he lifted the outstanding Syrian warrant for my arrest. Six years was a long time to be hunted. I was relieved. Now, if need be, I could travel freely to Syria. After the Israelis invaded Lebanon in June 1982, Kanaan became commander of Syrian forces in Lebanon as well as all militias in alliance with Syria. Two months later, in a moment of nervous danger, Abu al-Abbas asked Ghazi to save our lives.

A Favor for Hafez al-Assad

After leaving Lebanon in 1982, the PLF training facilities in the Syrian city of Homs were all that they had left. Ultimately, they would establish offices in Tunis near Arafat's Fatah offices. But Tunis would only accept a small slice of Palestinian commandos who were escorted into the desert and kept under armed guard. If the PLF did not have a camp in Syria, it would be difficult for them to train for military operations. Thus, Abu al-Abbas was quick to respond when the Syrian president asked him for a small favor.

One day, President Assad summoned Abu al-Abbas to his office on the hill overlooking Damascus. Hafez al-Assad was seated on a large chair of dark wood that was inlaid with mother of pearl in a traditional Arabic design. "My eldest son Basel is training to become an officer in the Army," said the Syrian president. "I want you to help me make a man out of him. I want him to get the same kind of training I got when I was young. Yet, this is difficult in Syria, because everyone treats him like a king. I want you Abu al-Abbas to train him in paragliding, with your boys."

Assad added that Basel should receive no privileges, but rather, ought to go through all the necessary drills, like any other Palestinian commando. "If he makes a mistake, feel free to correct him. If he disobeys an order, feel free to punish him," Assad added.

The young Basel, then in his late teens, was not yet the handsome, military officer whose poster—showing a young man of supreme confidence wearing airman's sunglasses and lounging casually in military fatigues while he looked directly into the camera—would still be found all over Syria thirty years later. At this point Basel was the first in line to succeed Assad as president. Assad needed to reach outside his normal circle to find someone who would attempt to instill the toughness that Assad sensed would be required to survive as head of the Syrian state.

Abu al-Abbas took Basel under his wing that summer. He saw promise in the young man, whom he described as "brave and dashing." What impressed him was Assad's desire to make a man out of his eldest son, by sending him to training in the rugged Palestinian camps and not to an elite institution similar to the Royal Military Academy Sandhurst in Britain where King Hussein had sent his son Abdullah or for a degree in Business Administration from Cairo University, as Husni Mubarak had done with his son Gamal. (Assad followed the later course with his younger son, Bashar, whom he sent to London to study ophthalmology.)

Abu al-Abbas gave his top PLF officers strict instructions: "Don't let him out of your sight for a single minute. This is the son of Hafez al-Assad. If something happens to him, we're dead!"

One evening, after a long day's work, Abu al-Abbas left Basel in the camp and drove back to Damascus. The young man was expected to have supper with the troops and go to bed early for tough training the next morning. No sooner had Abu al-Abbas arrived home in Damascus than his walkie-talkie's red light turned on: it was the camp commander calling with an SOS.

"What's wrong," snapped Abu al-Abbas.

"Basel," stuttered the officer, "Basel . . ."

Abu al-Abbas shouted back, "What in the world happened to him?" The officer replied, "No Comrade, he is okay. He took off in a plane, all by himself, in the middle of the night! He slipped under our nose. We didn't even see him."

Abu al-Abbas frantically rushed back to Homs, made sure that Basel landed safely, and arrested every single Palestinian officer on duty that night. He never told Hafez al-Assad, of course, and we don't know if Basel himself ever told his father. The young man was a gallant risk taker and many thought that he had the precise qualities needed to lead Syria. In the decade that followed, however, his elderly father found himself in failing health—yet never relinquished power. For his part, Basel was the heir in waiting. He died in January 1994 in a car accident while racing to the Damascus airport.

An Assassination Attempt

While Abu al-Abbas was commuting from Beirut to Homs, I was happy to live at home in Ras Beirut. I worked with my father, saw my mother often, and raised my two children. In the summer of 1982, after the Israelis put Beirut under siege, I needed a break. The airport was still open, so I flew to Cyprus with a friend of mine, the sister of Samir Sabbagh, deputy to Ibrahim Quleilat, a leading Sunni militia leader who was a Nasserist at heart and an ally of the PLO. Back in Beirut, Abu al-Abbas was with his colleagues at their office building in al-Fakhani. One day, Abu al-Abbas was preparing for lunch, but he was interrupted before he could take a single bite.

An informer tipped off the Israelis as to the whereabouts of Abu al-Abbas. An Israeli jet (probably an F-15 or F-16 although it could have been an F-4 Phantom) struck the PLF building in al-Fakhani with a missile. The detonation sliced the building in two. At the moment the missile struck, Abu al-Abbas happened to be on the tenth floor on side of the building that remained standing. When he came to his senses, my husband found himself looking through the dust and debris toward the interior of the building: Across where the interior offices and apartments of the PLF building should have been, he could see across the street to the facing buildings—they were in full view and below was a drop of 30 meters (100 feet). He and his comrades ran for the interior staircase only to see it crumble before their eyes. Their only hope was to slide with it. So they jumped out with their AK-47s awkwardly slung over their shoulders. As the groaning concrete, partially restrained by its reinforcing steel, sloughed, settled, and then fell to the ground, Abu al-Abbas and his comrades slid ten stories on this surfboard of concrete and debris. They suffered bruises, cuts and all types of injuries, minor and in some cases severe. It was a miracle that none of them were killed. When he reached the ground, Abu al-Abbas began running back and forth like a madman—searching for help.

Rule # 1 in the Lebanese Civil War: If you see somebody bleeding—look the other way and jet on out of there. Why? Because the assassins will surely strike a second time, this time killing you and him both. Stating it another way: when the Israelis struck from the air they would hit the very same target again approximately fifteen or twenty minutes later in order to kill survivors attempting to flee the wreckage as well as first responders. The Israelis had calibrated their procedures to achieve maximum damage and as high a body count as possible.

Abu al-Abbas tried waving to cars and passersby for help, but everyone just scrambled away, terrified by the sight of a huge blood-stained man covered with concrete dust and with an AK-47 over his shoulder. Suddenly, Abu al-Abbas heard moans from beneath the carnage. An Ethiopian woman was trapped and was doing her best to call out for help. Abu al-Abbas returned to the wreck and was pulling her from the debris when Israeli jets made another pass. The second strike finished off the PLF building and gave Abu al-Abbas a shrapnel wound in the head. This time, he forcefully stopped a car and asked to be taken to the American University Hospital (AUH). Right after sluggishly walking in, he asked for his doctor, Fouad Haddad, and then collapsed before being taken to the operating room.

I followed the unfolding events from the distance of Cyprus where I cried without recourse, because I had no way of knowing if my beloved was dead or alive. Before long, my friend's brother, Samir Sabbagh, received news about the strike. He called and told her that the attack was an assassination attempt on Abu al-Abbas. I took the first plane back to Beirut and rushed off to AUH to see him. As my taxi screamed through war torn Beirut, I sensed that I had changed. At this moment I knew that I wanted to spend the rest of my life with Abu al-Abbas.

Shortly afterward, an agreement was brokered by President Reagan's Middle East envoy Philip Habib that called for a truce. Under the terms of the agreement, 14,000 Palestinian fighters (including 6,500 from Arafat's Fatah) would withdraw to Syria, the Sudan, and primarily to Tunisia during the months of August and September 1982. The evacuation would be conducted under the supervision of the Multinational Forces in Lebanon and an international peacekeeping force with troops from the United States, UK, France, and Italy.

Abu al-Abbas, like Arafat, was scheduled to travel to Tunisia. It was a difficult decision for him to take because he feared that he would never return to Lebanon—and, indeed, he never did. He agreed to follow the PLO Chairman in full faith despite the colossal differences between them, differences which lasted until both men died in 2004. Occasionally, Abu al-Abbas even used the honorific term *"al-Ikhtiyar"* (Old Man) when referring to Arafat. I remember him often telling his troops: "Listen to what *al-Ikhtiyar* has to say. If a quarrel emerges between him and anyone else, follow Yasser Arafat!"

In those last days before the departure to Tunis, security on the streets of Beirut was unbearable. Since the destruction of his offices in Fakhani, Abu al-Abbas had moved his operations to another building nearby. The betting was that the Israelis would make a second attempt on Abu al-Abbas's life. Nevertheless, I traveled every day from my apartment in Ras Beirut to see Abu al-Abbas in his offices. Abu al-Abbas feared for my safety. He and Arafat predicted a wave of reprisals as soon as the Palestinian commandos and their leaders departed for Tunis by sea. A lot of people in Beirut were coming to the same conclusion and the main highway heading east into Syria was jammed with Palestinians and Lebanese Muslims where they were easy pickings for their enemies. How many were killed at Phalange checkpoints? No one kept track. But it is certain that they were vulnerable.

Which was more safe? Should we hide out in Ras Beirut or try to reach Syria? Abu al-Abbas pondered and then decided: We would make a run for the border.

An Escape to Syria

During the civil war in Lebanon, you always took a risk when you got on the road and drove—anywhere. And this applied to partisans from both sides. Any militia in a neighborhood of Beirut or a smaller town on the highway felt it their right to set up an impromptu checkpoint. Don't even mention the checkpoints set up on orders from their leadership. When men with guns were examining your documents, you felt utterly helpless. You could travel nowhere without those papers. And you had no way of knowing in advance who was managing a given checkpoint and what their frame of mind might be. At the beginning of the civil war in December 1975 in what has been called the Black Saturday massacre, a Phalange leader discovered the bodies of his son and three of his friends near the power plant in Christian East Beirut. The grieving father set up checkpoints on major roads nearby where Phalange soldiers inspected papers. Palestinians and Lebanese Muslims who happened to be driving through were stopped, ordered from their cars, and killed on the spot.

Others talked about the occasional Phalange checkpoints on the main escape route over the mountain into Syria. In one account the word "tomato" in Arabic spelled life or death for travelers attempting to cross the border. When stopped at a Phalange checkpoint, the travelers were asked to identify the common vegetable. If they pronounced the Arabic word as *"banadurra"* in the Syrian or Lebanese manner, they were allowed to. On the other hand, if they said *"ban-dora"* in the Palestinian manner they were terminated.[1]

On our ride out of the country, I was accompanied by my mother, my two children, and my brother Rami and his wife. (Rami had just returned from studies in the US.) Our strategy—well, we were in the hands of Ghazi Kanaan. If anyone could transport us to safety, it was Ghazi. Still, he was smart enough to avoid the main road heading east from Beirut over the mountain. Instead, Ghazi drove us north on the coastal road to Byblos, where we ate a picnic lunch on the beach in the August sun. Then our convoy of two cars drove farther north to the Syrian border. Once inside Syria , we were safe. We continued on to Damascus. Abu al-Abbas had given me the keys to his apartment in Rukn al-Din, and so I was all set.

As I waited for events to unfold in Beirut, I pondered the irony of my situation. In my youth, the Syrian government had seemed criminal for the way it used Palestinians as a pawn in its maneuvering with Israel. This was the second time in seven years, however, that I had saved my life by escaping into Syria. In my experience, Ghazi Kanaan was a man of chivalry. In 1982 he lived up to his word and did us an unforgettable favor.

The cease fire that began in August 1982 saved the lives of PLO leaders and their commandos. Yet, as far as Arafat and his colleagues were concerned, leading an armed struggle from faraway Tunis was the beginning of a long march into history. They would be deprived of access to enemy territory. They would have a difficult time obtaining weapons. They would have no battlefield. They feared that they would become couch revolutionaries who watched Palestine on TV from North Africa: a bittersweet end to a brave and once promising struggle.

Dancing on the Quay

Beirut. August 30, 1982. Arafat & Co. depart from Lebanon.

Two weeks after my escape to Syria, the Palestinian commandos launched forth on a journey to exile in Sudan, Tunisia, and Syria. *The New York Times* reporter Thomas Friedman described the event saying, "The PLO itself was never the quite the same after it quit Lebanon. And neither for that matter was the Arab world. Something in the Arab world died on August 30, 1982." Thousands of young men and women showed up at the port of Beirut, wearing the Palestinian *kufiyya*, sobbing their hearts out while crying, *"Allah ma'ak"* (May God be with you). It was the first time since 1948 that the Palestinians were driven from the Necklace States that encircle Palestine: Syria, Jordan, and Lebanon. As he walked onto the gangplank, Arafat made a gallant attempt to lift the morale of his men. A reporter asked him where he was heading. "To Palestine," he said. "To Jerusalem!" Alas, there was no sea route to Jerusalem, and Arafat knew it.

After leaving Beirut and before turning southwest toward Tunisia, the ship carrying Abu al-Abbas and Abu Jihad first headed north to the port city of Tartous on the Syrian coast. I took a car from Damascus to Tartous in order to greet the ship. The inhabitants of the local Palestinian refugee camps came out *en masse*. I stood with the crowds: small children, young men, women, and elders who carried photos of Arafat and waved the Palestinian Flag. When Abu al-Abbas stood on the gangplank, they began to sing and dance in celebration. I danced along with the crowd but couldn't help wondering, "What in the world are we celebrating? Defeat? Another exile?"

I waited a moment, and then a thought came to me. "We are celebrating defiance, power, and the ability to move onward and forward." I was unable to embrace Abu al-Abbas because he was swamped by the crowds. But I noticed that he was pale and fragile-looking, as though he were nearly overcome by fatigue after the Israeli siege. "How are you Mohammad?" My question floated in the air above the crowd. In my heart, I heard his response.

"I am tired. Very, very tired."

In Tartous, Abu al-Abbas disembarked from his ship and caught a car to Damascus and his place in Rukn al-Din. A week or so later, we were married on my thirtieth birthday: September 9, 1982. We visited the Sheikh, filled out the legal paperwork, and returned to our apartment in Rukn al-Din. Abu al-Abbas was not feeling well, so we wed without family, flowers, or champagne. My husband was still carrying shrapnel from the Israeli missile in al-Fakhani. Soon after, we traveled to USSR at the expense of the Soviet government so that Abu al-Abbas could recuperate.

Massacre at Sabra & Shatila

With Palestinian troops gone from Beirut, who would protect the Palestinian civilians in local refugee camps? Arafat had asked multinational forces from Italy, France, and the US who had escorted his men out of Beirut to return to the Lebanese capital to protect civilians. His call, unfortunately, fell on deaf ears. Arafat and also Abu al-Abbas did not trust the Israelis or the Christian Phalange who now had free reign. They sensed that something horrific was going to happen—soon.

Beirut. Tuesday September 14, 1982. Bashir Gemayel Is Assassinated.

About two weeks after the Palestinian forces left Beirut, the young Christian president Bashir Gemayel (in office for less than three weeks) was assassinated. He had been a cornerstone of Ariel Sharon's Lebanon invasion, and perhaps that is why he became a target for Habib Shartouni of the Syrian Social Nationalist Party (SSNP), an ultra-nationalist party which at the time was allied with the Syrians and Palestinians. In response, Christian militias immediately occupied all of West Beirut. The next day, they began a manhunt that was insane. They began arresting at random any Palestinian, Syrian, or Lebanese nationalist in West Beirut who was in the wrong place at the wrong time. In the process, they raided my father's office at the bank and attempted to arrest him.

Beirut. 12:00 Noon. September 15, 1982. The IDF surrounds Sabra and Shatila.

On Wednesday, the Israeli Army moved troops into West Beirut neighborhoods, a move that, according to the *New York Times* was "in violation of a ceasefire agreement with the United States."[2] Two of these neighborhoods were Sabra and Shatila. The IDF surrounded the two Palestinian camps, sealed off all exits, installed checkpoints to control access, and stationed snipers on adjacent rooftops. IDF troops situated on top of the Kuwaiti embassy had an unobstructed view of Sabra and Shatila. Later, Israeli tanks began firing into the refugee camp.

Beirut. 6:00 PM. September 15, 1982. The Phalange enters Sabra and Shatila.

According to Linda Malone of the Jerusalem Fund, at 3:00 PM on the 15th Ariel Sharon met with the Phalange militia and "invited" them to enter the Sabra and Shatila refugee camps, claiming that the PLO was responsible for Gemayel's assassination. Soon after, the operation took place, under the command of Phalange Party leader (and, ironically, a future Syrian ally) Elie Hobeika.

The Phalange sent 150 men into the Sabra and Shatila refugee camps. These were militia troops who had been recruited by Hobeika after their expulsion from the Lebanese Army for rowdy and undisciplined behavior. The pretext for entering Sabra and Shatila: The Phalange claimed that "two thousand PLO terrorists" had been left behind by Arafat.

Flashback:

> The Lebanese Civil War saw many provocations. Militias fought one another and killed civilians—by ones and twos and also in massacres. To simplify greatly, it was the Christian Phalange or Phalangists with their Israeli backers against left wing Lebanese Muslims (Lebanese Nationalists) and Palestinians with their Syrian backers. If you favor a complex view of history, consider ironies such as the point that the primary leader of the Christian Phalange, Elie Hobeika, later became a Syrian ally.
>
> Six years earlier, in January 1976, members of Hobeika's family were killed by PLO fighters in the Christian town of Damour located south of Beirut.

The PLO was responding to an attack two days earlier on the Karantina slum, a Muslim enclave within the larger Christian area of East Beirut.

The attack killed more than a thousand Palestinians and as well as Lebanese Muslims. Six weeks earlier, in December 1975, both sides had been involved in savage blood-letting on Black Saturday. When four dead Christian men were found in East Beirut, the father of one of the victims and other Phalange leaders set up check points, stopped traffic, and pulled from their cars Palestinian Christians and Lebanese Muslims. Three to six hundred died. The PLO responded. Vicious back and forth attacks followed.

By September 1982, there was evidence that Christian militias were just waiting for their chance to even the score. According to the Israeli Army newspaper, *Bamahane*, a Phalange official had asked an Israeli official two weeks earlier of their plan of operations toward Palestinian refugees after the departure of PLO fighters: "How to begin, by raping or killing?"

Beirut. 11:00 PM. September 15. Report: 300 killed in Sabra and Shatila.

Before midnight, Israeli headquarters in East Beirut announced that 300 people, including civilians, had been killed in Sabra and Shatila. The report was forwarded to headquarters in Tel Aviv and Jerusalem, where it was seen by more than twenty senior Israeli officers. At one point, a militiaman radioed a question to commander Hobeika: "What do we do with the women and children in the refugee camp?"

An Israeli officer could hear, on the militiaman's end of the line, Phalangist troops laughing—apparently at the question. The officer listened to Hobeika's reply: "This is the last time you're going to ask me a question like that. You know exactly what to do."

The orgy of killing in Sabra and Shatila lasted thirty-eight hours and took the lives of at least 800. Our best estimates are 1,800 to 3,500 dead. The latter figure was quoted by Israeli journalist Ammon Kapeliouk of *Le Monde Diplomatique*, and is largely accepted by Palestinian historians.

Beirut. Friday, September 17. Independent observers enter Sabra and Shatila.

While the camps still were sealed off, a few independent observers managed to enter. Among them was the Norwegian journalist and diplomat Gunnar Flakstad, who observed Phalangists during their cleanup operations removing dead bodies from destroyed houses. Many of the bodies found had been severely mutilated. Boys had been castrated, some had been scalped, and some had the Christian symbol of the cross carved into their bodies. Another foreigner who entered the camps after the massacre was Janet Lee Stevens, an American journalist, who later wrote to her husband: "I saw dead women in their houses with their skirts up to their waists and their legs spread apart; dozens of young men shot after being lined up against an alley wall; children with their throats slit, a pregnant woman with her stomach chopped open, her eyes still wide open, her blackened face silently screaming in horror; countless babies and toddlers who had been stabbed or ripped apart and who had been thrown into garbage piles."

As if the massacre was not enough, the international community added insult to injury at the UN General Assembly, on December 16, 1982 (two months after Sabra and Shatila). The Canadian Ambassador stated: "The term genocide cannot, in our view, be applied to this particular inhuman act." The delegate of Singapore added: "My delegation regrets the use of the term 'an act of genocide' . . . [as] the term 'genocide' is used to mean acts committed with intent to destroy, in whole or in part, a national, ethnic, racial or religious group." The US commented that, "while the criminality of the massacre was beyond question, it was a serious and reckless misuse of language to label this tragedy genocide."

Abu al-Abbas was by my side in Damascus just ten days after our wedding when we heard of the Sabra and Shatila massacre. There was nothing we could do. For years afterward, he would remember this event. "If this was not genocide," Abu al-Abbas would often ask me, shaking his head in disbelief, "then what is?"

Likewise, Palestinians all over the world received the news of Sabra and Shatila with shock, disbelief, and a sense of their own helplessness. I think especially of four Palestinian teenagers whose family and friends died here. Three years later, they booked passage to Haifa on an Italian cruise liner called the *Achille Lauro*.

1983: A Tête à Tête with the *Mukhabarat*

When the Palestinian leadership and 11,000 commandos left Beirut in August 1982, they were welcomed in many Arab countries including Sudan and Tunisia. For their part, the Tunisians put 1,100 Palestinian commandos in trucks and transported them to barracks in the desert surrounded by a fence and under continuous guard. Government ministers explained that only the political offices of the PLO—not training facilities of any kind— would be allowed in the capital city of Tunis and that commandos, even those housed in the remote desert camp, could not engage in military training: no artillery range, no obstacle courses, no tactical exercises. Why? The government explained that the visible presence of a Palestinian army in Tunisia would hurt the tourist trade.

Staying behind in Lebanon were 9,000 commandos based near Tripoli on the coast and in the Bekaa Valley. Some Palestinian leaders were welcomed in Damascus, and PLF training facilities apparently were still functioning in Homs. The larger group of Palestinian troops in the Bekaa Valley were kept under close watch by the Syrians, who were nervous about having foreign troops so close to Damascus.

Across the Mediterranean—to be exact 1,440 miles or 2,317 km to the west of Beirut—Yasser Arafat opened a Fatah office in Tunis, and Abu al-Abbas opened a PLF office nearby. The children and I joined Abu al-Abbas in Tunis. Yet both Arafat and Abu al-Abbas traveled frequently to nearby countries, including Syria. What was on Arafat's mind, nine months after Sabra and Shatila? He was still smarting from criticism that he had caved in to the US, France, and Israel by exiting Beirut under Israeli guns and leaving ordinary Palestinians with no protection except US promises—assurances that turned out to be a death warrant for 3,500 of them.

Damascus. April 25, 1983. A meeting between Arafat and President Assad.

Near the end of April, a meeting between Arafat and Hafez al-Assad ended in acrimony. Within Arafat's own Fatah faction, trouble was brewing. A dissident group composed of Fatah officers of middle rank found backing in Syria. The dissidents felt that Arafat's negotiated exit from Beirut was directly responsible for the slaughter at Sabra and Shatila.[3] They saw Arafat as soft and too ready to accept the peace plan that the Reagan administration was pushing.[4] Fatah rebels also charged that Arafat was appointing corrupt loyalists to positions of power rather than highly motivated freedom fighters.[5] In May, a rebellion broke out. A group led by Colonel Saed Abu Musa and supported by Syrian tanks began attacking the Beddawi and Naher al-Bared camps near Tripoli.[6]

Damascus. June 24, 1983. A meeting between Arafat and high Syrian officials.

In June, Arafat again met with officials in Damascus. After this meeting, Hafez al-Assad gave him twenty-four hours to leave the country. He left carrying nothing but the clothes on his back, followed by six aides. Some sources say that Syrians, at this point, attempted but failed to assassinate him. On June 27, Saad Sayel, the Arafat loyalist who commanded the PLO troops still in Lebanon, *was* killed—presumably by Syrian agents.

Tripoli. Mid-September 1983. Arafat returns to Lebanon.

A couple of months after leaving Damascus, Arafat flew to Cyprus, shaved his beard, donned a disguise, and traveled incognito to Tripoli where he joined his besieged PLO loyalists in the Beddawi and Naher al-Bared camps.[7] In the fall, Palestinian insurgents forced Arafat's loyalist troops from the Bekaa Valley to the camps near Tripoli. On December 21, Arafat and 4,000 of his fighters left Tripoli on five Greek ferries. Their ultimate destination was Yemen, Sudan, and several other Arab countries.[8]

In May 1983 in Damascus—in the middle of Arafat's breakup with Hafez al-Assad—Abu al-Abbas still had his apartment in Rukn al-Din and a staff who worked in other apartments nearby. As far as I can tell, PLF training camps were still functioning in Homs. By this time, it was clear to Abu al-Abbas that he had no substitute for Syria. Without their training camps near Homs, the PLF could not survive as an operational entity.

One day Abu al-Abbas was summoned to the office of his friend, intelligence chief Ali Douba. At this point, things were heating up: Palestinians eating breakfast in the Beddawi and Naher al-Bared camps near Tripoli could smell diesel fumes from Syrian tanks. Syria was offering sanctuary and cash grants to any Palestinian group willing to break with Fatah and challenge the authority of Arafat.

For his part, Abu al-Abbas was attempting to walk a thin line between Arafat and Damascus. Ali Douba was a ruthless man whose name sent shivers down the spine of Syrians. Hundreds of Palestinians and members of the Syrian Muslim Brotherhood had died in his jails over the previous decade. Nevertheless when Abu al-Abbas entered his office, he greeted my husband with a smile and signaled for him to be seated. He then began flipping through some papers, without saying a single word. Abu al-Abbas did not blink, even though he recognized that Douba was applying an interrogation technique common among members of Syrian intelligence: keep the suspect waiting long enough and he will be tortured into confession by his own apprehension.

"We have reports," Ali Douba said quietly to Abu al-Abbas at last, "that you are still in contact with Abu Ammar. Is that correct?"

Abu al-Abbas nodded, "Of course it is. He is the leader of our revolution!"

Douba banged his fist on the table. "This is unacceptable Abu al-Abbas," he snarled. "You cannot be working from Syria and keeping contact with Arafat. It's either us or *him*! You have to choose!"

"I hate to make hard choices," Abu al-Abbas gently explained. "But I can only choose to keep Arafat."

Soon after the meeting with Ali Douba, Abu al-Abbas was called to the office of Syrian vice-president Abdul Halim Khaddam in the Syrian capital, next to the Sibki Garden. Once again, he was grilled on his connections with Arafat. Khaddam was a hardcore Assad loyalist at this time. "Arafat is a liar," Khaddam said. "Not only that, he is also filthy and cheap. It is not in your interest to continue working with such a crook. He is a despicable character, with his miserable looks and pathetic *kufiyyeh*."

Abu al-Abbas stood up and pointed to a photograph hanging over Khaddam's head that showed Hafez al-Assad wearing a Russian *ushanka*. "Abu Jamal, allow me to tell you that Arafat's *kufiyyeh* is no less pathetic than the *ushanka* of your friend!"

This was the last time Abu al-Abbas ever saw Douba or Khaddam. It was also the last he ever saw of Hafez al-Assad. The working relationship between Abu al-Abbas and Hafez al-Assad had lasted two or three years. Now, Abu al-Abbas understood, he was *persona non grata*. A few days later, he left Syria, closing the door firmly behind him.

11
Life in Baghdad

IN SEPTEMBER 1982, THE ISRAELIS succeeded in forcing Abu al-Abbas and the PLO out of Beirut. On September 9, Abu al-Abbas and I married in Damascus. Shortly thereafter, Abu al-Abbas and I traveled to USSR to rehab his head wound. Then, in the first months of 1983, we moved our household from Damascus to Tunisia for what both Abu al-Abbas and I believed would be a brief exile before we returned to Beirut. Two years later in 1985—a year of intense back and forth attacks between Israel and the PLO—the *Achille Lauro* events unfolded. After Abu al-Abbas escaped from Italy thanks to the intercession of Italian prime minister Craxi, he traveled to Yugoslavia. He could not return to our home in Tunis because the Tunisian government was embarrassed by the *Achille Lauro* and declared Abu al-Abbas to be persona non grata. Instead, Abu al-Abbas accepted the hospitality of Saddam Hussein, traveled to Baghdad, and prepared a place for us. Less than a month after the *Achille Lauro*, the children and I joined him. This would be our home for the next seventeen years.

Iran-Iraq border. September 22, 1980. Iraq launches air attacks on Iran.

In September 1980 Iraq bombed ten Iranian airfields and, a day later, attacked Iran with armor and infantry along a 400 mile long front east of Basra. The bloodletting continued until 1988. Utter savagery was preoccupying Saddam and his men and their counterparts in Iran during these years. A million soldiers and civilians are thought to have perished. Yet, for those of us who lived in Baghdad and were too young or too old to be drafted, ordinary life continued.

1985: Our Villa Near Abu Nuwas Street

Saddam gave us a white-painted villa with a small yard that had several fruit trees in the central neighborhood of Karradeh Dakhel, a famous location in Baghdad since World War II—just across the Tigris from the Green Zone. Our villa had a main floor for living and an upper floor for bedrooms. The villa had been built in the 1950s and was previously occupied by an Iranian member of the Dawa Party (a religious party that now runs Iraq). After the Baathists came to power in 1968, they confiscated the house and evicted the inhabitants. Now it was ours to use as long as we liked. The villa provided a stable location for our family. It also had many hidden microphones, which was like adding to our family a demur and silent cousin who always listened but never had the impulse to speak.

Next door to the villa was an excellent family-owned sweet shop called Abu Afif that sold *baklava, man al salwa, basma,* and other traditional middle eastern delights. The shop has since survived and expanded. Find their website online if you want to see what tempted us every time we walked out our front door. We were less than a ten minute walk from Abu Nuwas Street, one of the city's oldest thoroughfares. Named after a great Arabic poet of the eighth century, it was developed in the 1940s and 1950s as a grand corniche along the Tigris.

Our favorite pastime was to stroll down Abu Nuwas Street where Abu al-Abbas loved the smell of the wood on which *maskouf*

Abu al-Abbas in Baghdad, 1986.

"Our villa had many hidden microphones." Abu al-Abbas and Reem in Baghdad, 1986.

Reem, Ali, and Abu al-Abbas at a wedding in Baghdad, 1987.

(fish) was strung on a wooden skewer and slowly broiled and blackened by the heat of the charcoal fire and seasoned by its smoke. Sometimes, after a stroll, we would eat at our favorite local restaurant, Khan Zaman, which served traditional Iraqi food. Abu al-Abbas especially liked their meat dishes and also loved *warak enab,* grape leaves stuffed with rice, spices, and meats. We both were crazy for *msakhan,* the traditional Palestinian dish that I had been eating since childhood.

I had started my own experiments with food as cultural fusion during our time in West Africa, and now I found time to explore my interest. In Abidjan, I had learned that they used peanuts to thicken their sauce. In Morocco, I had studied Oriental recipes. Later, when we moved to Tunisia, I got the chance to experiment with North African cuisine. On our travels to Algeria and Libya, to learn more about the nuances of North African food, I sought out restaurants that serve traditional dishes that were indigenous to the locale.

In Baghdad, I found that traditional food was a mix of Turkish, Persian, and Indian influences. This motivated me to develop a recipe of my own. I would cook Persian-style rice, soaking the rice for two or three nights, after which I would cook it for ten minutes in boiling water and add a lot of salt to give it a salty taste. I would then wash the rice under cold running water, and put it back in the cooking pot, without adding any water this time. I would cover the rice tightly and let it cook for two or three hours, on very low fire. This rice can be served plain or you can use it as a bed for meat, nuts, spices. The Iranians keep this dish very simple. I would sometimes add to the rice four things: pine nuts, minced meat, nutmeg, and cardamom. These ingredients would give this more of an Indian-spice flavor.

1986: Zafer al-Masri

In 1986 I gave birth to Ali in Baghdad. New life. Motherhood. I was a happy woman.

My children Ali, Reef, and Louai were all with us in Baghdad and we formed a tight family unit. We were normal people, respectful of religion but not fanatical or particularly observant. Abu al-Abbas drank a glass of wine over dinner, but never served himself a glass when alone or working. I did not cover in public. We loved Palestine. And we devoted ourselves to raising our children. Life was good, the new baby was strong—although surprises, sorrow, and grief were also part of our experience.

Nablus, West Bank (Palestine). March 2, 1986. Zafer al-Masri is killed.

In March we received word that my dear uncle Zafer—a very fine man of forty-five who was devoted to local government in Nablus—had been killed by an assassin's bullet. The *Christian Science Monitor* commented that the "quiet, gentle mayor" found himself in an impossible position as a pragmatic man on the ground trying to make government work for his friends and neighbors, a man whose politics were mainstream, which means that he was loyal to the PLO. My uncle was caught between the governance of Israeli authorities, the desire of Jordan's King Hussein to supplant the PLO, the insistence of Syria on controlling local governance in Palestine, and the national aspirations of local Palestinians. The *Christian Science Monitor* concluded:

Zafer al-Masri.

> Whether [Zafer al-Masri] was shot by the rejectionist Palestinian factions that have claimed credit for his murder or by some local thug is almost beside the point. Evil will have its way when good and just people leave the door ajar.[1]

My uncle was beloved. His public funeral in Nablus was attended by 200,000 mourners and his memory and example are still kept alive on his website. The death of my uncle brings sadness that lasts until today.

1986: An Interview with NBC News

New York. May 5, 1986. NBC Nightly News interviews Abu al-Abbas.

The spring following the *Achille Lauro* operation, NBC news arranged to do an interview with Abu al-Abbas in an "undisclosed" location. The highlights of the interview aired in May on NBC Nightly News and a longer segment aired on June 17 for a one hour documentary on the *Achille Lauro*.

According to the *Los Angeles Times*, the State Department charged that NBC was encouraging terrorism and termed the interview "reprehensible." Lawrence K. Grossman, NBC News president, pointed out that *Reuters* and the *Irish Times* also conducted interviews after the NBC interview was completed. As paraphrased by the *Los Angeles Times*, he stated that NBC had not "offered Abbas a platform for propaganda."[2]

The PLF in Baghdad

The life of Zafer al-Masri and his death put into bold relief the value of Abu al-Abbas and the PLF to Yasser Arafat. Perceived as too conciliatory toward the Americans, the PLO Chairman faced a revolt within his own Fatah group in 1983. Yet, if Arafat could still respond to Israeli attacks via the PLF, then he could maintain his profile as a freedom fighter. Could Jordan's King Hussein supplant Arafat as the leader of Palestinian aspirations? Could Syria's Hafez al-Assad? Not if Arafat was able to demonstrate to ordinary Palestinians that he was himself launching commando raids against Israel—fighting for justice on their behalf.

The PLF was one of several Palestinian groups that conducted military actions. It was common for the PLF to launch operations of high daring yet minimal success that other factions learned from and, in the case of hang gliders and rubber boats, implemented more successfully later on. The PFLP-GC under Ahmed Jibril, on the other hand, had plenty of Syrian money, training, and arms plus a thuggish love for violence. Compared to the PLF, it undoubtedly claimed more victims—among fellow Palestinians as well as the Israeli enemy. Yet the PFLP-GC was probably the least loyal to Arafat. We thought of them as instruments of Syrian foreign policy.

In contrast, the PFLP under George Habash was a noble group that I had worked for in Beirut and that supported the PLO. Habash was an ideologue, a Marxist philosopher, and excelled in the media war. After 1980, however, Habash was in declining health and gradually stepped back from leadership while a hard core group took control. When the Israelis invaded Beirut in 1982, the PFLP migrated to Damascus and apparently they began accepting funds from the Syrians—at the exact time that the PLF and Arafat were expelled from Syria for refusing to kowtow. When my uncle was killed in Nablus, the PFLP took credit for the assassination. One assumes that Syrian backing meant that the PFLP felt they could defy Arafat and the PLO.

What distinguished my husband's PLF among other Palestinian military groups was its utter loyalty to Arafat and the PLO.

Before Saddam invaded Kuwait, funds from Kuwait and the Gulf states were flowing into the PLO coffers. And Arafat was generous in providing for the PLF. Whatever needs Saddam did take care of were covered by Arafat and the PLO.

Algiers. April 20 - 25, 1987. Abu al-Abbas given "provisional" status.

International pressure following the *Achille Lauro* incident as well as sniping from the Talaat Yacoub splinter of the PLF and other

Palestinian factions seemed to say that the position of Abu al-Abbas on the PNC Executive Committee was lost. In a surprising development, however, the "unity" meeting of the PNC held in Algiers from April 20-25, 1987—rather than removing Abu al-Abbas from the Executive Committee—granted him "provisional" status. Another plus: the Talaat Yacoub faction of the PLF reconciled with the Abu al-Abbas faction. Yacoub assumed the role of leader and Abu al-Abbas was announced as his second in command. Still, Yacoub continued in Damascus with Syrian support and Abu al-Abbas stayed in Baghdad with Iraqi support. [3]

The PLF staff of 200 worked in several offices in a number of buildings in our Karradeh Dakhel neighborhood. If there was no single building for the PLF, neither was there a sign on any of their offices. Saddam was hosting the PLF, but he was not trumpeting its presence.

The PLF offices were simple spaces for working. They also included living quarters. Technology in those days was basic: phone (landline), fax, TV. The offices belonged to the Iraqi government, as did our villa and a number of the cars that PLF staff drove. We received free lodging, offices, automobiles, and passports—but no security detail, salaries, or pensions. Salaries and expenses came from Chairman Arafat. Still, if the PLF were to launch a major operation, it would require training facilities and cash to cover the costs of training. If Abu al-Abbas and the PLF were to reach again for eminence as a military force, they would need to conduct another big operation and they would need state backing to do so.

1987: The First Intifada

Gaza. December 9, 1987. The First Intifada begins.

Disturbances in northern Gaza near the Jabalia refugee camp sparked the First Intifada. The protest featured largely unarmed teenagers throwing stones at Israeli troops and armored vehicles. The Israelis deployed 80,000 troops to put down the uprising. According to some sources, 7% of all Palestinians under eighteen were injured. The First Intifada culminated in the Madrid Conference of 1991 and led to the Oslo Accords in 1993.

1988: A Feud Ends

Damascus, Syria. April 26, 1988. Arafat and Hafez al-Assad meet.

On the political front, in April Arafat traveled to Damascus for a meeting with Hafez al-Assad—the first time the two had seen each other since their feud erupted in June 1983. The First Intifada was in progress. The two leaders were forced to overcome their differences as the world watched Palestinian youths facing Israeli tanks in the occupied territories.

"If the feud had been settled two years earlier," I found myself thinking, "I wonder if my uncle Zafer would still be alive today?"

12
The Jerusalem Sea Operation

Algiers. November 1988. The Annual PNC Meeting.

ABU AL-ABBAS HAD BEEN LAYING LOW for three years since the *Achille Lauro* operation. Now, with chairman Arafat's blessing, Abu al-Abbas and I traveled from Baghdad to the annual Palestinian National Congress meeting which, in 1988, was held in the Algerian capital.

We flew from Baghdad to Algiers and rode in an official car from the airport to the Council Hall. We were accompanied by our son Ali, who was still a toddler. We had no idea what to expect. As we turned the corner to the Council Hall, we were thronged. Arafat waded through the crowd to meet us. When Abu al-Abbas stepped out of the car, Arafat embraced him. "The world press has doubled just because of you Abu al-Abbas," Arafat said. "All of them are here to catch a glimpse of the man behind the *Achille Lauro!*"

When Abu al-Abbas got out of the car, photographers rushed up to him and began clicking away. Our son Ali crawled from my lap out of the car and grabbed his father by the knee. Abu al-Abbas picked him up, embraced him, and then placed him next to me in the car's back seat—as the cameras flashed away. The next morning, photographs of Abu al-Abbas appeared on the front page of the Israeli dailies. One photo showed Abu al-Abbas bending to pick up his child. Another showed him embracing Ali. A third shows him placing Ali next to me.

The moment was one of elevation if not triumph. Abu al-Abbas, like all of us, had faced doubts and deep discouragement after the *Achille Lauro*. Now, despite the obvious errors of the operation, he saw that his efforts to challenge the injustice done to Palestine still struck a chord with ordinary Palestinians.

In this month, Talaat Yacoub, the schoolteacher who had joined with Abu al-Abbas to reestablish the PLF in 1977, died in Algiers of a heart attack.[1]

1988: Arafat's Honeymoon with the US

At the Palestinian National Council in Algeria in November 1988, Arafat famously marched into the conference room walking in uniform with a pistol on his hip like a military general who had just emerged from a victorious battle. As Abu al-Abbas and other comrades applauded, the PLO Chairman announced creation of the State of Palestine, with Jerusalem as its capital and himself as president and accepted all UN resolutions on the Arab-Israeli Conflict. This bold announcement was Arafat's way of agreeing, for the first time in twenty-three years as a resister, with the primary demand of Israel and the US: he was publicly accepting the right of Israel to exist.

As a member of Arafat's inner circle, Abu al-Abbas was consulted in advance on this and other major PLO initiatives. Although Abu al-Abbas was "in the next room" in Algiers before Arafat's 1988 speech, in the later meetings leading up to the honeymoon with the US, Abu al-Abbas was at home in Baghdad and in contact by phone. During these years when Arafat was in peace-making mode, he typically concealed his contacts with Abu al-Abbas to his English-speaking or French-speaking audiences whereas he trumpeted them to his Arabic-speaking audiences. Abu al-Abbas was a military commander and he gave Arafat "street cred" with ordinary Palestinians. Arafat saw Abu al-Abbas whenever he came to Baghdad, and the two men spoke frequently on the phone. As a member of the PLO's Executive Committee and a figure with a popular following among ordinary Palestinians, Abu al-Abbas possessed veto power—yet he seldom used it, preferring to support Arafat's decisions without making his reservations public. When Abu al-Abbas did have concerns, he would make them known. For his part, Arafat would listen to his comrade's views and take them into consideration. Yet Arafat made no apologies for his role as the sole decision maker.

Arafat called for a comprehensive Middle East Peace Conference and made a direct appeal to US president-elect George H. W. Bush to endorse the idea. This was something, Arafat believed, the Americans would not be able to refuse. Neither outgoing President Reagan or incoming President Bush, however, embraced the Arafat initiative. They said that it had "positive aspects" but fell short of being a serious proposal that merited full US support or commitment. They continued to refuse to recognize the concept of a Palestinian State. They laid down the condition that Arafat make an explicit statement, condemning all forms of "state terrorism."

As a result of his speech in Algeria, Arafat was invited to attend the UN General Assembly in New York on December 14, 1988. The US and Israel, however, objected and the Department of State refused to give Arafat a visa. George Shultz described him as "an accessory of terrorism." The UN protested the US ruling, and 154 countries proposed that the meeting be moved to Geneva instead of New York so that Arafat could attend.

Arafat traveled to Geneva via Stockholm where he met his friend, Minister Sven Anderson, who showed him a letter he had received from Shultz. The letter said that the PLO should issue a statement renouncing terrorism. Under much pressure, Arafat said that he would do it at the UN meeting. He reasoned that he and Abu al-Abbas would play a double role. Politically, the PLO would make nice with the Americans via Arafat, while militarily it would continue its war against Israel via Abu al-Abbas. Shultz had written the exact words he wanted Arafat to say. In his memoirs, Shultz said that the wording was the following: "The executive committee of the PLO, condemns individual, group, and state terrorism in all its form, and will not resort to it." Shultz added, "I received word that Yasser Arafat would make a speech at Geneva saying exactly that. I said that we would move promptly to be in touch with them—if he did say those words."

Arafat asked our friend, the legendary Palestinian poet Mahmud Darwish to write his UN speech for him. In the middle of poetic verse about the heroism of the Palestinians, Arafat carefully inserted the words Shultz wanted to hear—almost. The night before, Arafat had still found it hard to digest these words and so he made some minor edits. He did not take out words, but he rearranged them to make the statement ambiguous. And so it was that at his UN speech on December 14, Arafat renounced terrorism using text that he and Darwish had written. Still Shultz was not satisfied. In fact, he was angered by the changes that Arafat had made. He wrote, "I told President Reagan 'In one place, Arafat was saying *Unc* . . . *Unc* . . . in another *cle* . . . *cle* . . . He has yet to cry *Uncle*!'"

Swedish minister Sven Anderson came to see Arafat after the UN meeting. He explained that the US was still not satisfied, and that Arafat had to find another occasion to utter the precise words Shultz was insisting upon. Arafat was furious and refused the request. He rushed off to the dinner at the home of the Egyptian Ambassador to Switzerland, Amr Mousa. At dinner, Mousa convinced Arafat to return to the hotel, give a press conference, and to say what Shultz wanted him to say. Arafat agreed and at 2:00 AM called a press conference. Reporters from more than 800 news agencies attended. Arafat seemed irritable and was fiddling with the documents, waiting for the hall to be silent. Then he started reading from a small paper, "The executive committee of the PLO condemns individual, group, and state 'tourism'." He then looked back and said: "I am sorry, I meant 'terrorism'." When Arafat finished, he turned around and remarked to Mousa: "What more do they want me to do? Striptease?"

Four hours later, the US announced that it was ready for talks with Yasser Arafat and the PLO. Two comuniques were released, one by Reagan and one by Shultz. Both praised Arafat's statement. On December 15, the first

US-Palestinian meeting took place: the US ambassador in Tunis sat down with PLO representatives. Eight days later on December 23, Pan AM flight 103 was downed by a bomb over Lockerbie, Scotland. Arafat rushed to offer the US Palestinian intelligence support to help solve the crime. Arafat wanted to build bridges with the White House. At this point, the PLO and the Americans were having a honeymoon.

Gaddafi Makes Contact

While Arafat began his overture to the US at the November 1988 PNC annual conference in Algiers, Abu al-Abbas was heading in the exact opposite direction—with Arafat's blessing. At this same conference Abu al-Abbas made the first contacts that would lead to a military action against Israel that he hoped would be far more successful than the botched *Achille Lauro* affair.

On November 1, Gaddafi travelled to Algiers to take part in the annual Algerian Revolution celebrations. When Abu al-Abbas arrived for the PNC conference, Gaddafi sent word that he wanted to meet face-to-face. Not wanting to cross Saddam by consorting with a rival head of state and unsure of Arafat's attitude toward such a meeting, Abu al-Abbas ignored the invitation. Later, before the PNC conference was over, Gaddafi sent an envoy who requested a meeting with one of the aides of Abu al-Abbas. Away from the conference hall, at Nadi al-Sonobar, a swanky resort on the western shore of the Algerian capital, Gaddafi's envoy met with a confidant of Abu al-Abbas named Ziad al-Omar. The envoy invited my husband to visit Gaddafi in the Libyan capital of Tripoli to explore areas of mutual interest. Speaking through Ziad al-Omar, Abu al-Abbas declined on the grounds that such a meeting would displease his protector and his leader. "We cannot go without coordinating first with Saddam Hussein and Abu Ammar," Abu al-Abbas said.

Gaddafi was fickle. Not a reliable partner at all. There was no telling when he might retract his invitation, or withdraw political cover if Abu al-Abbas suddenly fell from grace or happened to cross one of the ever-shifting invisible lines that the Libyan dictator used to distinguish his friends from his enemies. Abu al-Abbas eventually sent word to Iraqi authorities that he was being stalked by Muammar al-Gaddafi. Saddam responded, via his deputy Tarek Aziz, "No harm in meeting him. Go ahead."

Saddam was the difficult one, Abu al-Abbas reasoned. Arafat would be much easier to persuade. One of Abu al-Abbas's men got on the phone with Abu Iyad, seeking Arafat's blessing to meet in Libya with Gaddafi. Abu Iyad confidently replied, "You must go. Take it while it lasts. Go quickly. Don't even think about it. I can assure you that *al-Ikhtiyar* won't mind."

Why Gaddafi Wanted to Strike Israel

To understand Gaddafi's motives in wanting to attack Israel, it helps to go back a decade. In 1979, well into his tenth year in power, Colonel Gaddafi adopted the title, "Leader of the Revolution," and began to finance revolutionary parties in all four corners of the globe. He wanted to nurture and develop these revolutions, to become their mentor. When they succeeded, Gaddafi hoped to take credit for their success (and, perhaps, to use them to do his bidding). As part of this policy, Libyan money began flowing at an increased rate to a variety of Palestinian groups via the conduit of the PLO. In response, in 1979 the US State Department placed the Libyan leader on their list of State Sponsors of Terrorism. When Gaddafi learned of his designation, his thugs attacked the US Embassy in Tripoli and set it afire. The Americans took offense, both the Jimmy Carter administration and that of Ronald Reagan.

President Reagan, who came to the White House in 1980, famously declared Gaddafi an "international pariah" and the "mad dog of the Middle East." In return, Gaddafi shut down the Libyan embassy in Washington, DC and threatened to join the Warsaw Pact. Gaddafi also strengthened his ties to the Soviet Union and gave funds to three anti-imperialist groups: the Red Army Faction in Germany; the Italian Red Brigades; and the Irish Republican Army. Reagan withdrew all US oil companies operating in Libya and in March 1982 imposed an embargo on Libyan oil. Relations hit rock bottom in April 1986. When a bomb detonated in the *La Bella* discotheque in West Berlin, which frequented often by US soldiers, three people died and seventy-nine Americans were injured. The US blamed Gaddafi and launched an air attack against Libya. The bombs targeted the Libyan leader's residence and, according to Libyan sources, killed his infant daughter. The Libyan Leader sought revenge for the US air bombardment by attacking Israel. To do this, he came knocking on the door of Abu al-Abbas in November 1988. By the following summer, Abu al-Abbas had received the OK from Saddam and from Arafat to see Gaddafi.

Tripoli, Libya. July 1989. Abu al-Abbas visits with Gaddafi.

Abu al-Abbas and his top lieutenants traveled to Tripoli, Libya on fake passports provided by the Iraqi government. They stayed at the Grand Hotel in Tripoli and were then flown to Gaddafi's hometown, Sirte, a dusty town lying halfway between Tripoli and Benghazi. Colonel Muammar al-Gaddafi, as always, was waiting for them in a large green tent and was wearing a colorful outfit of green, yellow, and orange cloth. He always took great pride in his hometown, frequently brought dignitaries here, and later held an Arab Summit in Sirte.

"I am upset with you Abu al-Abbas," he said upon greeting my husband, "You have spent your life between Lebanon, Syria, and Iraq. You have never come to Libya! Although we are home to all freedom fighters from around the world, you never once came to Libya!" Abu al-Abbas smiled, politely saying that he had never before been invited to Libya. The following conversation ensued between Abu al-Abbas and Gaddafi:

> **Gaddafi:** You are not the first fighter to come to Sirte. You are not the first to come to Libya. We have tried them all, brother Abu al-Abbas. Alas, all of them amount to nothing. They were, and still are, completely useless. We supported men who claimed to represent the resistance. They turned out to be agents of international imperialism and unpaid agents for the Zionists themselves. They were your own countrymen, Abu al-Abbas. All of them, however, turned out to be tailor-made for hotels (*fanadek*) rather than trenches (*khanadek*). Are you a man of hotels or trenches?
>
> **Abu al-Abbas:** We are ready for cooperation, Brother Muammar. We are open to working with anybody who believes in our cause: liberty and justice for the Palestinians. We are a resistance movement focused on destroying the State of Israel. You know us very well Brother Muammar. We don't need to explain ourselves to you. That is why you invited us to your great country, after all.
>
> **Gaddafi:** Indeed, I know everything about you, Abu al-Abbas. How is brother Saddam?
>
> **Abu al-Abbas:** Upset. Brother Saddam is upset. The Iranians are shelling Baghdad with missiles . . . .
>
> **Gaddafi:** God curse those wretched Persians . . . .
>
> **Abu al-Abbas:** But Brother Muammar—brother Saddam says that those missiles came from Libya. One of those Libyan missiles, in fact, landed right next to my house in Baghdad. It almost killed me and my family.
>
> **Gaddafi:** Libyan missiles? I sent those missiles to Hafez al-Assad, not to the Ayatollahs. They were meant for the Golan. . . to liberate Syrian territory. Yes, they are my missiles. They were never meant to land in Baghdad! The Syrians gave them to Iran, and Iran is using them against brother Saddam.

Gaddafi, of course, knew exactly the origin of these missiles. He was flirting heavily with the Iranians, using them in his proxy war with the United States, and did not really care where Libya's missiles were landing so long as they were keeping Ronald Reagan awake at night. Abu al-Abbas, it must be noted, was carrying a message from Saddam Hussein, who wanted to curb

Libyan-Iranian coordination. Gaddafi eventually agreed, asking in exchange for Palestinian help in tracking down—and killing—Libyan dissidents in Europe. Abu al-Abbas said, No, as Yasser Arafat had done before him. A decade earlier in the late 1970s, when Arafat turned down the Colonel's request, Gaddafi went mad and cut off all aid to the PLO. This time, he made the request halfheartedly, knowing beforehand that Abu al-Abbas would never become a "gun for hire" as Abu Nidal had been. The meeting ended on a positive note, nearly three hours later. Gaddafi offered nothing, and Abu al-Abbas asked for nothing. Gaddafi invited him to return to Libya on September 1, to take part in the 18th anniversary of the coup d'état that had brought him to power in 1969. That was a pompous annual event that was usually packed with anybody who was somebody in the Arab world. Gaddafi invited artists, writers, politicians, poets, scientists, and military leaders from the world over and rewarded each guest with a gift of cash, and a gold-plated Rolex carrying Gaddafi's picture and usually decorated with diamonds.

Tripoli, Libya. September 15, 1988. Abu al-Abbas Sees Gaddafi Again.

Abu al-Abbas did return to Libya, but only on September 15, two weeks after the celebrations had ended. He did not want to be part of the pro-Gaddafi chorus and made sure that he received no gift or favor that would put him in debt to the Libyan government. He was seeking financial support for one thing only: a new operation against Israel that would right the wrongs of the *Achille Lauro*.

1989: A Project in Libya

In the first months of 1989, the proposal of Abu al-Abbas was accepted. The operation was a "go" and was scheduled for May 30, 1990. Gaddafi presented the PLF with villas, automobiles, military experts, passports, and military camps in the Libyan dessert. Bases were dotted all over Libya, in Tripoli itself, in Benghazi, and Sirte. A total of 700 Palestinian staffers and commandos were flown in and out of Libya over the next eighteen months as the planning of the Jerusalem Sea Operation progressed. Abu al-Abbas spent entire days with no sleep, training with his men at the camps in Libya. In total, he held eleven meetings with Colonel Gaddafi, briefing him on military progress and preparations. Once, Gaddafi asked him to bring along the entire Political Bureau of the PLF. I also accompanied him several times to Tripoli, although I never met Gaddafi in person.

Once, I was asked to host Gaddafi and the entire Libyan command at a dinner at our house. Hours before dinner time, while I was slaving away in the kitchen, Gaddafi sent an official motorcade to escort Abu al-Abbas to the palace. I expected that the two men would have a brief conference and then show up together for dinner. They never did. I waited until nightfall, and when no word came from Abu al-Abbas, ugly thoughts began flowing through my head. I was certain that Abu al-Abbas had fallen into a trap and that Gaddafi had lured him into Libya to eliminate him, just as he had done with the Beirut-based Iranian cleric Musa al-Sadr back in 1978. I sat on the porch of our house, buried my head between my knees, and began to cry. Here I was, in the middle of nowhere, having lost any form of communication with my husband. I did not know a single soul in Libya. I sat there for what was seemingly an endless period, until I heard sounds of car wheels screeching along the pavement. The presidential motorcade was back, twenty-four hours after it had left our house. In the lead car I saw Abu al-Abbas, smiling as always.

"You will never leave me alone again like that!" I said. "Do you understand?" I was shouting and screaming, banging his chest in fury. The smile just expanded on his face. He was beaming and clearly had something amusing to say that he couldn't wait to get out. When we got inside, he recounted the following story:

"I was taken on an endless journey to see Gaddafi. I took every form of transportation you can imagine: trains, helicopters, cars, motorbikes, and rubber boats. I finally reached him in the middle of the dessert, seated before a huge stone that clearly was not the product of Mother Nature. It had been imported to its current location at Gaddafi's orders. Seated atop the stone, wearing florescent orange, was Brother Muammar himself. He waved to me, signaling that I should join. I climbed up the mammoth stone, and we sat there, gazing into the desert. The color of his dress reminded me of how he once showed up for a meeting with Arafat wearing a brownish-purple gown that resembled the color of the outer skin of eggplants. Arafat could hardly hold back his laughter, and would often tell us, 'Here comes the eggplant!' As I watched him gaze into the horizon, without saying a word, I too could barely hold back my laughter. He was mediating, Reem, and wanted me first to mediate with him. At any rate, you will never imagine what wanted from me. He said, 'Comrade Abu al-Abbas, we in Libya are working on an atomic bomb, and we want your assistance as Palestinians, in developing it so we can eliminate imperialism and Zionism!' He's crazy Reem! Absolutely crazy!"

What mattered to me was that Abu al-Abbas was happy, seemingly injected with enthusiasm and hope, two traits that I had not seen in him since the *Achille Lauro* and our days in Tunis. His eyes glimmered as he spoke of the new operation. He speculated on how painful it would be for the Tel Aviv government. The operation had to succeed. Everything depended upon it. With the enthusiasm of a sixteen-year-old, he would sit with me during the night and tell me how his troops would impose a stunning defeat and shatter the myth of the "invincible IDF."

The plan was to send four rubber-boats with sixteen commandos and another boat with fuel to the Nizanim beach, near Tel Aviv. The trip from Libya to Israel would take one day and a half, Abu al-Abbas said. As with the *Achille Lauro* Operation, his men were supposed to disembark on the seashore and engage Israeli security forces. They did not have orders to kill tourists or unarmed civilians, as the Western media said back then. The fighters were aged eighteen to twenty seven. They consisted of sympathetic Syrians and Palestinians from the refugee camps in and around Damascus, Beirut, and Amman.

The operation was supposed to coincide with the Arab League Summit in Baghdad, being hosted by Saddam Hussein. Both Saddam and Gaddafi wanted it to happen on the very same day as the opening ceremony, to force their radical agenda on the Arab world. The two men were personal friends, but stood on opposite ends of the political spectrum, with Gaddafi making common cause with the Iranians at a time when Saddam was pummeling them with missiles. Another irony: Gaddafi was the enemy # 1 in the eyes of the US, whereas Saddam was extremely close to the Americans at this stage, months before his August 1990 invasion of Kuwait. Saddam and Gaddafi both wanted to polish their credentials as Arab nationalists, and nothing would do that better than embracing the Palestinian Cause.

1990: The Jerusalem Sea Operation

Abu al-Abbas's second most prominent military action after the *Achille Lauro* was the Jerusalem Sea Operation. In Arabic, we call it the al-Quds al-Bahriya Operation. Although this action is well known, historians don't agree on its place in the jigsaw puzzle of the Arab-Israeli conflict. Abu al-Abbas himself originally had great faith in the operation, but was never satisfied with its execution.

The Israeli coast. May 30, 1990. Five rubber boats head toward shore.

The seaborne attack, as you might imagine, did not go as planned. Abu al-Abbas later explained that, per his agreement with Gaddafi, the Libyan mother ship was supposed to drop the PLF fighters and their rubber boats just a few kilometers from shore. Instead, they dropped the commandos far out at sea which meant that the Israelis had ample time to intercept the boats and to arrest or kill the PLF commandos.

Abu al-Abbas's liaison with Libya, Ziad al-Omar disputes the version of events given by Abu al-Abbas. He argues that Colonel Gaddafi had indeed lived up to his commitment and that the error was committed by the PLF itself. "One rubber boat actually made it to the shore north of Ashkelon," he explained. "If the Israelis knew of the operation before hand, they would have shot the rubber boats while they were still in the waters."

Ziad al-Omar also cited other complications. While sailing toward Israel, he explained, the outboard motor on one of the rubber boats broke down. The operation was delayed when the fighters and their weapons were transferred to another boat and the boat itself was scuttled. "The main mistake," said al-Omar, "was that the commandos forgot to bring a thick rope with them. Had they done that, they could have tied the damaged boat to the functioning ones, and pulled it safely and quickly with toward the shore. The need for rope completely slipped our minds." The Israeli Army was waiting for the commandos and arrested them before they could do any damage. They were released from Israeli jails ten years later, as part of the prisoner swaps that took place with Arafat after the 1993 signing of the Oslo Peace Accords.

Reasons for the Jerusalem Sea Operation

Plenty has been written about the Jerusalem Sea Operation of May 30, 1990 by Israeli historians and journalists, who analyzed it from the "terrorism angle" that western reporters typically use to frame their reporting on the Palestinians. Biographers of Muammar al-Gaddafi also refer to the Sea Operation as part of the Libyan leader's ploy to win popularity in the Arab world and inflict maximal pain on the US and Israel. From the Palestinian standpoint, however, the story is somewhat different. Yasser Arafat wanted the Sea Operation to succeed almost as much as Abu al-Abbas did. For the Sea Operation came at a critical time in Palestinian history. The intifada, which broke out two and a half years earlier in December 1987, was at its apex in the Occupied Territories at this time. But most veteran commanders like Arafat and Abu al-Abbas were watching from the distance of their exile in Tunisia or Iraq. The young Palestinian stone-throwers were gracing the stage inside Palestine and were making veteran PLO leaders look and sound old, distant, and utterly incapacitated.

In addition, the Soviet Union was on the verge of collapse, and Arafat was desperate for a back channel with Washington, DC. That door would never open, he was told, unless he took a firm stance against "Palestinian terrorism." In 1988 at the PNC conference in Algiers, Abu Ammar decided to do just that while simultaneously giving Abu al-Abbas carte blanche to pursue military resistance. Arafat only signed off on the Sea Operation *after* having established contact with the Americans. If Arafat's romance with the Americans collapsed, he would endorse the operation and lay claim to it. If they succeeded, he would forever distance himself from the Sea Operation, saying that it was the doing of Abu al-Abbas.

As it turned out, the Jerusalem Sea Operation destroyed the diplomatic bridge that Arafat had been building with the George H. W. Bush administration. In September 1991, Arafat dropped Abu al-Abbas from the PNC Executive Committee. In the eyes of the Americans, however, it was too little, too late. In fact, it came sixteen months after US Secretary of State James Baker uttered an oft-quoted rebuke directed at Yitzhak Shamir and, by implication, at Shamir's negotiating partners in the PLO.

A Telephone Number

Washington. June 20, 1990. James Baker suspends talks.

The brief honeymoon that Arafat cultivated with the US seemed tenable in December 1988. Five months later, however, it evaporated the moment that Abu al-Abbas launched five rubber boats toward the Israeli shore. After the Jerusalem Sea Operation, Secretary of State James Baker gave congressional testimony that included a sarcastic remark: "Our telephone number is 202-456-1414. When you are serious about peace, call us!"[2]

13
Early Retirement

I HAVE HAD AN UNUSUAL LIFE, a life demarked by many wars. Some, like Lebanon in 1975 and in 2006, or Iran-Iraq in the 1980s, I witnessed firsthand. Others, like the Arab-Israeli Wars of 1967 and 1973, I watched from a distance. More recently, I have stood witness to the US war on Iraq in 2003, the Israeli war on Gaza in 2008, the NATO war on Libya in 2011, and the ongoing war in Syria.

I have managed to escape Israeli and American missiles flying right past my head in Baghdad and run to bunkers in the middle of the night in Beirut. I grew up in Beirut. I have childhood memories here. And yet, in this city, I have seen men die between my two hands. In Gaza I have seen buildings crumble right before my eyes. In Syria I have seen children and women sobbing their hearts out.

I have lived through eleven wars and countless battles, and I don't know how many more wars I am destined to live through in the Middle East. In each of them I have suffered the death of friends, comrades, and fellow countrymen—often distinguished patriots. A part of my soul was taken with each of these senseless deaths. Beirut, Gaza, Baghdad, and Tripoli: Every one of the cities I have lived in or loved was pounded to dust by the Israelis, the Americans, or by Arab despots. One of the wars that I most detest—and in fact shiver every time I remember—was Saddam's occupation and liberation of Kuwait and the salvos of precision guided bombs that followed.

Although I was once an active member of the Palestinian resistance and the wife of a Palestinian commando, I have to admit: I hate war. I cannot imagine losing more friends and family in yet another battle. And, late at night, I imagine that our opponents in these conflicts share my grief. I have to admit that they, too, have lost children, women, and young men in the prime of life.

Teach the Children

In 1990, Iraq was on the verge of war. Saddam was about to do something crazy and the inevitable US response was easy to foretell. It seemed logical to take our children out of Baghdad and move them to a safer city. By now the civil war had ended in Lebanon, so I flew with my children to Beirut and enrolled them at the French school. I placed Ali, aged 4, in kindergarten.

1990: Iraq Invades Kuwait

Kuwait. August 2, 1990.

In the middle of the night the "glorious and invincible" Iraqi Army rumbled into Kuwait on the orders of Saddam Hussein. The reasons given for the invasion vary and have been debated to death by Middle East historians. One reason, no doubt, was Saddam's belief that Kuwait was stealing Iraqi oil through slant drilling. Another was Iraq's inability to repay $80 billion to Kuwait, borrowed during the Iran-Iraq War of 1980-1988. Saddam wanted to cancel the debt, expecting a reward for having battled the ayatollahs of Tehran on the behalf of the Arab Gulf for nearly a decade. To raise money for postwar reconstruction after ending his conflict with Iran, Saddam had pushed oil-exporting countries to raise oil prices by cutting back oil production in Iraq. Yet Kuwait curtly refused. Saddam also showed disdain for Kuwait's border, created by the British in 1922. One of the few things that Iraqis of all faiths, ethnic backgrounds, and political persuasions agreed on was that Kuwait was historically part of their country and should be a part of Iraq in the present day. For most of the century, Iraqi politicians had laid claims to Kuwait. In 1960, President Abdul Karim Qasim tried to occupy Kuwait but was prevented by the British Army and the Arab League. Saddam's ambitions were not new. They mirrored the mood in the Iraqi street.

On July 22, 1990, Saddam had complained to the US State Department about his relations with Kuwait through April Glaspie, the infamous US Ambassador to Baghdad. I remember Glaspie well. She hated my husband and would freeze whenever encountering him on the streets of the Iraqi capital. She would immediately complain to the Iraqi government about the presence of a terrorist in its territory. Yet Saddam Hussein would ignore her remarks. Officially, Iraq never admitted that Abu al-Abbas was a guest of Saddam Hussein, and the Iraqi press never, ever, mentioned him or carried his photograph. At one point in early 1990, Saddam told Ambassador Glaspie that he was thinking of invading Kuwait. Glaspie said that the US would not get involved and that this was an internal Kuwaiti-Iraqi issue, implying that President George H. W. Bush and Secretary of State James Baker would neither mind nor object. Soon after, Saddam invaded and occupied Kuwait in August 1990 declaring it the 19th province of Iraq, thereby sparking the famous international crisis.

President Bush responded cautiously at first. On the one hand, Kuwait was not Saudi Arabia. Also, Washington hated Kuwait's historic ties to the Palestinians. On the other hand, the US had heavy political, military, and private investment in Kuwait. Policymakers did not want further instability in the Persian Gulf. The invasion threatened to raise the price of world oil, and Americans considered that their economy, and that of the world, was at stake. Bush was talked into taking action by British Prime Minister Margaret Thatcher, who had been America's strongest European ally during the Reagan Administration. Britain had historical ties and investments in Kuwait, much more than the US, dating back to the British protectorate of the 1920s. As a result, Britain and the US decided to push for a UN Resolution to give Iraq a deadline to leave Kuwait by mid-January 1991.

Abu al-Abbas and I at the time were "hiding" in northern Iraq warned by Saddam's intelligence that the Israelis were planning to assassinate him, in retaliation for the recent operation. Yitzhak Shamir had appeared live on Israeli TV. "We will reach you Abu al-Abbas," he said, "regardless of what Baghdad bunker you are hiding in!" Abu al-Abbas of course loved it when the Israelis threatened him so bluntly. "This is testimony that what we are doing is working, and it's hurting them bad!" he would often say. "We cannot stay for more than two nights in a single place," he said to me, asking me to leave the house in haste, without packing much stuff. He added, "That is what the Iraqis told me, and I cannot but take their advice very seriously. Peres is furious. Take whatever belongings are absolutely necessary." I hated this line, "take what is absolutely necessary" because I had heard it too often. Abu al-Abbas had given me this same speech when we left Beirut for Syria in 1982, Syria for Tunisia that same year, and Tunisia for Iraq after the *Achille Lauro* Operation in 1985. I did not know if I would not ever return to see my home in Baghdad. I hated my wandering life, forever entering and then suddenly leaving different Arab cities. I lost most of my precious belongings along the way. And it was a nightmare for the kids to be carried off so abruptly, leaving behind their schools and friends.

We were whisked by Saddam's men into what is now known as Iraqi Kurdistan. We spent quick nights in Dahouk, Suleimaniyah, and Irbil. Of course, we were denied access to phones or fax machines for fear that the Israelis would intercept our calls. However Abu al-Abbas was allowed to bring along some of his security officials on our brief exile. "At least it's summer," Abu al-Abbas said, "and the children are out of school." He chuckled when he said this. It was characteristic of the man that he would always manage to find the bright side, no matter how gloomy our circumstances. "It's a well-deserved vacation," he said.

"My dear," I replied, "a 'forced' vacation is a better word!"

The Iraqis considered the Israeli threats "very serious" given that the sea operation had taken place only three months earlier. The Americans were also furious with Abu al-Abbas, who had spoken to CNN during one of his visits to Eastern Europe and put a $1 million bounty on Ronald Reagan's head. This, of course, was in response to the US President declaring from Japan that the US would pay $500,000 for the arrest or killing of Abu al-Abbas. Not only did this exchange embarrass the Iraqis, who until then, had kept up excellent relations with Washington, but it increased the chances that Abu al-Abbas would be assassinated by the Israelis or the Americans. We were running from Israeli ghosts with guns and were very far from Baghdad when Saddam invaded Kuwait on that fateful day in the summer of 1990.

Although much has been written about the role of Abu al-Abbas in the invasion and occupation of Kuwait, it remains nothing but market gossip. My husband was neither informed of the invasion nor did he endorse it. In fact, we heard the news together, when his bodyguard Abu Ali Kazem burst into our bedroom in the middle of the night, screaming hysterically, "Comrade wake up!" Abu al-Abbas grabbed his machine gun like a madman, as usual, certain that the Israelis were there to kill him. Guns and hand grenades were everywhere—even on corners of our bed. If I wanted to hold him before going to sleep, I often came across the cold metal of his pistol, or the rubber around his bombs. He put his finger to the trigger only to hear a dumbfounded Abu Ali blurting, "Saddam has invaded Kuwait!" We turned on the TV and learned the details like everyone else. Abu al-Abbas was tremendously upset by the news. "Only God knows what is in store for us," he said to me in private. "Abu Uday (Saddam) has dragged the entire Arab world into the unknown."

Abu al-Abbas's views on the occupation of Kuwait deserve elaboration, given that his supposed support for the invasion is one of the myths that has haunted him for years. In Baghdad, he later told Vice-President Taha Yassin Ramadan, "It seems that Mr. President has miscalculated." The face of the veteran Baathist turned crimson and he frowned at the audacity of such a remark. Saddam Hussein could not possibly go wrong.

"The liberation of Kuwait actually should have been the liberation of Palestine!" Abu al-Abbas continued. "We expected Abu Uday to concentrate on defeating the Israeli Army, not the Kuwaiti one! That would have been much wiser and it would have given him a grand standing in Arab history."

The Vice-President was taken aback, but Abu al-Abbas had more to say. When he continued, he referred to the "glorious" war that Saddam had fought against Iran from 1980 to 1988—with US support. This conflict is considered the longest conventional war in the last century and the most violent since World War II. "Please listen to me because I care for Iraq. See the victory you scored over Iran? It will vanish into thin air. It will evaporate if you stay in Kuwait. Everything that has been achieved in eight years of war will be wasted."

Since World War II, the Kuwaiti economy had relied heavily on foreign workers, many of whom were Palestinians. The Palestinians arrived in Kuwait, in large numbers, in three waves: 1948 after the *Nakba;* 1967 after the Six Day War; and 1975 after the onset of the Lebanese Civil War. One Palestinian who rose to fame from Kuwait was Arafat himself, who lived there and worked as an engineer in the 1950s. By 1990, it was estimated that 400,000 Palestinians were working in Kuwait, making up 30% of Kuwait's population of 2.2 million. Palestinians funneled money to their families inside the Occupied Territories and across the Arab world. The Emir of Kuwait maintained a warm friendship with Arafat and was always generous in supporting the PLO, both financially and politically.

Abu al-Abbas immediately saw the flaws in Saddam's invasion of Kuwait. He argued that it would have dramatic repercussions on the Palestinian Cause, and it would kill—forever after—any hope of receiving funds from the Kuwaitis. Abu al-Abbas advised Arafat against publicly siding with Saddam, but because Abu al-Abbas was a guest of the Iraqi government, he could not say the same to Iraqi officials. He did voice his displeasure with the occupation to his friend, Iraqi Deputy Prime Minister Tarek Aziz, knowing however, that this would be kept strictly between them and not reach the ears of Saddam Hussein. If Abu Uday found out, he would surely expel Abu al-Abbas and the PLF from Baghdad. If he got too angry, Saddam might even kill Abu al-Abbas and then blame it on the Israelis. Abu al-Abbas liked Aziz, whom he regarded as the most worldly of Saddam's men, and would often describe him saying: "He is a good man, yet his blind loyalty to Saddam gets in the way of his rational thinking."

Abu al-Abbas, however, did not have the luxury of saying, "No" to Saddam Hussein. By then, he had become a point of reference for journalists visiting Baghdad, and his opinions were widely circulated in the Arab press, making the Iraqis particularly sensitive to whatever he had to say.

Precisely as Abu al-Abbas predicted, two months after the January 1991 "liberation" of Kuwait by Saddam's forces, the Kuwaiti government expelled a total of 443,000 Palestinians, with orders never to return. Until this day, twenty-four years later, it has never forgiven the Palestinians for their support of the 1990 invasion. Neither, for that matter, has it forgiven Iraq although a decade has passed since the toppling of Saddam Hussein. Even today, the Iraqi government of Nuri al-Malki still feels Kuwaiti anger over 1990. For his part, Arafat never did apologize for supporting the 1990 invasion. Only in December 2004, shortly after Arafat's death, did his successor Mahmud Abbas offer regrets for the PLO's stance on the invasion.

1991: Surprise, Surprise!

Kuwait City. January 17, 1991. The US and coalition partners launch the Gulf War.

On a personal note, I brought Ali home to Baghdad with me after the initial invasion of Kuwait by Iraqi forces in August 1990. In the meantime, Reef and Louai continued at the French school in Beirut. The following January, just before the US military launched Operation Desert Storm in an effort to "liberate Kuwait," Abu al-Abbas sent Ali and me to Jordan for safe-keeping. The moment that the guns had fallen silent on the first of February, I began nagging my husband to allow me to return. All of my friends advised against it. "There is no electricity there," they pointed out, "no running water, and no basic commodities. People are dying. You cannot live in Baghdad for now. Just stay in Jordan." When I realized that my efforts to convince Abu al-Abbas were going to be useless, I turned to Arafat, who had briefly patched up his differences with King Hussein and was spending time in Jordan. I would visit his office daily and ask him to take me back to Baghdad. The first time I asked, Arafat exploded, "What's this! I tell you I cannot take you there. What will Abu al-Abbas say?" From my long experience with Arafat, however, I knew that I would finally get my way with him—and I did. He eventually agreed to ask Mashour al-Hadithi, the ex-Jordanian Army Commander, to take me with him to Baghdad. Hadithi had led the Jordanian Army in 1969, during the famous Karameh Battle. He had a soft spot for Palestinian nationalists, and agreed to take me along on a horrific road trip from Amman to Baghdad. When it came time to depart, I found that his son, also an officer in the Jordanian Army, was driving. Ali and I sat in the back seat.

The main road was completely empty, with not a single soul in sight. In the Iraqi wastelands, we would sporadically come across ragged Iraqi soldiers deserted in the wilderness, wearing what remained of their military uniforms. They had fled their positions and were caught between their fear of punishment by Saddam Hussein and their fear of being arrested by the US Army. They begged us for food "or a drop of water." Hadithi and I just shook our heads in disbelief. "Is this the Mother of All Battles that Saddam promised the world to behold?" Hadithi said. "Look at what has come of his troops?" At the border, we saw one van only driving ahead of us, a Jordanian relief agency sending aid to Baghdad. Hadithi turned to us in the back seat, caressed Ali's hair, then looked at me and asked, "My daughter, what takes you to Baghdad? Had it not been for Abu Ammar's insistence, I would never have accepted to bring you on this harsh journey. My son and I are officers, and this is part of our job. I am carrying a message to the Iraqis. But what forces you to undergo all this trouble to reach Baghdad?"

"My husband Mr. General," I replied. "I am going to see my husband. He is all alone."

"Are you not afraid?" he asked.

Referring to my earlier career with the Palestinian resistance, I proudly replied, "I am a commando myself. I am a *fedayee*."

Hadithi pointed to Ali. "Then what about this child?" He said. "Is he a *fedayee* as well? What crime has he committed to endure all of this pain?"

We reached Baghdad in the midst of a crippling electricity blackout. No streetlights, no cars, no telephones, and no pedestrians. It was a ghost town. We drove past Mansour Bridge to reach the Hanging Bridge of Baghdad only to find that it had been sliced in half by a US missile. I couldn't call Abu al-Abbas to come pick me up, as I wanted to surprise him, and also because phone service had largely been taken out. I was not sure if he was staying at the same location where I had left him, since we had not spoken to each other, due to the war, for an entire month. I asked Hadithi to take me to the house of Azzam Ahmed, one of the PLF's top officials, located on Abu Jaafar al-Mansour Street. When we reached Ahmed's house, we found that Abu al-Abbas had left the house due to the hot weather and was pacing back and forth on the sidewalk, chatting with friends. I will never forget the expression on his face when I got out of the car. I wonder how in the world I expected him to be happy at seeing me. He hurled all kinds of accusations against me, ranging from "careless and irresponsible" to "crazy and mad." But there was nothing he could do now that I was here. I stayed in Baghdad for two weeks and then realized that he was right—there was no water, no milk, and no diapers—I was forced to admit that I had been wrong in taking Ali on such a wild journey and to head back to Amman.

The invasion of Kuwait, and Iraq's defeat in the second Gulf War, had a drastic effect on my life, on that of Abu al-Abbas, and on Iraq. Kuwait turned off the tap for Palestinians and so did the other Gulf states. Iraq, crippled by defeat and the daunting sanctions that followed, could no longer provide support to Abu al-Abbas. Although Abu al-Abbas continued to reside in Iraqi territory, the Iraqis clearly were tired of playing host and longed to free themselves from what they thought of as a political burden.

The Children Return

After the fighting stopped, arterials were cleared of debris, and public services were restored, Ali and I returned from Jordan to our villa on Abu Nawas Street, and Reef came back from Beirut. For his part, Louai remained in Beirut. The following year, Abu al-Abbas's sons came from Canada to spend a year with us in Baghdad. Abu al-Abbas was surprised at how Americanized they had become, and so he enrolled them in school in Iraq in order to reawaken their experience with the language, customs, and traditions of the Arab world. This meant that four boys were now living with us—Reef, Khaled, Omar, and Ali.

1991: The Madrid Conference

Madrid, Spain. October 30, 1991. The Madrid Conference convenes.

By 1991 in Palestine, the First Intifada had fizzled out. Young men had grown tired of dying in a grossly imbalanced guerrilla war against the Israeli Army. By this time, Abu al-Abbas's belief in the ability of Palestinians to liberate their land by war alone was fading. Abu al-Abbas no longer had money, arms, or the political cover required to wage war. Peace rather than armed struggle was on everyone's mind. The Bush White House put its full weight behind the October 1991 peace conference in Madrid. They banned Arafat from the meeting because of his support for Saddam Hussein. With or without the consent of Arafat or of Abu al-Abbas, PLO representatives went to Madrid and took part in face-to-face talks with Israeli Prime Minister Yitzhak Shamir.

1992: Crossing Uday Hussein

Although most of the work of Abu al-Abbas was directed toward Palestine, occasionally he had an opportunity to assert his authority here in Baghdad. I am thinking specifically of an incident involving Saddam's son Uday Hussein. About this time, a middle-aged Palestinian woman came knocking on our door, seeking Abu al-Abbas's help. She was wearing the Islamic headscarf *(hijab)* and looked modest but respectable. "They told me to come to you," she said shyly, adding, "They said that you help Palestinians in need. My husband is Egyptian and he is in jail. I have no one to turn to but God and Abu al-Abbas."

The woman had four daughters with her, and all of them were ushered into the living room, where I served them coffee. What captured my attention were the large Cleopatra-like blue eyes of her eldest daughter, who was of university age. Her father had been jailed for "economic reasons" (in Iraq that could mean anything from money smuggling, to profiteering at the state's expense, to illegal arm, to drug deals). Somebody had advised her to seek Uday Hussein's help, saying that only Uday could get her husband released from jail. The mother committed the grand mistake of visiting Uday with her daughters. The next day, Uday sent an envoy to their house, inviting the eldest daughter to one of his "parties"—which were something closer to wild orgies, as the world only knows too well.

The mother curtly refused, saying, "My daughter doesn't go out alone at night, neither for Uday Hussein nor for anybody else." The next day, the envoy came insisting, and once again, he was turned down. On the third day he came carrying an open threat: "Either she comes to the party, or all of you will suffer a miserable fate!" Panicking, she left the house in the middle of the night, taking nothing but her daughters with her and walked from one place to another, seeking protection from Uday. She was finally directed toward our home by a mutual friend who said, "Abu al-Abbas will help you. He is the Palestinian 'ambassador' in Baghdad and has the ear of Iraqi officials."

Abu al-Abbas listened to her entire story. He then looked at me and winked, which meant, "Let's talk on the balcony." Our house was, of course, bugged from top to bottom by Iraqi intelligence. We felt as though we were living inside a microphone. When we were alone on the balcony, I said to him, "What are you going to do?" He smiled and lit a cigarette. "I am going to do the expected," he said. "I am going to help her get out of Iraq." I asked how he could escape Uday's wrath. Abu al-Abbas replied, "Saddam trusts me, and Uday fears his father. He would never go further on this matter, knowing that I can take the matter directly to the President. Saddam would never approve of it." Forty-eight hours later, the woman and her children were smuggled out of Iraq, on fake passports provided to them by Abu al-Abbas.

1993: Plastic Explosive in Kuwait City

Kuwait City. April 1993. Saddam tries to kill a president. Or does he?

In April 1993, George H.W. Bush visited Kuwait two years after launching the military effort to remove Saddam from Kuwait. He appears to have narrowly escaped with his life. Kuwaiti intelligence apprehended seventeen suspects, a Toyota Landcruiser packed with eighty kilograms of plastic explosive and a detonator, and ten smaller cube bombs (plastic explosive molded around a detonator). The suspects fingered Iraqi intelligence. The journalist Seymour Hersh and Ambassador Joe Wilson later expressed their skepticism.[1]

In June 1993, the US responded to the attempted killing by launching a cruise missile attack on a building in Baghdad occupied by Iraqi intelligence with cruise missiles. The US also dramatically tightened Iraqi oil sanctions by preventing Iraq from selling its oil on the international markets. The new sanctions regime caused immense hardships in Iraq. It destroyed the Iraqi economy and eroded state infrastructure. Unable to purify their drinking water, the elderly and the very young suffered. UN organizations estimated between 500,000 and 1.2 million Iraqis, most under the age of five, died due to the sanctions.

1993: The Oslo Accords

The Madrid Peace Conference led to the Washington talks between the Palestinians and Israel, and they in turn led to the secret Oslo Accords. Conducted without intermediaries, they led to an agreement signed on the White House lawn in September 1993. Before finalizing the deal, Arafat landed in Baghdad to brief both Saddam Hussein and Abu al-Abbas. He was clearly excited, seeing the seeds of Palestinian nationhood in-the-making. The same could not be said of Abu al-Abbas, who never for once took Oslo seriously. He told Arafat that he would never support such an agreement, nor would he ever stand in its way—out of respect for Abu Ammar's historic legacy and leadership. When we watched the live coverage of Oslo on TV, Abu al-Abbas began pounding his head, almost in a hysteric trance, and suffered blood pressure problems that forced us to call in the doctors. Nothing could have been more disturbing for someone of his stature than to see Yasser Arafat extending his hand to shake that of Yitzhak Rabin. What made things worse was that Rabin famously held back and only extended his arm after being "nudged" by President Bill Clinton.

As part of the Oslo Accords, Israel agreed to recognize Arafat as its peace partner and to recognize Palestinian autonomy in the West Bank and Gaza. Oslo sketched out a peace process with a two-phase timetable. During a five year interim period, Oslo envisioned a series of step-by-step measures to build trust and partnership. Palestinians would police the territories they controlled—by name—and cooperate with Israel in the "fight against terrorism."

The Palestinian Preventive Security Branch was established for this purpose, and amendments were made to the section of the PLO Charter that called for Israel's destruction.

The agreement did not lead to the halt of Israeli settlements nor did it make explicit reference to ending or even limiting them. On the contrary, settlements more than doubled after Oslo. During the seven years of the Oslo process (1993-2000), Israel's settler population increased by an unprecedented 111,000 settlers (42%), more than either of the seven year periods immediately before or after Oslo. Rather than make life easier for the Palestinians, the agreement with its roadblocks, checkpoints, and military personnel made travel back and forth between Israel and Palestine very difficult. To give an example: pre-Oslo, a student from Gaza wanting to attend class at Birzeit University, near Ramallah, could reach campus in an hour and a half. Afterward, he or she had to go to the Rafah Border Crossing, enter Egypt, fly out of Cairo Airport to Amman, and then drive through the Jordanian border into Palestine. This could take a day or more.

Oslo left Palestine fragmented, nevertheless, the PLO's emblem remained a map of the whole of pre-1948 Palestine. The emblem of Fatah was still a similar map covered by crossed rifles and a grenade. Because it failed to resolve the final status of Jerusalem and failed to end settlements the Oslo Agreement was a non-solution as far as we Palestinians were concerned.

An Evening with the Arafats

Shortly after the Oslo agreement was reached and before Arafat actually returned to Palestine from Tunisia, Abu al-Abbas and I were invited for family dinner at Arafat's house in Tunis. It was a cozy private affair, just two couples: my husband and I, and Arafat and his wife Suha. The future First Lady of Palestine prepared dinner and I helped. In the other room, the two guerrilla leaders talked politics. After supper, Arafat took out maps, spread them across the dinner table, and began explaining to us while pointing all over the documents, "*This* is going to become ours once again!" he said. "*That* is going to be given to us by the Israelis. See that point over there? It too will be with the Palestinians. All of this section will be ours." Arafat was very excited, and he believed every single word he was saying. I have never seen him so worked up in my entire life. Abu al-Abbas just nodded his head and said nothing. In his eyes, I saw disbelief.

When driving home later that evening, Abu al-Abbas said to me, "Either he is lying, or they [the Americans and Israelis] are lying to him." He quickly added, "Can it be true Reem? Can it be true that they are going to be giving us all of that? I don't trust them. I never did." The PNA, he believed, and all the trappings of nationhood that the PNA possessed—the flag, the national police, and the government in truncated Palestine—were nothing but an optical illusion.

Finding Jobs

After Oslo, Abu al-Abbas did not have military work to do. He once had been a fearless warrior. Now he was a silent partner in the project of Oslo—which he felt was doomed. Without a lot to do, Abu al-Abbas dragged through life rather aimlessly during these difficult years after 1993. Confident that Oslo was too good to be true, he never lost faith that he would one day see a political and military comeback. Abu al-Abbas would still go to his office on a regular basis, meet with comrades, read the newspapers, and lament the miserable state both of Iraq and the Palestinians.

Abu al-Abbas was the Shepherd. He was responsible for the 200 PLF staff in Baghdad and for smaller numbers in Lebanon, Tunisia. After Oslo, some returned to Palestine itself. As the new sanctions began to bite, times were tough for Abu al-Abbas and his PLF staff. Without funding from the PLO, we were high and dry. Iraq was crippled by sanctions, thanks to Saddam's decision to invade Kuwait, so Saddam had no money to spare.

The Iraqis gave members of the PLF permission to start their own businesses, and Abu al-Abbas helped to organize small businesses in Bagdad and other Iraqi cities. But he didn't have a businessman character or mind and consumer demand in these years was close to non-existent, due to the sanctions. Some of these businesses showed brief flickers of life, but in the end all of them failed.

Iraqi intelligence also tried to help by giving Abu al-Abbas a plot of land to cultivate. Abu al-Abbas spent more and more time at his "plantation." He grew vegetables for our dinner table and gave vegetables to his comrades in the PLF. The garden gradually became an obsession . . . but it was not a lonely calling. For Abu al-Abbas was joined in his agrarian efforts by Rocky, our golden retriever, who was a constant companion. Rocky went with his master on long walks along the river on Abu Nawas Street. Rocky sat guard beside the desk of his master when he was at work in the office. And Rocky patrolled the boundaries of the plantation when Abu al-Abbas was putting his hands into the soil.

Rocky's name recalled the most famous prize-fighter ever invented by Hollywood. A simple man from a working-class background, Rocky-the-prize-fighter succeeded by force of will and relentless desire. After his initial triumph years passed, he was forgotten and counted out—but then he surprised everyone by returning to triumph in one sequel after another. Our dog—by his very name—suggested that the bangs and bruises suffered in his career by Abu al-Abbas did not spell his defeat. The fighter was still alive within, looking for ways to make a difference.

1996: Arafat Calls a Meeting

Gaza. April 1996. Arafat convenes the PNC in Gaza.

What brought Abu al-Abbas back to life was Arafat's decision to convene the first session of the Palestinian National Council (PNC; also referred to as the "Congress" or "Parliament") following the signing of the second Oslo Accord in 1993. The Congress was made up of four hundred delegates who had composed the PLO during the long years of resistance in Lebanon, Jordan, and Tunisia. Some, like Farouk al-Qaddumi, refused to attend, claiming that this would legitimize Oslo, which he regarded as a grand concession to the Israelis. Many prominent names in the PLO were long gone. Some had been killed by the Israelis or their allies: Abu Jihad (Khalil al-Wazir); Abu Iyad (my father's friend); Kamal Udwan; and Abu Hasan Salameh (involved in the Munich Olympics operation). Others, like my husband Abu al-Abbas and Mohammad Salah Odeh (Abu Daoud) could not join the PNC because they were vetoed by Israel.

Abu Daoud was a prime architect of the 1972 operation at the Munich Olympics, in addition to being a member of the much feared Black September Organization which had arisen after the conflict in Jordan in 1970. Both he and my husband ranked high on the Israeli Army's Most Wanted List. Abu Ammar (Arafat) objected, however, telling the Americans: "If you want me to reign inside Palestine—if you really want me to reign, I need to have these two, Abu Abbas and Abu Daoud, on my side. If Abu al-Abbas decides to bring us down, Oslo will not pass. I absolutely *need* him in the PNC." As a result, under US pressure the Israelis lifted their veto. Now, for the first time in his life, Abu Abbas had permission to return home to Palestine. He would not return as a young revolutionary or a military commander, but rather, as a politician—an MP in the Palestinian parliament. It was a major career shift for Abu al-Abbas—and a difficult one.

1996: Abu al-Abbas Travels to Gaza

In preparing to travel to Gaza for the PNC Congress, Abu al-Abbas was nervous. He smoked heavily. He was excited and also tense. Abu al-Abbas had been born in a refugee camp in Syria after his family's expulsion from Palestine in 1948. Nevertheless, he was attached to the land in his lost home and he was afraid. Traveling to Palestine meant giving up the Palestine that existed in his dreams for the reality. He was afraid. What would he find in the land that he loved dearly? The Palestine that Abu al-Abbas returned to in 1996 was not even close to the one his parents had left behind in 1948. It seemed small. Its physical reality gave it solidity, but it lacked the expansiveness of the Palestine that had occupied his dreams for the previous fifty years. Over this time, Abu al-Abbas had paid local Palestinians to take photographs of his hometown in Tiret Haifa on Mount Carmel and send them to him. Often they charged him ludicrously high amounts. Still, he always was happy to pay. Abu al-Abbas would spent long hours neatly placing the photos side-by-side, fitting them together like the pieces of a puzzle, trying to create a panoramic view of the landscape. He would memorize every single tree, balcony, street corner. This was a psychological exercise—no doubt—to convince himself that it was "almost" as if he was still in Palestine. Indeed, Abu al-Abbas dreamt of a heroic comeback. This post-Oslo return, however, was not what he had imagined. Now, he was chained to the wills and whims of the Israelis. The comeback he had longed for was something completely different. He dreamt of marching into a liberated Palestine like a knight in armor. He wanted to see cheering women and children on both sides of the road. The picture in his mind was taken from accounts of Saladin, the great general of the Arab armies in the middle ages, who had marched into Jerusalem after defeating the Crusaders.

Unlike Saladin, Abu al-Abbas had to pass checkpoints manned by IDF troops where the Israeli Flag fluttered in the breeze. He had to get Israeli stamps on his documents before crossing into his own land. Add to this the larger point that Abu al-Abbas was not allowed to return to his native village near Haifa, nor was he returning to historic Jerusalem, Haifa, or Acre. Instead, his comeback was limited to the Gaza Strip where he was allowed to stay while the Congress was in session, since he was traveling on something similar to a tourist visa with geographic restrictions. These constraints were painful, to say the least. But Abu al-Abbas put them aside and savored the point that now, for the first time, he was able to set foot on historic Palestine.

Gaza City. May 10, 1996. CNN interviews Abu al-Abbas.

CNN Correspondent Rob Reynolds reported that, for Abu al-Abbas, ". . . times have changed, and now, he offers advice on reaching a lasting peace in the Middle East . . . . He spends his days rushing from meeting to meeting, lunching with officials of the new Palestinian National Authority, networking, listening and making suggestions . . . . He now says the time for armed struggle has ended, but not the struggle itself. 'The purpose of armed struggle is not simply to kill . . . its purpose is to reach a political goal,' Abu al-Abbas said."[2]

14
A Final Journey to Palestine

Palestine. June 2000.

ABU AL-ABBAS AND I MADE A TRIP to Palestine at the end of June. Camp David talks were to begin on July 11. Little did we know that the talks would fail on July 25 and that the Israelis would pull the visa that enabled Abu al-Abbas to travel in Palestine. This road trip would be the last time Abu al-Abbas saw the land that he so cherished. It would be his final good-bye. Our trip through Palestine would also be our last travel together. This time we traveled beyond Gaza into the historical cities of Palestine: Jerusalem, Haifa, Ramallah, Nablus, and Mount Carmel—where Abu al-Abbas's native village, Tiret Haifa, is located. Ours was a journey of self-discovery, pain, and farewell.

2000: Twenty-four Hours on the Road

We visited all of these places in a twenty-four-hour-long road trip with friends. Our son Ali was fourteen now and rode with us, getting a firsthand lesson in the history, geography, and politics of Palestine. Back then, there were no roadblocks separating Palestinian and Israeli cities and no concrete Separation Barrier. We would drive through checkpoints without being required to stop. We glanced at the Israeli Flags fluttering beside the highway and we saw the young Israeli Army soldiers standing at a distance, carrying automatic weapons. They would stare at us, and we would stare back. Certainly, we were disgusted at their presence yet we knew that we were incapable of doing anything about it. They were young men in their late teens, in the prime of life, and reminded me of our boys about the same age who were stationed at PNA (Palestinian National Authority) buildings in Gaza and Ramallah.

Abu al-Abbas was in a meditative mood on this trip. He lapsed into long silences where, judging from the glimmer in his eyes, a million thoughts were going through his mind. What was he thinking about? His life, his cause, his legacy, his future. In these years after Madrid and Oslo, we were living out a new chapter in Palestinian history—and Abu al-Abbas did not like it. He never believed that "Palestinian sovereignty and autonomy" were on the minds of Israeli decision-makers in Tel Aviv. As it turned out, thanks to Ariel

Sharon, the Oslo Accords fell apart just six years after Arafat returned from Tunis to Gaza—and only a couple of months after our twenty-four hour road trip through Palestine.

One of the thoughts that went through my mind during our road trip was that, as Palestinian families in exile, we failed to consider the people who actually lived in Gaza today. Instead of making a humble entry into the city, one that fit the simplicity of its inhabitants, we came in as though we were liberators, honking our horns and waving from the windows. In reality, however, we never really "liberated" Gaza. Palestinian officials who flocked from Tunisia, Jordan, Iraq, Lebanon, and Syria arrived with plenty of money and purchased comfortable villas for their families—which stood empty much of the time. PLO officials would visit Gaza to attend periodic meetings of the Palestinian Council or to spend summers on the beach. Few PLO members became permanent residents. Gaza City was overcrowded. The infrastructure was crumbling. Public health was poor—periodically some form of contagion would break out.

The PLO brass contributed little or nothing to the Gaza City's infrastructure or to improve life here in any way. They led from above, rather than below. They hired Gazan youth as drivers, bodyguards, and errand boys instead of putting them in proper schools and universities. PLO officials acted like lords, and expected the young men of Gaza to obey their every command. They seemed to think that this was their due reward for the careers they had spent in the Diaspora "liberating" Palestine. To my eye, it was the Palestinians who endured in Gaza—who never left their homeland and put up with the daily misery of occupation—who were the real champions of the Cause.

The highlight of our road trip, of course, was Mount Carmel. A coastal mountain range in northern Palestine (now part of Israel). Archaeologists have discovered ancient wine and oil presses at various locations in the mountain, and Israelis have transformed it into a tourist destination because it is so convenient to Haifa, located on Mount Carmel's northern slope. The Carmel range is approximately 6.5 to 8 km wide, sloping gradually toward the southwest and forming a steep ridge on the northeastern face. Abu al-Abbas's native Tiret Haifa, or al-Tira for short, is located 7 km south of Haifa. Modern reference books refer to it in the past tense, "al-Tira *was* a Palestinian town." For Abu al-Abbas and me, it was, still is, and will forever remain, a "Palestinian town." It is made up of five *"khirbets"* (Arabic for "ruin" or "ruin on a hill") including "Khirbet al-Dayr" where the ruins of St. Brocardus Monastery are located. Tiret Haifa was attacked by the Haganah on April 21, 1948 because it was providing logistic and military support to Palestinian fighters in Haifa. On April 25, the city was shelled by the Israelis, forcing its original civilian population to flee. It was occupied by Israelis in July 1948. By February 1949, the town's original population had been savagely expelled and replaced with two thousand Jewish settlers who were flown in from Europe.

What struck us when driving through was a small shack in a tiny street next to where his family home had been, just past an intersection of two large trees, which Abu al-Abbas knew from the photos he had gathered over the years, of Al-Tira. The aging trees were much older, clearly, than the state of Israel itself. An orthodox Israeli Jew was now living there, amidst rubbish and flies, catering to a few ill-fed and dirty hens. Clad in black with long hair locks, he looked like a typical Jewish fundamentalist—or at least, the kind of stereotype we had of them for many years. The years had been harsh on him, carving deep wrinkles around every corner of his face and neck. We drove up to ask for directions. Abu al-Abbas, of course, spoke with an Iraqi dialect. The elderly Jews eyes lit up as he asked, "You Sir . . . You are from Iraq?" Abu al-Abbas nodded, surprised that an Israeli would recognize the tough Iraqi accent. "I am originally from Mosul," the Jewish man said proudly, patting his own chest to add emphasis to his claim. The famous close knit Jewish community of Mosul had been composed mainly of laborers and shopkeepers with a few exceptional merchants. All four thousand of them had immigrated to Israel in 1951. This man was very nostalgic about Mosul, having spent his childhood and early youth in Iraq. Clearly he had nothing but fond memories of Iraq. It meant more to him than the rubbish dump he had ended up with inside Israel. He began asking specific details about Mosul, speaking with an Iraqi accent of course, and Abu al-Abbas responded with specific questions about al-Tira. The two men from different backgrounds discovered a bond. Each reminded the other of a bygone era. Here was one Palestinian, fed up with life in Iraq and longing to return to Palestine, versus an Israeli Jew, fed up with life in Palestine and longing to return to Iraq. Each one had paid the price for circumstances of life imposed upon them.

Palestine. September 28, 2000. The Second Intifada begins.

Shortly after our return to Baghdad, in late September 2000, the Second Intifada broke out in Jerusalem. It was triggered by the provocative visit of Ariel Sharon to the al-Aqsa Mosque although Israelis would later say that Arafat used this as a pretext to launch a protest that he felt would once again catch the attention of the world and bring gains for Palestinians.

Months later, Sharon translated his al-Aqsa foray into election as Prime Minister of Israel.

The Second Intifada was a repeat of 1987. Abu al-Abbas had no control over what was happening inside the Occupied Territories, as young Hamas militants dominated the streets of Palestine. Nor did Arafat have control. In any case, shortly after the protests began Arafat was besieged by Sharon—confined to his compound in the West Bank city of Ramallah. The Second Intifada, it must be mentioned, failed to move the minds and hearts of the international community, as the first one had done. Why? The Second Intifada was dominated by Islamists carrying guns, whereas the First Intifada was led by young, unarmed youth, confronting tanks with nothing but stones and bare chests.

15
The Iraq War

2001: The Middle East Conflict Comes to America

New York and Washington, DC. September 11, 2001. The 9/11 attacks.

ONE YEAR AFTER THE ONSET of the Second Intifada, the horrific 9/11 attacks brought down the World Trade Center in New York City and crashed airliners full of passengers in Washington and Pennsylvania. More than 3,000 innocents died. These attacks were shamefully carried out by Osama Bin Laden, an Arab Muslim representing neither Arabs nor Muslims. Bin Laden hijacked both identities and committed crimes in their name.

The advent of political Islam in the Middle East was a new layer of East-West conflict in the region—and now within the US itself. Nevertheless, the challenge of political Islam had roots in a core problem that had festered for fifty-three years: the failure to achieve a fair-minded solution to the *Nabka* of 1948.

Oil & Water

After 9/11, the entire world held its breath while those of us who lived in the Middle East waited for the US response. The perpetrators of 9/11 were Osama's guys who mixed with Saddam like oil and water. According to the theory that "the enemy of my enemy is my friend," Saddam should have been back in bed with the Americans—and we should have been safe in Baghdad. But the Americans did not know their history. Or they chose to ignore it.

Saddam was a Baathist—not an Islamist. And Islam as a political ideology was probably the greatest current day threat to his power. That is, if you could discount the possibility that past enemies might reassert themselves. In this category, count his arch-enemy Iran, and the Shiite majority whose southern tribes Saddam had savagely suppressed after Iraqi troops withdrew from Kuwait in 1991. Then there were the Kurds in the north that Saddam had gassed—and whose 1991 revolt he had crushed.

The Baath Party was secular and political, not Islamist. It was created by the two Damascus schoolteachers Michel Aflaq and Salah al-Din al-Bitar whose example had suggested to the teenage Abu al-Abbas in Damascus that politics was a possible career. Aflaq was a Greek Orthodox Christian and Bitar was a Sunni Muslim. Both men were middle class sons of Damascus grain merchants, both were educated in France, and both had a philosophical bent. The Baath ideal that they developed was one of socialism and unity among people of all backgrounds in Arab lands. Where did Islam fit in? Islam was celebrated as a common culture for people of all ethnic and religious backgrounds who lived in the region. The point of Baath ideology was Arab Nationalism—which means a secular focus: land reform, elevating women into professional and political positions, and helping minorities and the poor participate in the national economy.

When Saddam was running Iraq as the number two man to his cousin Ahmed Hassan al-Bakr, he spent ten years beginning in 1968 implementing measures that showed what Baath socialism could look like in practice. He nationalized Iraq's oil industry and used oil wealth to give every conceivable stakeholder a slice of the pie. He nudged two dominant political constituencies: First, the old Iraqi aristocracy once affiliated with the monarchy; Second, the mosque. Beside these two groups, he created space for a secular base of non-elite families lifted into economic well-being—something that approached a middle class. In a dramatic move to modernize the country, he provided free education through college, subsidized agriculture, distributed land to small farmers, rebuilt the country's infrastructure, and gave women entry to professional and government careers. Syria and Algeria had tried to do some of these things, but they lacked Iraq's oil wealth. Saddam accomplished what no other Arab nation had been able to do. He deserves credit for spreading his country's wealth. Still, Saddam pursued progressive policies as an antidote to Iraq's tendency to fragment along sectarian and tribal lines. He was, in effect, consolidating a political base on which he could found his rule.

Saddam celebrated Aflaq as the founder of Baathism. Yet Saddam seemed to feel that he was vulnerable to attacks from Islamists based on the idea that Baath ideology had a Christian origin. This may be why, when Aflaq died in Paris in 1989, Saddam announced that Aflaq had converted to Islam on his deathbed—which was news to family members who had actually been *at* his deathbed. Saddam gave Aflaq a Muslim burial in a massive tomb in the Green Zone that is built in same style as a mosque.

Life on Abu Nuwas Street

As the years passed, our life in the villa near Abu Nawas Street continued. Our children went back and forth to school and then to jobs. In time, even the most loved children do grow up and start their own lives. Omar and Khaled went back to Canada, while Reef attended the Anglo-American University in Prague. Meanwhile, upon graduation back in Lebanon, Louai enrolled at my alma mater, the Lebanese American University (LAU) to study Business Administration. Eventually Ali studied at Concordia University in Canada. Louai finished university in 1997, Reef in 1998, and Ali in 2009.

As for work, Reef became an entrepreneur with start-up projects in Prague. Louai went into banking like his uncle and grandfather. As we are writing this book, Ali is still studying and has developed a rap music routine on the subject of Abu al-Abbas.

With the passing of time, Abu al-Abbas and his good looks suffered from too much food, too little exercise, too many Marlboros, too much drinking—and a life of stress. Still, his charm only increased. He loved his children, all of them, and doted upon them. Abu al-Abbas managed to attend the graduation of Reef and Khaled from high school in Baghdad but he couldn't attend Louai's (as he was unable to return to Lebanon). Similar problems prevented him from attending their university graduations.

In Baghdad, we had a mix of cars. Some were PLF property, others were given to us by the Iraqis. Abu al-Abbas loved 4-wheel-drive cars and his favorite was a silver Range Rover. As for me, I had a white 1994 Toyota.

By 2001, Saddam had upgraded our technology. Now, Abu al-Abbas had the use of two Thuraya phones (satellite phones) and full Internet access—both were reserved for Saddam's top guys. Totalitarian Arab regimes, it must be noted, were very late to allow the Internet. In Syria at this time the Internet was banned on the grounds that it "threatened national security." Anyone in Syria caught evading government restrictions and browsing the Internet via a Lebanese connection had his dial-up line disconnected and was fined heavily. A second offense could bring jail time.

Information was dangerous to security states such as Syria and Iraq. Under Saddam, the people of Iraq were supposed to know nothing more than what "Abu Uday" wanted them to know. In Iraq, the Internet only became available to ordinary Iraqis after Saddam's downfall in 2003.

While most Iraqi officials used the Internet for email and online discussion, Abu al-Abbas was enchanted with it as a tool of knowledge. In the pre-Google era, Hotbot, AltaVista and Yahoo!—first generation search engines—became part of a morning schedule that took Abu al-Abbas into the pages of the Israeli and US press where he would spend hours browsing *Maariv*, *Haaretz*, and the *New York Times*.

"Why don't you learn to use the computer?" Abu al-Abbas would urge me, "Try it. It's not as difficult as you imagine!" I was computer illiterate in those days. During the weeks that preceded the US invasion of Afghanistan, Abu al-Abbas spent more time than usual online. He liked to read reports and studies posted on the websites of US and Israeli think-tanks. He focused on the neocons surrounding Bush, Paul Wolfowitz chief among them. Abu al-Abbas, almost prophetically, predicted the military actions of the George W. Bush administration and how this would change the Middle East.

2001: The US Invades Afghanistan

Afghanistan. October 7, 2001. The US launches air strikes.

The US struck Kabul, Kandahar, and Jalalabad in the autumn of 2001. We waited over the next fourteen months as the Bush administration pushed for a second step in its war on terror: the invasion of Iraq.

In September 2002, George W. Bush argued before the UN Security Council that Saddam Hussein had links to al-Qaeda and was developing weapons of mass destruction. Then the UN Security Council passed Resolution 1441 which authorized resumption of weapons inspections and threatened "serious consequences" for non-compliance. France and Russia, two Security Council members, said that they did not consider the term "consequences" to include the use of force against the Iraqi government. John Negroponte, US Ambassador to the UN, said that the resolution contained "no hidden trigger" for an invasion. In retrospect, he was lying—to put it mildly.

In February 2003, the International Atomic Energy Agency (IAEA) said that it found "no evidence" of the revival of a nuclear weapons program in Iraq. When addressing the UN General Assembly that month, US Secretary of State Colin Powell tried to win UN support for an invasion, presenting images of what he said was a "mobile biological weapons laboratory." In mid-February 2003 as the US was sending materiel to staging depots in Kuwait, anti-war protests broke out in more than 800 cities across the world, attracting anywhere between six and ten million people. According to the Guinness Book of World Records, they were the "largest protests in human history." George W. Bush completely ignored them and (along with the UK, Spain, Australia, Poland, Denmark, and Italy) increased the pace of his country's mobilization.

On March 17, Bush gave Saddam and his two sons Uday and Qusay, a forty-eight hour deadline to surrender and leave Iraq. More stubborn and outrageous than the US President, of course, was his Iraqi counterpart, who refused to budge. UAE President Sheikh Zayed Bin Sultan offered Saddam asylum in Abu Dhabi, but Saddam did not have the wisdom—or guts—to accept. The world remembers his outrageous statements including a challenge to Bush: "Let us see who falls first!" Why would the US empower Iran by attacking Iraq? Didn't the Americans fear Saddam's supposed WMDs? Saddam did not believe that the Americans would make good on their threats. I recall speaking to a Kurdish friend who worked for Iraqi Intelligence about the state of mind of Saddam, weeks before the invasion. I asked him, "Our Uncle (as we referred to Saddam)—how is he?" He shook his head in dismay. "Our uncle is spending his time in al-Awja (his native village in Tikrit), having propped up a tent (in traditional Arabic genre). He brings in old women to tell him folk stories and Iraqi myths. He then rolls over laughing."

My Kurdish friend was saying, "Saddam Hussein is absolutely clueless. He has no idea of what is happening around him!" Saddam was arguably the only person in Iraq who thought that an invasion was not in sight. The skies were dark with the threat of war. Every single one of us in Baghdad could see this much. So could everyone else in the region. A decade earlier when the US invaded Kuwait in 1991, there had been a UN resolution to authorize the military action. Now, in 2003, the UN was shunted aside. This war consisted of two madmen—Bush and Saddam—gambling with the fate of the region and the lives of millions.

2003: The Iraq War

Shortly before the war started, in February 2003, I went to Beirut to enroll my seventeen-year-old son Ali in school and visit my father, whose health was deteriorating. My eldest Louai was now working between Baghdad and Beirut, while Reef was doing business in the Czech Republic. When the war started, as Abu al-Abbas understood, Baghdad would not be safe. In previous wars he had insisted that I remain by his side, and we lived through them together. This time, however, he gave me a bundle of papers, "Take them with you Reem. You never know what will happen." I went through them: birth certificates of our children, real estate papers, bank statements, diplomas, passports, and documents related to our twenty years of marriage. Their sight brought shivers down my spine. "Why Mohammad, are you giving me all of this? Is this our last time together?"

Abu al-Abbas cracked a smile. "No my dear," he reassured me. "We'll be together soon. It's safer, however, to take them with you to Lebanon."

With tears running down my cheeks, I got into a car that would take me to Damascus where I could catch a taxi to Beirut. I had seen my husband for the last time.

The road to Damascus was hauntingly dark, with no street lights, no headlights. Taxi drivers and truck drivers alike relied on moonlight and the light of the stars to navigate the narrow highway linking the capitals of the two greatest Muslim Empires in history. Usually I would take sleeping pills before traveling to kill the seven or eight hour car drive. This time, however, I refrained. I did not want to sleep. I sat upright, my heart churning, as I watched the dirt slopes and sand dunes pass before me, one after another. Iraq had been my home for a little more than seventeen years. I was leaving it behind.

Escape, Or Not

Abu al-Abbas sent his family to safety in the face of the US invasion that he predicted, but he did not do the most basic things to ensure his own escape. For one thing, he could have gotten in touch with old friends in positions of power in Syria such as Ghazi Kanaan who might have been in a position to gain him sanctuary. At least he could have verified their current phone numbers. He might have gotten in touch with contacts in Beirut who were close to Hezbollah and could conceivably have asked the Iranians to grant him asylum.

I suppose that Abu al-Abbas did not want to give Saddam's intelligence service the slightest hint that he was thinking of jumping ship. Perhaps Abu al-Abbas felt that a US invasion would develop over a couple of months' time, which would give him space to maneuver when Saddam and his intelligence services were preoccupied with their own survival. Saying this another way, perhaps Abu al-Abbas was surprised by how quickly Saddam's forces melted before the advancing US troops.

Another reason for the hesitation of Abu al-Abbas is that, from a legal standpoint, he had no reason to run. Thanks to the Oslo Accords, he was granted immunity for any military actions prior to 1993. He had been in military retirement since then, and the US did not have a warrant for his arrest. The need to keep up the appearance of loyalty unto death toward Saddam and the lack of a legal basis for his arrest may have been just enough, in the mind of Abu al-Abbas, to prevent him from preparing a way for his own escape.

I think that there is also a deeper reason for the unwillingness of Abu al-Abbas to plan his escape. This was his belief in the utter rightness of his life devoted to Palestine. Abu al-Abbas was utterly convinced that he had led an honorable life. He expected the world to acknowledge this point. He did not want to run like a hunted man because he was not a criminal, he was a man of principle. Of course, pride also entered in. Abu al-Abbas preferred to give out favors rather than to ask for them. He did not feel like begging the Syrians or the Iranians—for anything. They, in particular, should recognize his stature as a Palestinian resister. To his mind, a mere mention of his name at the Syrian or Iranian border should be enough for him to gain access. When Abu al-Abbas was a young schoolteacher in Damascus, he showed up late the first day of work—intentionally. He carried a sheaf of political writings on Palestine as his sole excuse. Even as a twenty-year-old he demanded respect as an advocate for justice in Palestine. On this point, little had changed in the attitude of Abu al-Abbas during the interceding three decades.

The real question: Had the world changed around Abu al-Abbas? Was the son of Hafez al-Assad, for example, as ready to support Palestinian resistance as his father had been?

A Trip to Nowhere

Cairo. February, 2003. A phone call from Egypt.

The Egyptian government invited Abu al-Abbas to Cairo where they asked him to mediate a feud in the Palestinian Territories between Fatah and the Islamic group Hamas. "This is the wrong battle with the wrong opponent," he would often say. "Instead of squabbling with each other, the two Palestinian factions should be taking issue with the Israelis."

Abu al-Abbas wanted to put out fires in the Palestinian Territories. He realized that the dream of a decisive military victory against Israel was long gone. What *was* attainable was to bring peace and stability to the Palestinian Territories. Mediation among Palestinian groups was a role for which he was uniquely qualified. It was the type of second act that Abu al-Abbas had been waiting for.

At this point, Arafat was in a difficult situation—the IDF had him under siege in his compound in Ramallah. "All sides trust and respect you Abu Al-Abbas," said Egyptian Intelligence Commander Omar Suleiman. "This is your job, to help bring internal peace in Palestine."

Abu al-Abbas enjoyed hearing these words. For this was the first real cooperation—if the word applies—between Abu al-Abbas and the Mubarak regime since the *Achille Lauro* episode of 1985. Indeed, Abu al-Abbas could have been a uniting force in this situation, since he had excellent relations at the time with both sides of the dispute: Mohammad Dahlan, commander of Preventive Security in Gaza, and Sheikh Ahmed Yassin, the aging spiritual founder of Hamas. Yet Abu al-Abbas still had little trust in Husni Mubarak. "Stay in Cairo," the Egyptian authorities said to him, "and delegations from Palestine will travel back and forth to meet you under auspices of the Egyptian government." Abu al-Abbas toyed with the idea, but the Bush Administration swiftly vetoed his participation, asking Mubarak to drop the idea altogether. As a result, Abu al-Abbas returned to Baghdad. Had he stayed in Cairo, his life might have been saved. Just weeks later, the US invaded Iraq.

Baghdad. April 9, 2003. US forces take control of the Iraqi capital.

Twenty-four days after the US invasion of Iraq, the mighty army of Saddam Hussein collapsed and American forces entered Baghdad. Saddam's troops threw down their guns, abandoned their posts and replaced their military uniforms with civilian clothes to avoid being recognized by the Americans. The Iraqi President and his family fled the capital. Saddam went into hiding in the Anbar province, while his wife and children headed to Syria. In Damascus, Saddam's sons Uday and Qusay were stripped of their money and sent back to Iraq where they were killed in July 2003.

For his part, Abu al-Abbas was trapped in Baghdad with his top aide Bilal Qasim and bodyguard Mohammad Zaidan. Preparing for the worst, his PLF men had rented three apartments in different locations in the capital to hide PLF weapons, documents, and senior officials. Twenty-four hours before Baghdad was occupied, PLF officers rushed Abu al-Abbas to one of these safe houses, a very plain residential building in Saadun Park that would be unlikely to arouse suspicion. He stayed for one night with no electricity, since the Americans had switched off the city's power to aid their hunt for Saddam and his cronies.

Mohammad was the bodyguard of Abu al-Abbas and also happened to be his second cousin. At this point, Mohammad came to see him. "Comrade," he said solemnly, "Baghdad has been occupied!" Abu al-Abbas nodded. He had predicted the US invasion and occupation. Yet he still was surprised at how swiftly the city and the country as a whole had fallen.

On the Iranian border. April 10, 2003. Abu al-Abbas seeks refuge in Iran.

At about eight the next morning, Abu al-Abbas grabbed both of his Thuraya phones, some cash, and several travel documents. He closed the villa door on his dear Rocky who whined and barked as his master departed without him, then left the keys with a neighbor. A few minutes later, Abu al-Abbas along with Bilal Qasim and Mohammad Zaidan were traveling northeast on the Baqubah highway which headed northeast through suburbs and then desert into the Diyala Province. While zig zagging toward the Iranian border, he and his two companions passed right by US troops, Bradley armored personnel carriers, and M-1 tanks—within shouting distance of combat: the American front had splintered into small units conducting mopping up operations. In the confusion, no one stopped them. They saw city blocks pounded to dust and clouds of smoke over villages that until recently had been almost mythically peaceful and quiet. Roads were torn apart by mortar and bomb craters. Bodies lay in the streets, rotting in the blazing sun. No one in Iraq dared to venture out to retrieve their dead for burial.

Abu al-Abbas and his companions passed through Baqubah and Miqdadiyah to the small town of Khanaqin and then traveled another 10 km to the border crossing itself. It was past noon when they arrived. Abu al-Abbas and his comrades were seeking refugee with the mullahs of Tehran—rather ironic since Abu al-Abbas, as a secular military commander, had never really liked these guys. Of course, Saddam had waged a bloody war against Iran and like the mullahs even less than my husband.

Abu al-Abbas had three passports on him, two Thuraya satellite phones, $10,000 in cash, and his firearm. One passport was his official PNA document. Another passport was Iraqi, which described his profession as "Consultant." This document had expired three days earlier. A third was a fake Yemeni passport with the name "Khalil Abdul Rahman." Abu al-Abbas did not carry a bag or travel kit. He had grown a full beard and was dressed in a traditional Arabic gown like those worn by the tribes of northern Iraq. This garb, he reasoned, might make it easier to "disappear" into the Iraqi dessert. Mohammad carried an additional $3,000. When arriving at the border, Abu al-Abbas distributed 25,000 Iraqi dinars (at today's rates, about $20) to Iraqi officials who stamped his passport and those of his two companions.

They passed through Iraqi border control without hindrance but were stopped by the Iranians. Bribing them would be difficult, if not impossible. The Iranian border station was empty, since few if any Iraqis traveled into Iran in the three weeks that had passed since the Americans entered Iraqi territory on March 20. Tehran had given no indication that it was willing to offer sanctuary or even safe passage to any of Saddam's men. The officer on duty addressed them in Persian saying, "You will not pass through here. The Sudanese Ambassador to Baghdad was stopped right here, at this same border crossing, for three entire nights. We only let him through after getting orders from our Ministry of Foreign Affairs. Take your passports and go to Syria."

Abu al-Abbas was a wise man who was used to planning operations and realized that any delay in these critical circumstances could be deadly. He immediately turned around and headed back into Iraq.

Baqubah, Iraq. April 11, 2003. Abu al-Abbas turns toward Syria.

After driving southwest for a couple of hours, Abu al-Abbas reached the home of a friend in Baqubah, capital of the Diyala province, 50 km northeast of Baghdad. While he rested, Abu al-Abbas sent his companions back to the Iranian border to make one last attempt at entering into Iran via a smugglers' path, if one could be found. Mohammad and Bilal returned in darkness and reported that travel into Iran was impossible, as every inch of the Iraqi-Iranian border had been planted with mines—some dating back to the 1980s. They took a meal with their Baqubah friend and then, after midnight, headed north. In the cold of early morning they reached Mosul and then took a highway heading east and north toward a remote crossing on the Iraqi-Syrian border, an hour's drive from any town.

Unlike Iran, Syria had welcomed scores of official and semi-official Iraqis. In addition to Saddam's wife Sajida Toulfah and their two sons, Damascus had reportedly given asylum to Vice-President Izzat Ibrahim al-Douri and a handful of top generals, who arrived with trucks of gold and cash. "They carried such riches," as Iraqis said later, "that they could have opened the doors of heaven—not just Syria."

Others, however, like my husband, were not that lucky.

Flashback to 1963:

When the Baath Party took power in Syria on March 8, 1963, the three young officers who held primary power appointed the older Amin al-Hafez its first president as a way of reassuring the populace that experienced hands were running the government. Three years later al-Hafez, a Sunni, was overthrown in a palace coup lead by Alawites with support from Druze backers of the regime. Syria has been ruled by Alawites ever since. For his part, al-Hafez served a stint in the Mezzeh prison before being expelled to Lebanon in 1967. A year later he began a life in exile in Baghdad with generous support from Saddam. His favor with the Syrian regime continued on its downward arc. Syrian courts sentenced him to death in absentia 1971.

Now, al-Hafez was stranded at the Syrian border—and had been for weeks. This was his punishment, no doubt, for his criticism years earlier of the late president Hafez al-Assad from the safety of Baghdad. Also, his 1971 death sentence needed to be sorted out. Ultimately, he was allowed to cross into Syria. He settled in Aleppo where he lived until his death.

It was eight in the morning when Abu al-Abbas and his crew arrived at the Syrian border. It was April, the sun was shining, yet it was still cold in the shade. After passing through Iraqi border control, Abu al-Abbas was stopped by the Syrians, who asked for documents and then made Abu al-Abbas and his entourage wait.

For his part, Abu al-Abbas had no money on him aside from the $10,000—certainly not enough to bribe the Baathist officers on duty. He had plenty of friends inside Syria. Ghazi Kenaan, commander of Syrian troops in Lebanon, was still in a position of power. But Ghazi and Abu al-Abbas had not spoken in years. Pride kept Abu al-Abbas from making the call to Ghazi. As his bodyguard Mohammad said later, "Comrade Abu al-Abbas did not even have the phone numbers of Syrian officials who might have assisted him." Earlier that morning, Abu al-Abbas had asked his aides to contact Nasser Qandil, the Lebanese MP who was close to Syrian President Bashar al-Assad. Qandil had been a frequent visitor to Baghdad in 2000-2003, where he joined many other Arabs in making money from the UN Oil-for-Food Program. Yet even Qandil, who was a good friend of the Assad regime, failed to get a green light for Abu al-Abbas. Hence, when the American troops crashed into Baghdad, Abu al-Abbas was forced to run for the border—any border—and now he was in the middle of nowhere passing forged documents to the *shebab* at Syrian border control. After waiting a couple of hours, Abu al-Abbas gave up on the incognito approach and told one of his aides, "Go in and tell them who I am."

Abu al-Abbas was an idealist, a Palestinian warrior—a dreamer until the very last moment—and this had not changed since his confrontation with the school director in Damascus in 1968. When Abu al-Abbas was fired from that position, he had made calls to important people all over Damascus, pleading for assistance—as recognition of his work in the Palestinian underground. Now, once again, Abu al-Abbas needed help from important men in Damascus. Syria was a country that had boasted of embracing the "resistance" for years and had created the "Steadfastness Front" with Arafat in the 1970s. Surely, it would not close its doors before a Palestinian commando. As it turned out, the name of Abu al-Abbas did raise eyebrows, but not in the way that he had hoped.

In an hour a man returned with their documents in hand. But it was not a border control official, it was "Khaldoun" (we'll use this name to protect his privacy), a military intelligence officer who had now taken over. In the ten hours that followed, Abu al-Abbas was to find his career, his hopes—his very life in the hands of Khaldoun.

The intelligence officer introduced himself, greeting Abu al-Abbas with respect and directing him to a waiting room on the Syrian side of the border. He then returned their documents to Abu al-Abbas's entourage and motioned for them to continue into Syria. Mohammad Zaidan, Abu al-Abbas's bodyguard, was free to enter Syria but chose to stay with Abu al-Abbas. "I'll never leave you," he said, "until we pass together into Syria or perish together in the Syrian Desert."

Khaldoun invited the two men to rest for a bit in a nearby room. "We need to get clearance from Damascus," Khaldoun explained. "It will take some time."

The room had two steel beds and was cold and damp—but their vehicle had disappeared into Syria and this room was certainly better than sitting in the rocky sand wilderness. Then Khaldoun sent border control men with trays of hot tea and strong Arabic coffee. He came another time to reassure them. *"Mafi mushkila abadan,"* he said, No problem whatsoever. Clearance, Khaldoun suggested, was just a procedural matter. Yet Abu al-Abbas was not convinced. Anyone who knows Syrian domestic politics, understands that—once military intelligence is involved—approval would need to come directly from President Bashar al-Assad. And for his part, less than three years into office, Assad may have hesitated to make such a decision on his own. He did not know Abu al-Abbas, even though my husband had once enjoyed a good working relationship with Hafez al-Assad. I suspect that the young Syrian President consulted with the Americans. Did the Americans also contact Israel?

In late afternoon, Khaldoun opened the door and delivered Bashar's answer. "Prepare your belongings," he said. "We are taking you to Damascus at 7:00 PM." Mohammad Zaidan, Abu al-Abbas's bodyguard, was relieved. But Abu al-Abbas was more cautious. He never took Syrian officials at face value. He had learned from his long experience with the Baath regime that they often said one thing and then did the exact opposite. Before long, a white van with thick black curtains arrived at the border crossing. Transport to Damascus? Khaldoun motioned for the two men to board. In the back, Abu al-Abbas saw four grim-faced soldiers carrying AK-47s. Where had the friendly uniforms gone, the ones who brought them coffee and tea earlier in the day? *"Assalamu Aleikum,"* Abu al-Abbas said, "Greetings upon you." They grunted a reply. Abu al-Abbas began to fidget. This seemed more like an arrest than a guarded escort. Khaldoun climbed into the passenger seat next to the driver. Something was different now ... with Khaldoun. Maybe it was the pistol which he carried in his right hand.

Khaldoun signaled the driver to travel down the road toward Damascus. As they drove away, Abu al-Abbas looked to Mohammad. "Give me a cigarette," he said, lifting his eyebrows just slightly. Anyone who knew Abu al-Abbas understood his meaning, "Something is wrong. I am starting to worry!"

A few minutes later, Khaldoun motioned the driver to take a cut off road, not much more than a dirt track, that looped back to the border. When the van reached the no-man's land between the two nations, Khaldoun called for it to stop, then held his gun in the air and ordered Abu al-Abbas and Mohammad to step out of the van.

Mohammad and Abu al-Abbas got out of the van and stared into the twilight. The Iraqi border was a couple of kilometers away, a walk of thirty to forty minutes. By now, Abu al-Abbas had been on the road for thirty-six hours with no proper rest. He was weak, about to collapse.

"Abu al-Abbas," Khaldoun intoned, "Syria cannot protect you any longer or tolerate you on our territory. We are sorry. You must return to Iraq." Abu al-Abbas looked around, only to see that the four soldiers had formed a line and were standing firm, with fingers on the triggers of their assault rifles.

"I *cannot* return to Iraq," Abu al-Abbas explained. "The country is up in flames—occupied by the Americans. They have a bounty on my head! They want to kill me!"

Khaldoun said nothing.

"We don't want to stay in Syria," Abu al-Abbas continued. "Send escorts with us and we will go directly to the Damascus airport."

Khaldoun was impassive, stone-cold.

"If you don't want to let me in," Abu al-Abbas continued, "then at least take me back to the border crossing where I came, not here in the middle of nowhere."

At this point, Khaldoun walked up to him, still holding his gun in his right hand, and looked him straight in the eye. "Comrade Abu al-Abbas," he said, "You must return to Iraq. And, if you try to come back, I swear that *we* will kill you!"

Khaldoun then pointed to a distant light and said, "See that over there? That is the Iraqi border. *Yala!*"

The last words had been spoken. It was time to start walking. Or should they run? To Abu al-Abbas it seemed odd that Khaldoun had driven them to this desolate location. If his intentions were good, why not just send them walking back on the highway toward Mosul? On the highway, surely, they could catch a car or a taxi. To Abu al-Abbas, this was a setup: the Syrians intended to shoot them from behind and then blame it on desert tribes or bandits. What to do? Abu al-Abbas calculated that if they managed to cross the first 600 meters, then bullets would injure but not kill them. They would need to march quickly.

Abu Abbas and Mohammad walked as fast as they could, waiting for the sound of the AK-47s. Abu al-Abbas was tall and bulky—all six feet two inches (190 cm) of him. He stomped and stumbled across desert sand and rock in his now dusty Arabic garb. Just before they reached the first border mark, he and Mohammad heard the Syrian van's engine start up and turned to see Khaldoun and his goons disappear over a rise into Syria. They were alone now, wandering in the desert, but still alive.

Abu al-Abbas stopped to rest while Mohammad tore apart Abu al-Abbas's Iraqi passport. The chill of the April night had set in. Before resuming their march, Abu al-Abbas buried one of his Thuraya phones in the sand. Only Iraqi officials carried such devices during and after the war, and either it or the passport would blow his cover. With his remaining phone, Abu al-Abbas called his brother in Damascus and said, "I was unable to come through into Syria. I am returning home to Baghdad."

At last, Abu al-Abbas and Mohammad reached the Iraqi side of the border which did have a small shack and a single light but was otherwise uninhabited. While they were wondering what to do, they heard and then saw a battered 4-wheel-drive powering across the sands and broken dirt of the desert. The driver stopped when he saw them and jumped out of his vehicle. He was an older man of noble bearing who wore a red *kuffiah* and a flowing white cotton robe. He seemed to be a local sheikh. "What in the world are you doing here?" he asked. "You are in the middle of nowhere."

Abu al-Abbas addressed him with an accent, saying, "Oh, noble sheikh. We are Yemeni jihadists who came here to fight the US infidel occupiers of Iraq. We are seeking shelter from the US Army."

The driver introduced himself as one of the leaders of the powerful Shummar tribe whose nomadic presence in this desert predated the Sykes Picot agreement after World War I that divided the land into national boundaries—some tribal members lived in what was now Saudi Arabia, others in Iraq, and others still in Syria. The sheikh took Abu al-Abbas and Mohammad to his headquarters—a tent filled with tribesmen and goods. "According to our tradition," the sheikh explained, "you may stay with us for three days. You may eat, sleep, and rest. Once three days have passed, you must tell us more about yourself, or leave." After a day with the sheikh, Abu al-Abbas and

Mohammad were rested and ready to return to Baghdad. In the meantime, one of the sheikh's men had discovered their Thuraya phone. The sheikh quickly understood that they were Saddam's guys and, therefore, too hot to handle. They needed to leave immediately. The sheikh enlisted local smugglers who arranged for the two men to travel as far as Mosul in a car packed with women and children and then to Baghdad in a truck carrying international medics. Eight hours later, they were once again walking the streets of the war-torn Iraqi capital.

Apaches

Abu al-Abbas headed first to the home of his colleague and friend, Faisal Zaki. He rested and changed out of his dusty tribal garb. Then he spoke to me in Beirut via Thuraya. I briefed him on the talks of my father with a senior Hezbollah chief who was close to the party's secretary-general Hasan Nasrallah. This man was Hezbollah's liaison with the Palestinians, and he had lobbied on Abu al-Abbas's behalf with top officials in Iran. They agreed to grant him asylum, and Abu al-Abbas began preparing to return to the Iranian border the very next morning. He did not want to spend too much time in one place. Soon he left for another residence in Baghdad, this one owned by a Jordanian friend. A few minutes after his departure, Faisal Zaki's house was raided by US troops who had just intercepted his Thuraya call. Faisal did not have means to communicate with Abu al-Abbas, to warn him that the Americans were now on his track.

At around 4:30 AM, Abu al-Abbas was startled awake. Police cars on the street in front and choppers hovering over the house were sending flashing blue lights into his bedroom. The helicopters flew at such a low elevation that the roof was almost torn off. The entire house began to shake—as if an earthquake measuring eight on the Richter Scale was rumbling through Baghdad. Abu al-Abbas could hear and feel the advance of the one hundred eighty US troops encircling the house accompanied by thirty Bradley armored personnel carriers and six Apache helicopters. He walked out of his bedroom, rather submissively, and sat down on the living room couch, helplessly waiting for his arrest. Mohammad was sleeping on a mattress. When he heard the noise he grabbed his firearm and jumped to attention, but was stopped short by Abu al-Abbas, who seemed to be saying, "What's the use?" The American GIs smashed the door of the house in a scene that could have been lifted from a Hollywood action flick—more Rambo than Rocky. Carrying M-4 rifles with sophisticated attachments, the soldiers pointed their weapons, painting the chest and head of Abu al-Abbas with their lasers. They screamed orders. "Hands up! Take one step back. Sit down!" Abu al-Abbas put up no resistance. Both he and Mohammad were handcuffed

Reem and her sons. From left to right: Reef, Reem, Ali, Louai. Rocky the dog also escaped Baghdad.

and escorted out at gunpoint, only to see that the Americans had arrested the entire neighborhood before breaking into their house like a pack of wolves.

Mohammad recalled the event saying, "I was dragged out forcefully and a black ski-mask was pulled over my head with a small hole for my mouth and two very small holes for me to see. The neighbors and I were lined up against the wall while police dogs snarled and barked at us, as if they were trying to bite off a limb or a finger. Women and children wept hysterically. I caught a final glimpse of Abu al-Abbas—spotting his white *galabiya* (cotton gown) in the crowd. Nearby, two US officers were going through black & white photos of Abu al-Abbas. The senior officer looked closely at one of the pictures, and then said, 'Yup. That's him alright. We got 'em!' That was the last I ever saw of Abu al-Abbas."

US Detention

"We were loaded into military trucks that drove four hours to an unknown destination," Mohammad continued. "We realized later that we were still in Baghdad, held at Saddam International Airport."

Abu al-Abbas, as Mohammad went on to explain, was kept in a cell with a group of senior Iraqi officials that included ex-Interior Minister Saadun Shaker and ex-Prime Minister Saadun Hammadi. Others included Abed Hammoud, a pro-Saddam journalist, and Aseel Tabra, a business associate of Uday.

In Beirut, I heard that US troops had ransacked our villa and carted away our belongings. All the mementos of our life together were lost. And I wondered about Rocky. Had the US troops killed our dog? At last I was able to reach our neighbor. "After the American troops pulled everything out of your house," she said, "I tip-toed back in when no one was looking. I found Rocky—alive. He was tied to a tree in the courtyard, in rough shape, hungry and thirsty and looking confused. Do you want him in Beirut? I'll figure out a way to get him to you."

From his jail cell in Baghdad, Abu al-Abbas asked me about the fate of Rocky and rejoiced when I told him that Rocky was still alive. The family was good, everyone had survived, and our dog had made it through the invasion and occupation and now was with us in Beirut. Thanks to the ministrations of kind fate, Rocky had survived the Americans and this suggested that Abu al-Abbas might well do the same.

From his jail cell in Baghdad, Abu al-Abbas asked me for books. I went to a bookstore in Beirut but all I could find were volumes on political, historical, and philosophical topics. "Would books of this type," I wondered, "be allowed by US prison authorities?" Instead, I bought him a full collection of the world-acclaimed Abbasid era poet al-Mutanabbi. Abu al-Abbas had often said, "I regret not having had the time to read his complete works, because he was an avant-garde political and religious philosopher."

Abu al-Abbas in US detention, 2003.

"Perhaps now is the time," I said to myself. I hoped that al-Mutanabbi would provide him comfort, companionship, and entertainment in jail.

Abu al-Abbas was the only member of the group to serve prison time and die in jail—although he was neither given a trial nor access to an attorney. He was not sentenced to death by the Americans. In fact, there was no US warrant (or Israeli warrant) for the arrest of Abu al-Abbas, since his "offenses" had been committed prior to 1993 and he had been granted amnesty under the Oslo Accord. Abu al-Abbas wasn't terminally ill. He nevertheless died suddenly at the age of 56 on March 8, 2004.

I was having dinner at one of the restaurants of Old Damascus, with Syrian businessman Munzer al-Kassar, a good friend of Abu al-Abbas. His driver walked in halfway through the meal and whispered something into his ear. Munzer's face turned white, as if he had seen a ghost. "What's wrong Munzer?" I said, taking the matter rather lightly at first. I could see an icy cold stare in his eyes as he looked back at me, but he refused to say a word. My phone then rang and it was Abu al-Abbas's brother, who almost never called me. "Is it true?! Is it true that he died?!" Munzer angrily grabbed the phone and dressed him down: "Of course it isn't. What's wrong with you man? Al-Arabiya TV has just denied the rumor!" The rest didn't require much explanation. I knew that Abu al-Abbas was gone.

Taking control of myself, I asked Munzer, "How did he die?" He yet again dismissed it completely, insisting that it was nothing but a baseless rumor, the product of an imaginative journalist at some Arabic satellite TV. When I got home, I turned on al-Arabiya. True, on their news bar they were denying rumors that Abu al-Abbas had died. Reuters apparently was the original source of the story. Yasser Arafat had also denied it and so had the PLO offices in Tunisia. BBC, however, insisted that it was true. Minutes later, the Doha-based al-Jazeera TV called up asking for an interview. The director of news began the conversation by offering his condolences. "Please, don't say it! Let us wait to be sure first. I just telephoned Ramallah, and I am waiting for confirmation from President Arafat." He went silent for a moment, taken aback that I—Abu al-Abbas's wife—was still in the dark. "Madame, I assure you, it is true, alas. I am so sorry. We confirmed it through the International Red Cross."

I then got a telephone call from a Swiss official at the Red Cross (ICRC), who ironically had met Abu al-Abbas just that morning. ICRC officers had relocated to Amman after their offices were destroyed in Baghdad and they made twice monthly visits to US and Iraqi prisons. I had sought his help a few days earlier to find out how to deliver packages to my husband. The Swiss gentleman said, "I regret that I met your husband today. He had a strong impact on me—he was so commanding, and so confident. He was living in a cell with nine former Iraqi officials, whose names I cannot reveal. All I can tell you is that they were moaning and laughing and groaning, like mischievous little children. They refused to accept their fate and were creating daily tantrums in jail. Abu al-Abbas was the only real leader among them, lifting their spirits, organizing their affairs, and planning for the day after he would walk out of prison. He was a fighter until the very last moment of his life."

This account was later confirmed to me by Aseel Tabra, the business associate of Uday, who was confined with my husband and who was the last person to see Abu al-Abbas before the doctors arrived and performed their check-up. "They walked in carrying a stretcher," Tabra said, "but Abu al-Abbas refused to lay on it, insisting that he could walk into the medical room. I bid him, 'Good luck!' and watched him walk down that long corridor. The minute he entered the medical exam room, I saw him collapse. I said to myself, 'Rest in peace Abu al-Abbas. The palm [an Arabic term for a tall bulky man] has fallen.' I knew that only death could bring him down. If he fell, that meant he was dead!"

Was it a coincidence that Abu al-Abbas and three other Palestinian leaders who had lived within reach of Israeli arms for decades suddenly died in 2004? Two were overt assassinations. Two others could have been the result of poison. Here are the facts: Abu al-Abbas died of unknown causes in early March 2004. Sheikh Ahmed Yassin was killed by a rocket from an Israeli helicopter on March 22, 2004. Abdul-Aiz al-Rantisi was killed by a missile fired from an Israeli helicopter on April 17, 2004. On November 11, 2004 Yasser Arafat died of unknown causes.

It's as though a decision was made in Tel Aviv to cleanse the Palestinian resistance of aging leaders who had proven over many years to be too difficult, too stubborn. You be the judge.

Yarmouk

Many years later, after an al-Jazeera TV documentary on the mysteries of Arafat's death, a Swiss lab said that Arafat might have died through poison: Polonium 210. A Russian and a French lab, however, could not confirm this evidence. Abu al-Abbas never had the honor of a TV documentary inquiring as to the cause of his death. His body was laid to rest in the Martyrs' Cemetery at the Yarmouk Refugee Camp in Damascus in March 2004 without an autopsy. I cannot say for sure if he was murdered, since I was not with him during his final hours. What I do know, however, was that he did not suffer from a serious illness. It seems strange that four prominent Palestinian leaders—including the legendary Arafat—died in the span of six months. Sharon was Prime Minister of Israel at this time, and he had pledged to kill each of these Palestinian leaders over the years. Arafat's widow Suha believes that Sharon made good on his promise. She believes that Sharon was behind the death of Arafat. And I suspect that Sharon was responsible for the death of my husband. It was only natural

The casket of Abu al-Abbas in the Yarmouk refugee camp, Damascus 2004.

Reem at her husband's funeral in Yarmouk.

that Abu al-Abbas would be a target, after the years he had spent struggling against the occupation of Palestine.

The career of Abu al-Abbas included military errors and, occasionally, fiascos such as the *Achille Lauro*. Perhaps the West still considers him "a class A terrorist." I nevertheless knew an Abu al-Abbas that others never experienced. I was his political disciple, his companion, friend, and wife.

All that is left for us in Palestine are "symbols" of our Cause. They include the olive branch, the orange orchards, the Dome of the Rock, the al-Aqsa Mosque—and the legacy of men like Abu al-Abbas, Abu Jihad, Abu Iyad, and Abu Ammar. Those living in the Occupied Territories and the Diaspora have labeled them the "last standing wall" of Palestine. The "state," which they had dreamt of for decades, was systematically destroyed by Sharon and so was Greater Palestine. The Palestinian National Authority (PNA; established in 1993 by the Oslo Accords as an interim governmental body), barricaded from outside and divided from within, has also crumbled as chaos now prevails in the Occupied Territories. Whether the world likes it or not, these "Class A terrorists," as the Americans have labeled them, have become symbols for the Palestinians—a legend since Fatah launched its first attack in Israel on January 1, 1965 and the Palestinian Revolt began. These men, through military struggle and then via Oslo, restored Palestine to the map of the world. Maybe it was not our vision of Palestine . . . but it *was* Palestine, nevertheless.

For long years Palestinians could not travel and had to wait for hours at airports and to endure lengthy questioning. Now they were issued local PNA passports, and could now fly from their own airport in Gaza. They earned a home to live in, a civil service to join, a police force to bring order to their lives, a government that they could ask for help, and a leader to follow. Now, Palestinians had a parliament, a constitution, an independent judiciary, a social security program, along with their own schools and national universities.

Why have we lost the fruits of Oslo? The reason is our weakness and the incitement, madness, and corruption of Sharon. Abu al-Abbas and his generation did for the Palestinians what Zionism did for the Jews after World War II. Arafat, Abu al-Abbas, and their comrades brought Palestinians out from the obscurity and persecution of the 1950s, from the misery of the refugee camps into the world as key players in international affairs. For forty years, these leaders were the center of gravity in Palestinian politics. Power went where they went: Amman, Beirut, Tunis, Gaza, or Ramallah. Everyone is to blame for the death of Abu al-Abbas as well as that of Arafat: Israel, the US, and Arabs. We were not nearly strong enough. We allowed the Israelis to put Arafat under siege . . . to detain him in his office from 2001 until 2004. We allowed Abu al-Abbas to rot in a US jail in 2003 and 2004.

When walking behind my husband's coffin at his funeral in Damascus, women threw rice as a gesture of farewell as I sobbed my heart out. I cried for my husband, for our lost Arab nationalism, and I cried at the thought of American troops roaming freely in Baghdad. I refused, however, to write a political obituary to the Palestinian Struggle, the cause that Abu al-Abbas fought for so aggressively. That generation, the men that Palestinians call the "superhuman people," is gone. The Middle East will never be the same without them.

Epilogue
A Note on Terror

THIRTY YEARS AGO, IRREGULAR WARFARE—some would call it "terror"—was a technical term that described a military tactic used in asymmetric conflict. In the version of the American war of independence portrayed to school children in the 1950s, when irregular forces among the American revolutionaries concealed themselves in the forests and shot into the exposed ranks of uniformed British soldiers marching past—they were simply being effective, even though they were breaking the gentleman's rules of contemporary warfare. They engaged in terror as a tactic. Yet, this tactic did not suggest that the irregulars were the villains in this conflict. Inflicting terror, in another sense, has always been the object of combat. One side wins, not by killing all the troops of the enemy but by demoralizing them. A winning attack succeeds when the enemy becomes confused, is unable to see a path to victory, and begins to fear for its survival. Commanders are unable to govern their troops. Panic sets in. And the rout is on.

In the modern era, "terror" is used to designate combatants who are evil. In the currently prevailing definition, any tactics used by combatants that have a just cause can not be terror. Conversely, all manner of tactics used by the opponents of justice are termed "terror." As a Palestinian, it's always bothered me that the western media assumes that irregular forces in the Middle East—unlike those fighting in the American Revolution—were in the wrong. As a mother and as a civilized human being, I have always bridled at the assumption that Middle Easterners are themselves immune to the effects of unrestrained violence—call it "terror," if you like.

Zafer al-Masri: The Death of a Good Man

I've mentioned the shock and sorrow we felt at the death of my uncle Zafer al-Masri. To me, his killing was a grand act of terror. It's helped assuage my grief to some extent to understand more about his death. This type of violence exists in context. The details are important. In this case, my uncle was a victim of many things, chief among them Syrian meddling in Palestinian affairs.

Zafer al-Masri was one of the notables of Nablus who ran for the city's municipal elections in 1976 with the full endorsement of Arafat. The Syrians, however, did not want to have Arafat's man in office in Nablus, so they worked for his downfall from day one. Bassam al-Shakaa, a Syrian-backed figure, became president of the city's municipality, and my Zafer became his deputy. Shakaa was close to Damascus and Zafer was close to Arafat. The balance held for six years, until the Israelis dismissed the Nablus Municipality altogether in 1982. At this point, an Israeli military governor took over and for three and a half years the city was under martial law. In 1985, the PLO sought to restore local governance by referring to a Jordanian law that delegated power, in the absence of a municipality, to the largest elected body in Nablus until an election could be held. In this case it was the Nablus Chamber of Commerce, which was now headed by Zafer al-Masri. Weeks later, my uncle was gunned down while walking to work.

A TV Movie Starring Karl Malden

Four years after the *Achille Lauro* operation, a made-for-TV movie called *The Hijacking of the Achille Lauro* was released. It stared Karl Malden and Lee Grant. Malden was a famous American actor who had appeared alongside Marlon Brando twice, in *A Streetcar Named Desire* and *On the Waterfront*. Surely, his new film was not to be missed. Abu al-Abbas and I decided to watch it on TV from our villa in Baghdad. We took a deep breath and resolved to view the movie with open minds, more like movie critics than participants in the events in the film. It was a horrible movie, however. What I remember most was the depiction of my husband on screen—a very unflattering and flawed portrayal by Nabil Hakkim—an obscure actor with an Arabic accent and no other dramatic credits. I saw the film as character assassination perpetrated by the Western media.

For his part, Abu al-Abbas was amused and chuckled through the film. He was not surprised by the slant of the movie. "The American and European media," he said, "sometimes sounds like a public relations firm that works for Israel and the CIA." In one scene, Abu al-Abbas was shown talking on the telephone with one of his aides. Behind him was a mosque and the sound track was delivered a sonorous Muslim *athan* or call to prayer. It was the director's way of saying, "Abu al-Abbas is a Muslim and Muslims are terrorists!" Abu al-Abbas, however, was a secular-minded Muslim who respected the faith but did not attend mosque or fast during Ramadan. In a restaurant, he drank beer or wine with his meal and, later in the evening, he might well drink something harder. The actions of Abu al-Abbas were motivated by politics. He did not "hate the infidel." He simply wanted the Israelis to give back the land that they had stolen in 1948.

A letter from Abu al-Abbas to his son Ali, January 2004.

It struck me that this TV movie was trying to make a simple problem—a dispute over land—into an intractable religious conflict. It's as though the movie were saying, "As long as there are Muslims there will be terrorists. They are crazy with hatred and have no identifiable grievances that can be satisfied at the negotiating table. All that we can do is to fight—to the death." Politically motivated commandos such as Abu al-Abbas who sought to attack military objectives and who avoided civilian casualties as much as possible were a far cry from intractable religious warriors.

Be careful what you ask for. Fifty-three years after the *Nakba*, the open wound of Palestine still had not been healed and the rational, political-and-military approach of leaders like Abu al-Abbas had been largely discredited. Across the Arab world, people were saying to themselves, "The secular approach utterly failed to resolve the injustice of Palestine. So, what will?" Suddenly, the horrific 9/11 attacks in New York brought religious warfare to the international stage, forever linking terrorism and Islam in the mind of the Western public. What should have been most frightening to the West: the new villains were not presenting demands. They wanted something far larger than a fair shake on a real estate deal that had gone bad in 1948.

Letters from Prison

Since we are talking about terrorism and terrorists and asking whether these terms apply to Abu al-Abbas as opposed to Osama bin Laden, I thought it might make sense for the reader to see into the interior life of our family. I am providing below an English translation of two letters that Abu al-Abbas wrote after his capture by US forces in 2003. Please recall that Ali is our youngest, eighteen years old at the time he received this letter, a student with a budding hobby as a rap artist.

Baghdad. January 16, 2004. Abu al-Abbas writes to his son Ali.

In the name of God the most Gracious, the most Merciful,

My beloved son Ali,

This is the first time I write to you in particular, while you are at the age of 18, one year after we last met. I was glad to hear your remarks in the letter you sent to me, with your mother and Louai. In those remarks I found a high sense of responsibility, and high moral spirit that I pray to God, will strengthen.

My dear son: I don't know how long my absence will be but I do know that life never pursues one single path. It is often marked by severe ups-and-downs. What is important is to always be optimistic, and to place before our eyes very high and noble goals; not letting life pass without achievements. Noble goals require effort, sacrifice, and knowledge. That knowledge will only be obtained through reading and experience. The more knowledge you obtain, the closer you are to success.

That is why it is imperative that you pay attention to your studies this year and to improve yourself by reading and interacting with society. You need to respect your family, your parents, your grandparents, and your brothers. You need to check on them, visit them, and help them when needed. You need to stay in touch with your relatives and friends.

I have full faith in your morals and your ability to carry responsibility like a man. First and foremost, however, you need to succeed in your studies this year.

Please pass my regards to your great Mother and to Louai, Reef, Khaled, and Omar—who are dear to my heart. Also pass on my regards to all my friends and yours.

At any rate, we have been told that the Red Cross is trying to obtain permission to arrange for family visits. This requires follow-up from your Mother.

Sorry for the short letter. I will write others, and you try to write one for me. I pray to God that he grants you success. To you all I extend my love, and to your dear Mother. I am proud of all of you and hope to meet, *inshallah,* soon.

PS: My weight is now 95 kg [205 lbs]—no extras, and my letter has to be like that as well.

Baghdad. January 15, 2004. Abu al-Abbas writes to me from US detention.

Dear Reem,

I got your letter, the beautiful clothes, and the books. The best thing was your photos. I was surprised to see Rocky [our dog from Baghdad] standing amidst the family in Beirut. I was very glad to receive letters from the boys, especially Ali's emotion-filled beautiful one. God bless you all.

I am well, thanks to God. We are allowed to write one letter per week. That is why I write to you every two weeks because I also write to friends who correspond with me from Baghdad. I will write in response to the children's letter. As for Ali, I think that if he studies business [administration] this would be good because it fits with his personality. Louai ought to remain a free bird, for now. As for Reef, Omar, and Khaled, I pray that all their ambitions come true.

I don't need additional clothes although some Marlboro Light cigarettes would be nice, along with nuts and other "light" things. The *marron glacé* never reached me. Apparently some things are not allowed here.

My greetings to your father, to Rabouha [my mother Rabiha], Rami, Malak, Nour, Rifaat, Rana, her husband, and daughters. How are our friends? It's been a while since I last heard from them. How is the family in Palestine, Syria, and Lebanon? I hope that they are all in best conditions.

Nothing new from here. I am still waiting for updates. After two months, one year will have passed since my incarnation—new know-how to add to the many experiences in life. Personally I am good and trying to maximize benefit from time. I miss you all and send you my love. Until we meet again, *inshallah*.

PS: I got the letters and stuff you sent me on 10 February. Please send me more books.

9/11

With the TV movie on the *Achille Lauro* and the other coverage in the Western media, the name of Abu al-Abbas was forever after linked to two words: "Wanted Terrorist." Only that now, after 9/11, the word "terrorist" has been redefined to suggest irrational thinking motivated by an intractable and twisted religious belief.

Abu al-Abbas was never a terrorist, and he drew a distinction between the PLF's "limited, historical goal" of liberating Palestine—a war that he felt was justified—and the 9/11 attacks which he condemned. He termed the 9/11 attacks as the start of a "borderless, limitless religious war on America and Israel, and Americans and Jews."[1]

Abu al-Abbas was idealistic, but never irrational. He respected religious belief, but he was not observant and did not consider himself to be motivated by religious doctrine. The phrase "holy war" had no bearing on his life and actions. A war began in 1948 with the *Nakba*. And that war has never been concluded. More than sixty years later, we still do not have a peace agreement. Everyone in the world is against war. War brings destruction and death.

The casket of Abu al-Abbas is raised by the crowd in Yarmouk cemetery, Damascus March 2004.

Young men are killed, civilians are killed, children are killed. People are starved, the economy is wrecked, the environment is ravaged. Tell me, what is good about war? Yet human beings continue to have wars because they are unwilling to work out their differences in other ways. Once a war starts, every victim is a profound loss and a crime against civilization. Is it really much better that a young man in uniform is killed rather than a civilian, or a mother or a child? Is it really much better that hundreds of people are killed anonymously from the air when a bomb lands than it is when three or four are killed up close and in person?

Neither Abu al-Abbas nor I ever exulted in military action. What motivated us was the desire for justice in Palestine. Abu al-Abbas welcomed a genuine peace. When Oslo came along, he was deeply suspicious and felt that it was too good to be true. He had the capability of undermining the Oslo accords. Yet, out of loyalty to Arafat and to err on the side of the possibility that Oslo was genuine, he let Oslo pass and joined the process as a Palestinian Member of Parliament.

I was always proud of my husband. And I continue to admire him as the tenth anniversary of his death approaches. Abu al-Abbas was a man of principle, talent, dedication, and character. Some will call into question his luck as a military commander, since both the *Achille Lauro* and the Sea Operation were beset by snafus. Yet no one will doubt his bold thinking and his imagination as a tactician. My life with Abu al-Abbas had its ups and downs and was filled with enough intrigue and weaponry for a Hollywood action thriller. Its hero, however, would be Abu al-Abbas himself, not our opponents. Abu al-Abbas was a man who bravely lived in the shadow of death for thirty-five years. He was a man who could not be intimidated. After each close call, he continued to act according to his principles: military operations focused on weakening Israel and the liberating Palestine. With an unwavering determination and an ambition that knew no bounds, he lived—and died by this sacred dream—a dream that is still largely unfulfilled.

I stood beside Abu al-Abbas during twenty-four years of turmoil from 1980 until his arrest and death in US custody in 2004. I watched him evolve as a husband, a politician, and a military commander during our life together in Lebanon, Syria, Tunisia, and finally Iraq. I am writing this book as my way of saying, "Good-bye my mentor, my friend, my love."

Resources

End Notes

To the Reader
00.1 Anonymous. "Abu Abbas," *The Telegraph* (March 11, 2004).
Preface
0.1 Lansford, Tom. Political Handbook of the World 2012. (Thousand Oaks, California: Sage Publications, page 1634.
0.2 Anonymous. "Abbas Key Strategist in Palestinian War," *Chicago Tribune* from the *New York Times* News Service (Oct 14, 1985).

1. Something Went Horribly Wrong
1.1 Bohn, Michael K. *The* Achille Lauro *Hijacking: Lessons in the Politics and Prejudice of Terrorism,* (Washington: Potomac Books, Inc, 2004), pages 148-151.
1.2 Ibid.
1.3 Interview with Bassam al-Achkar (September 20, 2012).
1.4 Interview with Bassam al-Achkar (September 20, 2012).
1.5 Earlier PLF operations include: September 16, 1978, the PLF tried and failed to attack an Israeli squad in Kiryat Shmona; March 7, 1981, they also tried and failed to launch a hang glider attack against the Israeli Army in Haifa; April 16, 1981 they failed to take hostages from Haifa in a balloon attack.
1.6 Anonymous. "Abu Abbas," *The Telegraph* (March 11, 2004).
1.7 Interview with Bassam al-Achkar (Beirut - September 20, 2012).
1.8 Before re-establishing the PLF in 1977, Abu al-Abbas had been a member of the Syria-backed Popular Front for the Liberation of Palestine-General Command (PFLP-GC). He parted ways with its chairman and founder, Ahmad Jibril, when the PFLP-GC backed Syria's attacks on Arafat in Lebanon during the civil war in 1976. Along with the late Talaat Yacoub, Abu al-Abbas revived the Palestine Liberation Front (PLF) in Lebanon on April 24, 1977.
1.9 Interview with Bassam al-Achkar (Beirut - September 20, 2012).
1.10 Ibid.

2. Aboard the *Achille Lauro*
2.1 Interview with Bassam al-Achkar (September 20, 2012). It was a fancy car that had been parked in our garage in Tunis, with gold trim on the interior. Abu al-Abbas and I drove around in it once, but then it disappeared, and I never asked him where it had gone. I later found out that the weapons used for the operation had been hidden in its gas tank.
2.2 Ibid.
2.3 Ibid.
2.4 Ibid.
2.5 Wallach, John & Wallach, Janet. *Arafat: In the eyes of the Beholder,* (New York: Citadel Press, March 1997), page 324.

2.6 Ibid.
2.7 Interview with Bassam al-Achkar (September 20, 2012).
2.8 Interview with Bassam al-Achkar (September 20, 2012).

3. Mubarak Gives Us a Ride
3.1 Interview with Bassam al-Achkar (September 20, 2012).
3.2 Clines, Francis. "U.S. Heads Off the Hijackers: How the Operation Unfolded," *New York Times* (October 12, 1985).
3.3 Ibid.
3.4 Ibid.
3.5 Keller, Bill. "Aides Say Reagan Put End to Troop Standoff," *New York Times* (October 19, 1985).
3.6 Friedman, Thomas. "Israelis Say Tape Ties Top P.L.O. Aide to Ship Hijackers," *New York Times* (October 17, 1985).
3.7 Anonymous. "The Klinghoffers Sue P.L.O. for $1.5 Billion," *New York Times*, November 28, 1985.

4. Abu al-Abbas: A Rebel with a Cause
4.1 Johnston, David. "Leader of 85 *Achille Lauro* Attack Dies at Prison in Iraq," *New York Times* (March 10, 2004).
4.2 Anonymous. "Abbas Key Strategist in Palestinian War," *Chicago Tribune* from the *New York Times News Service* (October 14, 1985).

5. Rifaat al-Nimer & Our Family
5.1 For more on my mother's school: www.palfriends.org.

6. Operation Gamal Abdul Nasser
6.1 Anonymous. "Talaat Yacoub, a Palestinian Leader, Dies," *New York Times* (November 19, 1988).
6.2 Anonymous. "Israeli Navy Hits Back after Raid," *Glasgow Herald*, (Monday, April 23, 1979).

7. My Life in Politics
7.1 Castañeda, Jorge G. *Compañero: The Life and Death of Che Guevara*. New York: Vintage, October 27, 1998, page 291.
7.2 Cooley, John K. (1973). *Green March Black September: The Story of the Palestinian Arabs*. London: Frank Cass & Co, page 135.

9. Our Time in West Africa
9.1 "Abu Abbas," *The Telegraph* (March 11, 2004), (http://www.telegraph.co.UK/news/obituaries/1456489/Abu-Abbas.html).
9.2 Joffe, Lawrence. "Abu Abbas," *The Guardian* (March 10, 2004).

10. The Lebanese Civil War: 1975 - 1982
10.1 Gharavi, Maryam Monalisa. "Pronunciation as Death Sentence," *The New Inquiry* (October 31, 2012).

10.2 *The New York Times*, January 12, 2014, "Israeli Hawk Sought Peace His Way" by Ethan Bonner.

10.3 Friedman, Thomas L. "P.L.O. Leader Lists Demands to Quit Tripoli," *New York Times* (November 13, 1983).

10.4 Treaster, Joseph B. "Arafat Says Syria and Libya Have Joined Tripoli Battle," *New York Times* (November 04, 1983).

10.5 Cowell, Alan. "4,000 Palestinians Evacuate Tripoli on Greek Vessels," *New York Times* (December 21, 1983).

10.6 Muir, Jim. "Syria pulls strings in Palestinian clash. Arafat rival gets upper hand in battle for Beirut camps," *Christian Science Monitor* (July 7, 1988).

10.7 Abruish, Said K. *Arafat: From Defender to Dictator.* New York: *Bloomsbury Publishing*, October 15, 1998, page 183.

10.8 Cowell, Alan. "4,000 Palestinians Evacuate Tripoli on Greek Vessels," *New York Times* (December 21, 1983).

11. Life in Baghdad
11.1 Zelnick, Robert, "How the Rug Was Pulled from under Zafer al-Masri," *Christian Science Monitor* (March 11, 1986).

11.2 Sharbutt, Jay. "NBC Lets Justice Dpt. See Interview with Abu Abbas," *Los Angeles Times* (June 17, 1986).

11.3 Lansford, Tom. Political Handbook of the World 2012. (Thousand Oaks, CA: Sage Publications, page 1634.

12. The Jerusalem Sea Operation
12.1 Anonymous. "Talaat Yacoub, a Palestinian Leader, Dies," *New York Times* (November 19, 1988).

12.2 James G. Smart, "Yitzhak Shamir (1915-2012): Not the Only Terrorist Elected Prime Minister of Israel," Washington Report on Middle East Affairs (September 2012).

13. Early Retirement
13.1 The Office of the Inspector General, Department of Justice, "The FBI Laboratory: An Investigation into Laboratory Practices and Alleged Misconduct in Explosives-Related and Other Cases," April, 1997, Part II of Section D (http://hnn.US/article/1000#sthash.KkhwAwfY.dpuf).

13.2 Reynolds, Rob. "Abu Abbas: from terrorist to peace advocate," *CNN* (May 10, 1996), (http://www.CNN.com/WORLD/9605/10/abu.abbas/).

Epilogue: A Note on Terror
1. Johnston, David. "Leader of 85 *Achille Lauro* Attack Dies at Prison in Iraq," *New York Times* (March 10, 2004).

Notes on Illustrations

All photos, unless otherwise noted, are from the collection of the Rifaat al-Nimer family.

Other photo/illustration credits:
1. Alberto Korda photo of Che Guevara 1960: Editorial use granted to the public by the photographer. (Image # 7.7).
2. Images controlled by Palestinian Organizations are used under a Creative Commons license and can easily be located by an Internet search.
3. Cover background: Palestinian Flag by Garyck Arntzen, London (=GaryckArntzen; twitter.com/GaryckArntzen). Cover photos, the collection of the Rifaat al-Nimer family.
4. Other, see below:

    6.1   PFLP 10th anniversary poster, 1977. Credit: PFLP.
    7.1   PFLP poster   72
    7.2   PFLP logo   72
    7.3   PLO logo   73
    7.4   Fatah logo   73
    7.5   PLF logo   73
    7.6   PFLP-GC logo   72
    9.1   PLF poster: "Operation Martyr Kamal Nasser." Credit: PLF.
    9.2   PLF poster: "Heroes of the Kamal Jumblatt Operation." Credit: PLF.
    10.1 Cover of a PFLP publication. Credit PFLP.
    11.4 Zafer al-Masri photo courtesy of the Zafer al-Masri estate: www.zafermasri.com

Glossary

(Find a Glossary with names from Palestinian History mentioned in *The Curse of the Achille Lauro:* www.cunepress.com. Click on "Free" in the header.)

Further Reading

Abbas, Mahmud. *Through Secret Channels: the Road to Oslo* (London: Garnet, 1995).

Abu Iyad. *My home, my land: a narrative of the Palestinian Struggle* (New York: Times Books, 1981).

Abu Sharif, Bassam. *Arafat and the dream of Palestine: An insider's account* (London: Palgrave Macmillan, 2009).

Abbas, Mahmud. *Through Secret Channels: the Road to Oslo* (London: Garnet, 1995).

Abu Iyad. *My home, my land: a narrative of the Palestinian Struggle* (New York: Times Books, 1981).

Abu Sharif, Bassam. *Arafat and the dream of Palestine: An insider's account* (London: Palgrave Macmillan, 2009).

Antonius, George. *The Arab Awakening: The story of the Arab National Movement* (London: Hamish Hamilton, 1969).

Ashrawi, Hanan. *This side of peace: A personal account* (New York: Simon & Schuster Macmillan, 1996).

Atwan, Abdel Bari. *A country of words: A Palestinian Journey from the refugee camps to the front page* (London: Saqi Books, 2008).

Avnery, Uri. *My Friend, the Enemy* (London: Zed Books, 1985).

Baroud, Ramzy. *My Father was a Freedom Fighter: Gaza's Untold Story* (London: Pluto Press, 2010).

Bohn, Michael K. *The Achille Lauro Hijacking: Lessons in the Politics and Prejudice of Terrorism* (Washington, DC: Brassey's Inc, 2004).

Cobban, Helena. *The Palestinian Liberation Organization: People, Power, and Politics* (Cambridge: Cambridge University Press, 1984).

Doumani, Beshara. *Rediscovering Palestine: Merchants and Peasants in Jabal Nablus 1700-1900* (Berkley: University of California Press, 1995).

Ferber, Elizabeth. *Yasir Arafat* (Brookfield: Millbrook Press, 1995).

Fisk, Robert. *Pity the Nation: Lebanon at War* (Oxford University Press, 2003).

Fisk, Robert. *The Great War for Civilization: The conquest of the Middle East* (New York: Doubleday, 2007).

Friedman, Thomas. *From Beirut to Jerusalem* (New York: Farrar, Straus & Giroux, 1990).

Ghanem, As'ad. *Palestinian Politics after Arafat: A failed national movement* (Bloomington: Indiana University Press, 2010).

Green, Stephan. *Living by the Sword: America and Israel in the Middle East 1968-1987* (London: Faber & Faber, 1988).

Haikal, Mohamed. *Sphinx and Commissar: The rise and fall of Soviet Influence in the Middle East* (London: Collins, 1978).

Hirst, David. *The Gun and the Olive Branch: The roots of violence in the Middle East* (New York: Thunder Mouth Press: Nation Books, 2003).

Hirst, David. *Beware of Small States: Lebanon, battlefield of the Middle East* (New York: Nation Books, 2010).

Iskandar, Adel & Rustom, Hakem. *Edward Said: a legacy of emancipation and representation* (Berkley: University of California Press, 2010).

Jenkins, Vlad. *The Achille Lauro Hijacking* (President and Fellows of Harvard College, 1988).

Kassir, Samir. *Being Arab* (London: Verso, 2006).
Kassir, Samir. *Beirut* (Berkley: University of California Press, 2010).
Khalaf, Issa. *Politics in Palestine: Arab factionalism and Social Disintegration 1939-1948* (NY: State University of New York, 1991).
Khalidi, Rashid. *The Iron Cage: The story of the Palestinian struggle for Statehood* (Boston: Beacon Press, 2006).
Khalidi, Walid. *All that Remains: The Palestinian Villages occupied and depopulated by Israel in 1948* (Washington, DC: Institute for Palestinian Studies, 1992).
Nazzal, Nafez. *The Palestinian Exodus from Galilee 1948* (Beirut: Institute for Palestinian Studies, 1978).
Lansford, Tom ed. *Political Handbook of the World 2012* (Thousand Oaks, California; Sage Publications, 2012).
Peres, Shimon. *Battling for peace: Memoirs* (London: Weidenfeld & Nicolson, 1995).
Said, Edward. *Reflections on Exile and other Essays* (Cambridge: Harvard University Press, 2000).
Said, Edward. *The Politics of Dispossession: The struggle for Palestinian Self-Determination 1969-1994* (New York: Pantheon Books, 1994).
Salibi, Kamal. *A House of Many Mansions: The History of Lebanon Reconsidered* (London, IB Tauris, 1988).
Seale, Patrick. *Abu Nidal: A gun for Hire* (New York: Random House, 1992).
Sanchez, Jonathan. *State of Failure: Yasser Arafat, Mahmoud Abbas, and the Unmaking of the Palestinian State* (London: Palgrave Macmillan, 2013).
Shlaim, Avi & Rolan, Eugene (ed.). *The war for Palestine: Rewriting the history of 1948* (Cambridge: Cambridge University Press, 2001).
Shamir, Yitzhak. *Summing Up: An autobiography* (London: Weidenfeld & Nicolson, 1994).
Sharon, Ariel. *Warrior: An autobiography* (New York: Simon & Schuster, 2001).

Index

Abu al-Abbas (detail)
Abu al-Abbas, and Arafat 14-15, 22, 114, 131, 132, 133, 152-154; treatment from wounds 16, Achille Lauro operation 20-33, and Klinghoffer 31-32, 39, and Egypt 32, 35-39, 168; and Syria 33, and Craxi 37; and mother 44, life in the camps 44-45, schoolteacher 46-47, joins underground 47-51, 64; and PLF 65-67, 128-129, 101; Operation Gamal Abdul Nasser 67-69, Jerusalem Sea Operation 139-141; meets Reem 91-92, 103; marriage 147; and Abu Nidal 107, assassination attempt 109, 112-114; and Hafez al-Assad 109-112, 111, 115, 116, 122-123, 171-173; life in Baghdad 124-125, 146, 153, 163-164; and media appearances 127, 156; and Gaddafi 134-138; invasion of Kuwait 143-146, and Uday Hussein 149-150, becomes member of parliament 154-155, visits Gaza 157-160; refugee attempt in Iran 169, arrest of 174-175; US detention 175-176, death of 1760178, views on terrorism 182-185; correspondences from jail 184-185

A
al-Abbas, Abu Ismail, 41, 44
al-Abbas, Ali: 131, 142, 147-149, 156, 162, 164, 175, 182, 184, 200
al-Abbas, Latifa, 41, 44
Abbas, Mahmud, 65, 70, 147
Abdul Latif, Ibrahim Fatayer, 19
al-Abed, Hussein, 20
al-Abras, Ahmed, 67, 69
Abu al-Abbas, 12, 15-20, 24, 26, 35, 44, 50, 81, 87, 91, 94, 99-100, 103, 106-107, 117, 122, 128, 134, 136, 138, 143, 145, 147-148, 150, 152, 154, 166, 170-172, 177, 179-180, 182, 187, 201
Abu Ghazaleh, Rashed, 54
Abu Iyad, 70, 80, 81, 86, 92, 105, 108, 134, 154, 178
Abu Jihad, 64, 70, 105, 108, 116, 154, 178
Abu Yaghi, Sami, 78, 86
Abu Nidal, 23, 40, 106, 107, 137
Abdul Rahman, Khalil, 18, 20, 168
Achille Lauro, 13, 19-20, 22, 25-26, 30, 32-34, 73, 127, 131, 139, 144, 182, 194, 197, 201
al-Achkar, Bassam, 19-20, 28-30
Aflaq, Michel, 46, 89, 160, 161
Aleppo, 16, 44, 103, 110, 170
Algeria, 126, 131-132, 134, 161
Amal Movement, 60, 194
Amanpour, Christiane, 12, 145
American University of Beirut, 42, 48-49, 61-62, 65, 70, 78, 100-101, 196
American University Hospital, 114
Amman, 25-26, 52, 54-55, 71, 82, 139, 147-148, 152, 177, 180
Anderson, Sven, 132-133
Arab Bank, 54, 97
Arab Communist Organization, 83-84, 86, 90, 92
Arab League, 14, 21, 35, 41-42, 48, 53, 72, 139, 143, 194
Arab Nationalist Movement, 49, 65, 72
Arafat, Suha, 152, 178
Arafat, Yasser, 7, 11-12, 14, 20-22, 24, 31, 33, 40, 59-60, 70, 72, 92, 104-106, 108, 110, 114, 121-122, 128, 131, 133-135, 137, 140-141, 148, 151, 154, 177-179, 192, 200, 206
Argov, Shlomo, 106-107
Army of Deliverance, 42
Aslan, Abdul Majid, 67-68
al-Assad, Basel, 111-112
al-Assad, Bashar, 112, 170-171
al-Assad, Hafez, 16, 20, 82, 86, 89-90, 96, 98-99, 110-112, 121-123, 128, 130, 136, 169, 171-172
Aziz, Tarek, 134, 146

B
Baath Party, 46, 65, 83, 160, 169
Baghdad, 8-9, 11, 33, 44, 54-55, 89-94, 98, 102, 124-126, 128-129, 131-132, 136, 139, 142-151, 153, 159, 161, 163, 165, 167-168, 170-171, 173-177, 180, 182, 184-185, 190, 193, 195-197, 201, 206
al-Bakr, Ahmed Hasan, 89, 91, 161
Baker, James, 141, 143
Baq'a Camp, 30
Barak, Ehud, 39
Battle of Karameh, 67, 71, 81-82, 105, 147
Beddawi camp, 121
Beirut, 2, 8-9, 11, 17, 19, 23, 42, 48-49, 54-

55, 58-66, 69-71, 73-76, 78-81, 83, 85-87, 92, 94-105, 108-110, 112-121, 124, 128, 139, 142, 144, 147, 149, 165-166, 174, 176, 180, 185, 188, 190, 192, 196, 199-200, 206
Beirut Bank for Commerce, 59, 101
Beirut University College, 76, 101
Begin, Menachem, 81, 98, 106
Bernadotte, Folke, 42
Berri, Nabih, 104
Birzeit University, 152
al-Bitar, Salah, 46, 160
Black September Organization, 154
Bourguiba, Habib, 40
Brando, Marlon, 182
Bsisso, Atef, 81
Bush, George HW, 132, 141, 143, 144
Bush, George W, 163-164, 167

C
Cairo, 14-15, 21, 25-26, 32, 35-36, 38, 48, 54, 72, 77-78, 82, 90, 112, 152, 167-168, 194, 196
Camp David Accords, 21, 98
Carter, Jimmy, 135
Chatah, Mohamad B, 109
CIA, 23
Clinton, Bill, 151
Costandi, Samia, 101, 102, 103
Craxi, Bettino, 34, 37, 38-40, 124

D
Dahlan, Mohammad, 167
Damascus, 6, 15, 20, 30-31, 45-51, 54, 60-61, 64-66, 71, 85-86, 88-91, 96, 98, 103, 110-112, 116-117, 120-124, 128-130, 139, 161-162, 166-168, 170-173, 176, 178-180, 182, 185, 192-193, 206
Damascus International Fair, 85
Damascus University, 46, 48-49
Darwaza, Izzat, 54
Darwish, Mahmud, 133
Darwish, Samir, 65
Dayan, Moshe, 81
De Gaulle, Charles, 66
Douba, Ali, 122-123
al-Douri, Izzat Ibrahim, 169

E
Egypt, 13, 19, 21-22, 35-36, 38, 40, 43, 59, 62-63, 65, 78, 84, 98, 152, 167-168, 195
Eitan, Rafael, 107

F
Farouk, King of Egypt, 43, 48
Fatah Movement, 8, 11, 14, 21, 67, 70-73, 80-81, 85-86, 89, 91, 95, 98, 105-106, 110-111, 114, 121-122, 128, 152, 167, 180, 191, 193-195, 206
Fatah Revolutionary Council, 106
Flakstad, Gunnar, 119
France, 66, 100, 114, 117, 121, 163
Friedman, Thomas, 116

G
al-Gaddafi, Muammar, 16, 134-137, 140
Gaza Strip, 10, 20, 22, 43, 48, 59, 81, 130, 142, 151-152, 154-159, 168, 180, 199
Gemayel, Bashir, 108, 117-118
Gemayel, Pierre, 105, 107
al-Ghadban, Ali, 76, 77-81, 84-87, 91-92, 100
al-Ghadban, Louai, 85, 97, 126, 147, 149, 162, 164, 175, 184-185
al-Ghadban, Mohammad, 75-100
al-Ghadban, Reef, 90, 95, 97, 109, 126, 147, 149, 164, 175, 184
Glaspie, April, 143
Glubb, Faris, 109
Glubb, John Bagot, 109
Grant, Lee, 181
Great Britain, 143-144
Guevara, Che, 11, 74-76

H
Habash, George, 48-49, 65-66, 72-73, 76, 100, 108, 128
Habib, Philip, 114
Haddad, Fouad, 114
Haddad, Wadih, 48-49, 100
al-Hadithi, Mashour, 147-148
al-Hafez, Amin, 89, 169
Haifa, 20, 41, 43-44, 65, 101, 120, 155, 157-159
Haig, Alexander, 106
Halab, Abu Ahmed, 67
Hamas, 69, 159, 166-167
Hammad, Nimer, 39
Hammadi, Saadun, 174
Hammoud, Abed, 175
Hariri, Saad, 109

al-Hasan, Hani, 26-27
Helou, Shadia, 70
al-Hindi, Amin, 81
Hezbollah, 69, 174, 195
Hobeika, Elie, 118-119
Homs, 109-112, 120, 122, 126
Hourani, Ali, 86
al-Hout, Shafiq, 65, 72
Howe, Geoffrey, 33
Husni, Farouk, 37
Hussein, Qusay, 164, 167
Hussein, Uday, 149-150, 164, 175, 176
Hussein, King of Jordan, 63, 82, 84, 112, 127, 128, 147
Hussein, Saddam, 91, 107, 124, 128, 129, 134, 136, 139, 143, 145-149, 151, 163-165, 168-169
Hussein, Taha, 54, 195
al-Husseini, Abdul Qader, 42
al-Husseini, Amin, 42, 54

I
International Atomic Energy Agency, 163
International Red Cross, 20, 176, 184
Iran, 164-168, 169
Iraq, 89-91, 93-94, 126, 129, 134-135, 143-144, 146-147, 149-151, 153, 159, 161-165, 167-169, 172-175, 177, 196, 198
Israel, 8-9, 12-13, 15, 18-25, 30-33, 35-39, 41-43, 48, 53, 59, 65-69, 71-73, 77, 80, 82-84, 88, 96, 98-99, 101-102, 104-114, 116-117, 119, 121, 124, 128, 130, 132-140, 142, 144-146, 151-155, 157-160, 167, 171-172, 178-180, 182, 186-187, 189-190, 192-197, 199-200
Israeli Defense Forces, 20, 25, 28, 30, 32, 43, 67, 71, 84, 101, 107-109, 118-119, 139-140, 145, 149, 154-156, 157, 167
Istanbuli, Akram, 79
Italy, 17-18, 26, 34-35, 37-40, 114, 117, 124, 163

J
Jackson, Michael, 17
Jaffa, 20, 42, 44
Jibril, Ahmed, 46, 49, 64-66, 72-73, 92, 96-97, 105, 128, 187
Jerusalem, 9, 42, 52-55, 59, 64, 116, 118-119, 131, 137, 139-141, 152, 155, 157, 159, 190, 194, 199

Jordan, 19, 25-26, 29-30, 33, 41, 43, 49, 52-55, 58-59, 63, 67, 71, 79, 82, 84, 96, 104, 110, 116, 127-128, 139, 147-149, 152, 154, 158, 177, 180
Jumblatt, Kamal, 11, 61, 67, 102, 104, 191, 195
Jumblatt, Walid, 61, 195

K
Kanaan, Ghazi, 110-111, 115-116, 165, 170
Kamal, Wasfi, 53
Kapeliouk, Ammon, 119
Karami, Rashid, 104
al-Kassar, Munzer, 175-176
Kazem, Abu Ali, 145
Khaddam, Abdul Halim, 122-123
Khoury, Colette, 110
Khoury, Ramzi, 21
Khrushchev, Nikita, 63
Klinghoffer, Leon, 13, 29, 31-32, 38-39
Klinghoffer, Marilyn, 31
Kuwait, 9-10, 59, 65, 129, 139, 142-147, 149-151, 153, 161, 164-165, 197-198

L
Lahad, Antoine, 106, 107
Lebanese Civil War, 9, 16, 44, 59-60, 82, 85, 98, 104-105, 109-110, 113, 118, 146, 189, 195, 197
Lebanon, 2, 8-9, 11, 15-17, 19-21, 23, 31, 33, 41-44, 48-49, 53-55, 58-71, 73-76, 78-88, 91-122, 124, 128, 136, 139, 142, 144, 146-147, 149, 153-154, 158, 163, 165-166, 170-171, 174, 176, 180, 185-190, 192-193, 195-197, 199-200, 206
Libya, 9, 23, 59, 109, 126, 134-140, 142, 190, 195-197, 206
Litani River, 43, 67, 105

M
Malden, Karl, 181
al-Malki, Nuri, 147
Malone, Linda, 118
al-Masri, Rabiha, 2, 7, 44, 55-58, 61-63, 97, 184, 200
al-Masri, Sabih, 97
al-Masri, Zafer, 126-128, 130, 180-181
al-Molqi, Majid Yusuf, 19
Mousa, Amr, 133

Mubarak, Husni, 21, 35-37, 39-40, 112, 166-167
Muhsen, Zuheir, 60
al-Mutanabbi, 175

N
Nablus, 52-55, 57, 102, 127-128, 156, 180-181
Naher al-Bared camp, 121
Nakba, 42, 49, 65, 104, 146, 183, 185
Nasrallah, Hasan, 69, 173
Nasser, Gamal Abdul, 48, 58, 63-64, 67
Nayef, Mohammad Kheir, 86
Neirab Refugee Camp, 16, 44-45, 103
Negroponte, John, 163
al-Nimer family, 55-58
al-Nimer, Rana, 2, 55, 184, 200
al-Nimer, Rami, 55, 115, 184, 200
al-Nimer, Rashed, 53, 80
al-Nimer, Rifaat, 52-63, 79-81, 85, 92, 10-102, 184
al-Nimer, Sudki, 53

O
Odeh, Mohammad Salah, 154
al-Omar, Ziad, 134, 140, 200
Operation Gamal Abdul Nasser, 67-69
Operation Kamal Jumblatt, 67, 102
Operation Wooden Leg, 30
Oslo Accords, 34, 130, 140, 151-157, 165, 175, 178-179, 185-186

P
Palestine Liberation Front, 8-9, 11, 14, 18-21, 24, 26, 33, 49, 64-69, 72-73, 92, 96-97, 101-102, 109-114, 121-122, 128-129, 131, 137, 139-140, 146, 148, 153, 163, 168, 186, 188, 191-192, 194-197, 206
Palestine Liberation Organization, 11-14, 17-18, 20-24, 26, 30-31, 38-40, 46-47, 49, 59-60, 64, 66-67, 71-73, 82-84, 91, 96, 104-105, 107-108, 113-114, 116, 118-120, 122, 124, 127-129, 131-135, 137, 140-141, 146-147, 149, 152-154, 158, 177, 182, 191-194, 197
Palestinian National Authority, 12, 153, 157, 169, 179-180
Palestinian National Council, 14, 32, 59, 131, 154, 192
Palestinian National Fund, 59, 192

Palestinian Students' Union, 53
Peres, Shimon, 69, 144
Phalange Party, 105, 108, 115-119
Popular Front for the Liberation of Palestine, 8, 11, 42, 49, 64-66, 69, 72-76, 84, 92, 96, 106, 128, 191-194
Popular Front for the Liberation of Palestine – General Command, 11, 49, 64, 66, 69, 72-73, 92, 96-97, 128, 188, 191-193
Powell, Colin, 163

Q
Qabbani, Nizar, 78
Qabbani, Tawfiq, 78
al-Qaddumi, Farouk, 78, 154
al-Qaddumi, Lutof, 24
al-Qaddumi, Nabila, 78
Qandil, Nasser, 170
al-Qantar, Samir, 31, 67-69
Qasim, Abdul Karim, 143
Qasim, Bilal, 167-168
al-Qawiqji, Fawzi, 42
al-Qudsi al-Bahriya Operation, 139-141
Quleilat, Ibrahim, 113

R
Rabin, Yitzhak, 151
Ramadan, Taha Yassin, 145
Ramallah, 152, 156, 159, 166, 176, 179
al-Rantisi, Abdul-Aziz, 177
Reagan, Ronald, 17, 22, 24, 29, 31, 36, 38-39, 114, 121, 132-133, 135-137, 144-145
Revolutionary Front for the Liberation of Palestine, 75, 77, 192

S
Sabbagh, Samir, 112
Sabra and Shatila, 19, 73, 117-120, 121
al-Sadat, Anwar, 21, 35, 67, 77, 98
al-Sadr, Musa, 138
Safad, 44, 48
Said, Edward, 63
Salam, Saeb, 104
Salameh, Abu Hasan, 105, 154
Saudi Arabia, 42, 55, 58, 84, 107, 143, 173
Seale, Patrick, 106
Shaath, Ali, 58
Shaath, Nabil, 58
Shachar, Eliyahu, 68
al-Shakaa, Bassam, 180

Shaker, Saadun, 174
Shamir, Yitzhak, 42, 141, 144, 149
Shapiro, Charles, 68
Sharif, Omar, 63
Sharon, Ariel, 107-108, 117-118, 157-159, 178-179
Shartouni, Habib, 117
Sheeha, Mohammad Giath, 86
Shibli, Omar, 66
Shouman, Abdul Hameed, 54
Shultz, George, 132-133
al-Shuqayri, Ahmad, 59-60
Six Day War, 19, 48-49, 53, 59, 65, 71-72, 146, 194
Soviet Union, 34, 66-67, 74-75, 117, 135, 140
Spandolini, Giovanni, 40
Stevens, Janet Lee, 119
Suleiman, Omar, 166
Syria, 6, 9, 15-16, 20, 23, 29-31, 41-51, 53-54, 58-61, 64-67, 71, 73, 79, 82-86, 88-89, 91, 94, 96, 98, 101, 103, 109-112, 114-117, 120-124, 127-130, 136, 139, 142, 144, 155, 158, 161-163, 166-168, 170-174, 176, 178-180, 182, 185-188, 190, 192-193, 195-196, 201, 206
Syrian Social Nationalist Party, 117, 192, 195

T

Tabra, Aseel, 175-177
Tel Aviv, 105-107, 119, 138-139, 157, 178
Thatcher, Margaret, 33, 144
Tiret Haifa, 41, 44, 155-157
Touqan family, 53
Toulfah, Sajida, 169
Tripoli (Lebanon), 69, 120-122
Tunisia, 17-18, 20-22, 24, 40, 59, 114, 116, 120-121, 124, 126, 140, 144, 152-154, 158, 177, 187, 197

U

Udwan, Kamal, 154
United Nations, 42-45, 48, 106, 120, 132-133, 144, 151, 164-165, 171, 198
United States, 2, 7, 9-12, 17-19, 21-25, 32-33, 35-40, 42, 44, 53, 55, 59, 61-63, 73-81, 85-89, 91, 93-94, 97-99, 106, 108-109, 114-118, 120-122, 124-126, 128, 131-136, 138-149, 151-154, 157, 159, 161-169, 173-177, 179-180, 184-187, 189-190, 195-197, 206

V

Victoria College, 63

W

Wallach, Janet, 30-31
Wallach, John, 30-31
Washington DC, 24, 31, 34, 36, 98, 135, 140-141, 143, 145, 151, 161, 188, 190, 199-200
West Bank, 20, 43, 52, 58-59, 127, 151, 159-160
Wihdat Camp, 30
Wolfwitz, Paul, 163

Y

Yacoub, Talaat, 66, 73, 92, 108, 128-129, 131
Yarmouk Refugee Camp, 30, 45-46, 60, 66, 103, 110, 178-179
Yassin, Ahmed, 69, 167, 177
Yusuf, Said, 67
al-Yusufi, Fihmi, 85

Z

Zaki, Faisal, 173
Zayed Bin Sultan, UAE President, 164
Zayn al-Din, Farid, 53
Zaidan, Mohammad, 167-171
Zedong, Mao, 74
Zueiter, Akram, 53-54
Zureik, Constantine, 42, 48-49, 100

Acknowledgements

This book is the product of a lifelong dream. I promised to myself to write this book in remembrance of Abu al-Abbas shortly after he died in Baghdad in 2004, ten years ago. It could never have been completed, however, had it not been for the monumental support I received from family and friends.

I start off by thanking my mother, Rabiha al-Masri, my brother Rami, his wife Malak, and my sister Rana. All of them were hands to hold and shoulders to cry on over the long years narrated in this book and the decade of its creation—when fate was taking painful strikes at me. If it were not for them, I would have collapsed years ago. I thank my good friend Roula Amin for reading the manuscript before it went to print and offering her detailed input on Palestinian affairs, polishing the book into its final form.

My husband's ever-loyal comrades took the time to see me for interviews, refreshing my memory of events that have been forcefully suppressed, perhaps by virtue of how painful they were. I thank Ziad al-Omar, Abbas Jumaa, Bassam Achkar, Bilal Qasim, Mohammad Zaidan, and Ambassador Nimer Hammad.

My friend Ali Chakaron worked closely with me, as my book coincided with a TV documentary he was creating on the *Achille Lauro* Operation. My friend, the Syrian historian Sami Moubayed helped as a writing coach. He also edited and developed the work, offering his expertise on Palestinian affairs which are dear to his heart. Scott C. Davis, the Founder of Cune Press (publisher of *Searching Jenin*) and a writer on Syria also helped edit the manuscript. This book is as much theirs as it is mine.

REEM AL-NIMER is the widow of Abu al-Abbas, the leader of the Palestine Liberation Front (PLF) which worked under the umbrella of the Palestine Liberation Organization (PLO) and Yasser Arafat.

Reem hailed from landed Palestinian notability. She was born in Nablus and raised in Beirut where her father was a prominent banker. At age eighteen, she enrolled in Yasser Arafat's Fatah Movement and, after a year, she joined a succession of ever more committed Palestinian resistance groups.

At this time of her life, Reem had an earnest desire to oppose Israeli military action with force. Her book, *Curse of the Achille Lauro,* traces her growth over thirty years' time to an understanding that war, in the end, does not create the desired result. It requires reconciliation to make peace.

Reem's marriage to Abu al-Abbas took her to Algiers, Baghdad, Damascus, Tripoli, and Tunis. She witnessed or participated in the major events of Palestinian history from the mid-1960s. Reem and her children survived eleven wars including the 1982 siege of Beirut by Israeli forces.

Reem's husband, Abu al-Abbas, died in US custody in 2004.

www.ingramcontent.com/pod-product-compliance
Lightning Source LLC
Chambersburg PA
CBHW052027070526
44584CB00016B/1931